THE KEY TO SPECULATION ON THE NEW YORK STOCK EXCHANGE

JACK GILLEN

Copyright 2009 by Jack Gillen

No part of this book may be reproduced or transcribed in any form or by any means, electronic or mechanical, including photocopying or recording or by any information storage and retrieval system without written permission from the author and publisher, except in the case of brief quotations embodied in critical reviews and articles. Requests and inquiries may be mailed to: American Federation of Astrologers, Inc., 6535 S. Rural Road, Tempe, AZ 85283.

ISBN-10: 0-86690-594-4
ISBN-13: 978-0-86690-594-7

Cover Design: Jack Cipolla

Published by:
American Federation of Astrologers, Inc.
6535 S. Rural Road
Tempe, AZ 85283

www.astrologers.com

Printed in the United States of America

DEDICATION

This book is dedicated to my mother,
Angelina Gillen,
who's been a positive force throughout my life.

The Key to Speculation Story

Jack Gillen's fascination with astrology began in the early 1960s. This led him to question the ability of astrology with regard to speculative events. He shared some of the findings through predictions made on radio shows and in print media. After being convinced, in 1970 he compiled a summary of each speculative subject in his book *The Key to Speculation*.

At the 1970 American Federation of Astrologers convention in Miami Beach, Florida, at the Fontainebleu Hotel, he shared his findings with other astrologers and convinced them he was onto something that was unprecedented. The first book in The Key to Speculation series was *The Key to Speculation for Casino Games*, and the final book, in 1980, *The Key to Speculation for Greyhound Racing*.

After the release of *The Key to Speculation on the New York Stock Exchange*, Robert Cooper of the AFA was extremely fascinated by this stock market material and was very ambitious in getting this book before the public. It was because of his efforts that this book did not fade away, as did all the others in the series.

The Saturn return has come full circle once again; Kris Brandt Riske of the AFA entered into a contact to republish the book in an updated version. This book has already become a classic among astrologers. *The Astrology Encyclopedia* by James R. Lewis credits *The Key to Speculation on the New York Stock Exchange* for bringing financial astrology to what it is today.

Contents

Chapter I. The Planets	1
Chapter II. The Planetary Aspects	47
Chapter III. The Planetary Signs	55
Chapter IV. Panics and Crashes	59
Chapter V. Accidents and Their Effect on the Dow-Jones Industrial Averages	73
Chapter VI. Death and Illness of World Leaders	75
Chapter VII. Sensitive Degrees of the Sun and Moon	79
Chapter VIII. Year-End Rally	95
Chapter IX. Dow-Jones Predictions	103
Chapter X. Analyzing the Corporate Chart	113
Appendix I. Birthdates of Stocks on the NYSE	141
Appenidx II. New and Full Moons	201
Appendix III. Planetary Data	217

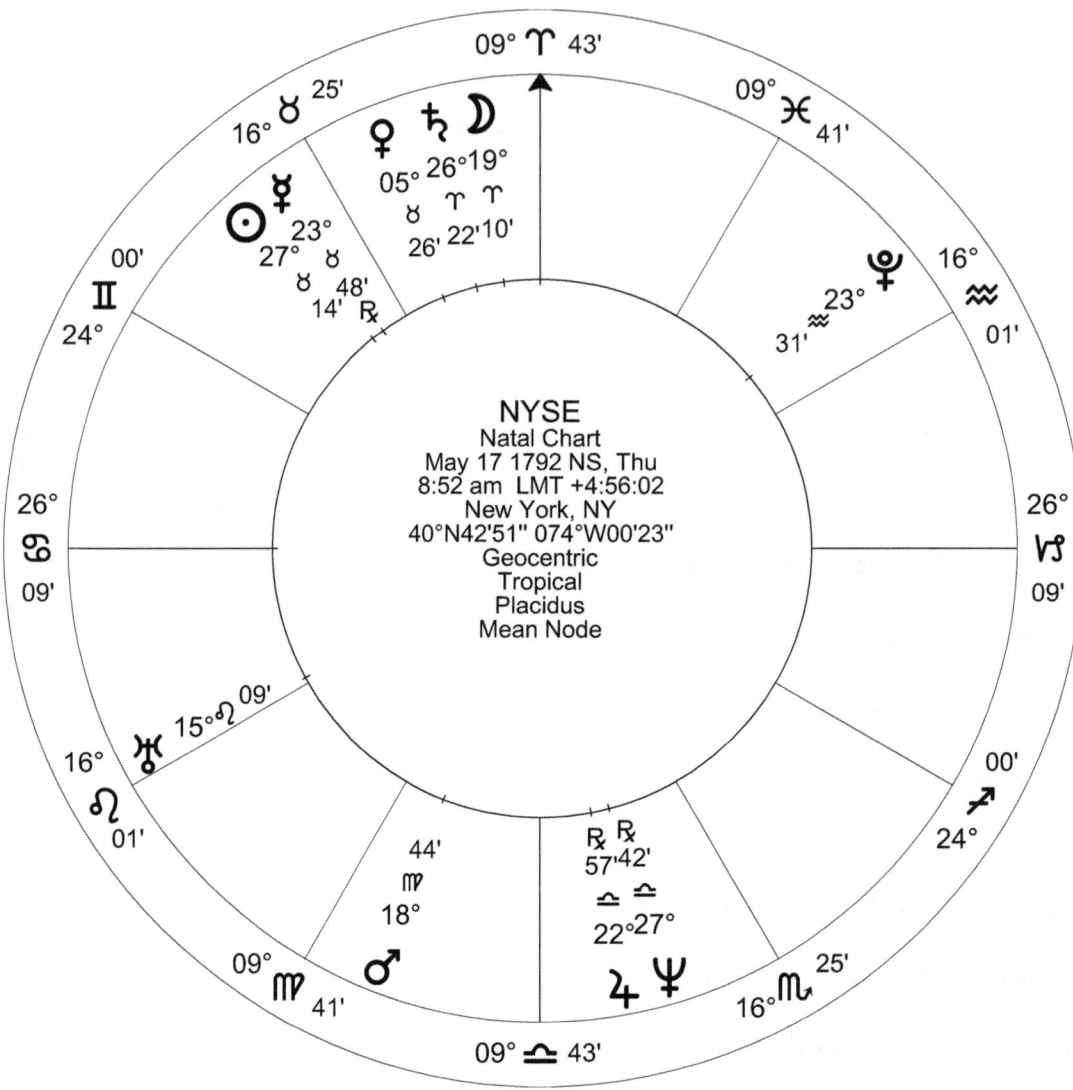

New York Stock Exchange

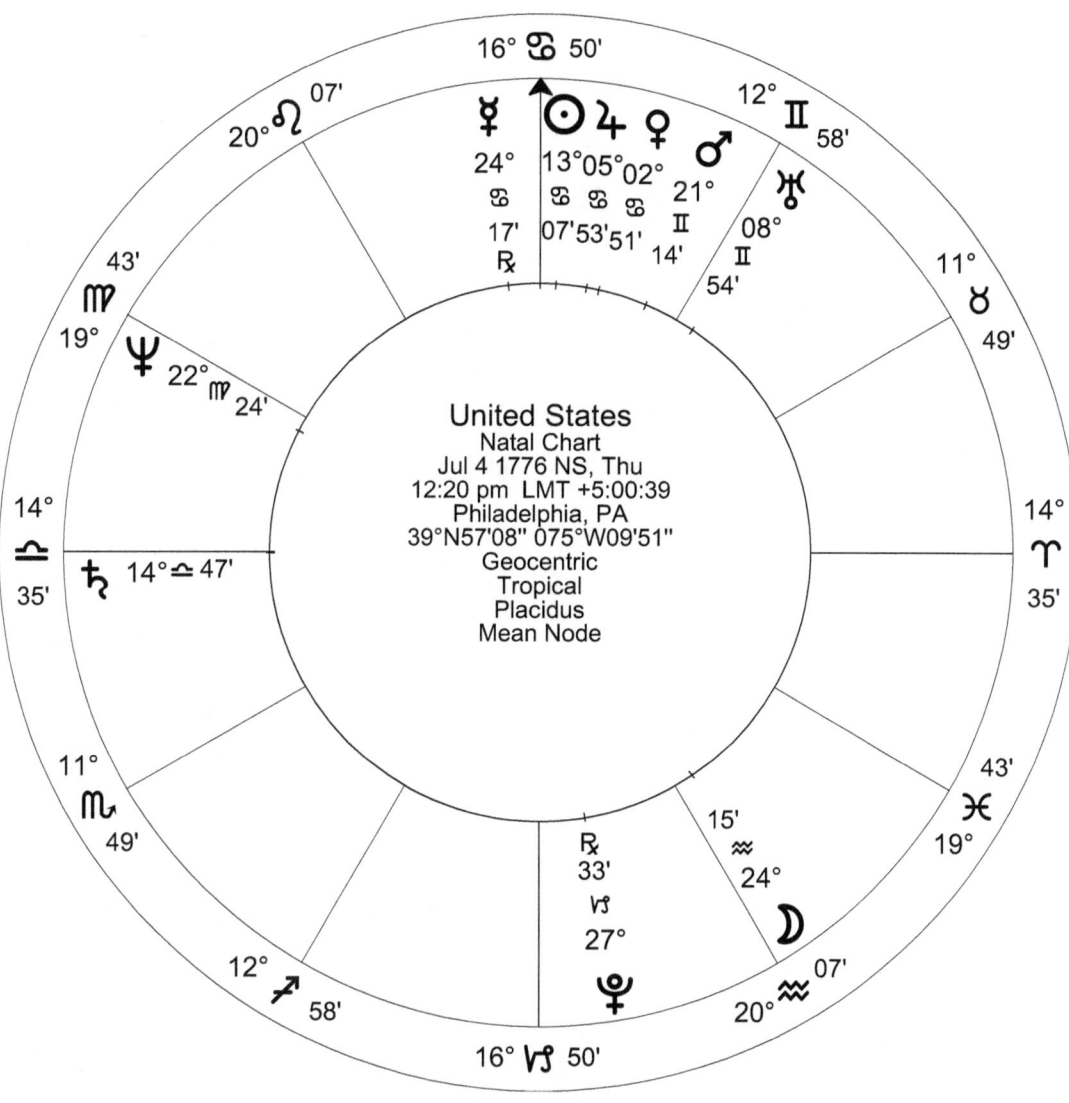

United States of America

CHAPTER I

THE PLANETS

Sun

The Sun is an energy planet. It gives and takes energy. A solar cycle is 365.25 days. It affects the stock market every 30 days, as the Sun transits through the 12 signs of the zodiac. The Sun also has an 11-year solar cycle in which Sun-spot activity peaks, followed by five and a half years of solar flares, a period of more or less calm with respect to the Sun's surface. And during this period the Sunspot areas emit a wide range of intense radio and electromagnetic radiation of various types, affecting people and conditions of the planet Earth. This has been researched not only by astrologers but by astronomers. It has a definite effect on the stock market, commodities, and other areas related to the stock market.

As in all living matters it seems to affect mundane things like corporations and the stock market in the same way. This is to say that with regard to the birth month and the birth date, six months prior to the birth date the solar cycle is high, giving energy and pushing the related company forward. The Sun also is a planet associated with the ego . . . appearance and personality. Six months prior to the birth date, the company is brought out before the public. The birthdate to six months after, the energy flow is low . . . it becomes weaker . . . and this affects the stock market in the same way.

As an example, the stock market was born May 17, 1792. So the months of May through November relate to low activity, affecting the market's price and structure. As we go from December through May, we go through the high cycle, the up period of the Sun. But there are many cycles of the Sun that affect different areas of the stock market as the Sun affects each house with relation to the buying public. In each six-month period of the year we will also find a close relationship between price, movement and volume from Aquarius to Leo, or from February to the last two weeks of July. Looking at example 1, we find that the birth month and the Sun cycle six months prior to the birth month is at a high level; six months after the birth date, it is at a low level.

In Example 2 we take the Midheaven aspect to the Ascendant. We can see in Example 2 that the chart of the stock exchange starts its up level in the sign of Aquarius and its down level begins in the sign of Leo. So these are the two breaking points within a year: under Aquarius and under Leo as the Sun transits these signs. The low part of the chart, which is the Nadir, is the sign of Libra. This will generally be the low point of the year, as October would always represent low price, low volume, in which the opposite point to the Midheaven is Aries. This would be affected by the planet represented at the Midheaven. However, in April, under no afflictions, this would be a great month where records would be set in the areas of volume and prices.

As we start with Aquarius, this would run from the last two weeks of January through the first two weeks of July. However, as the cycle proceeds through Pisces, which is a weak sign, it would represent a weak month for volume. From the latter part of March through April and May, and even into June, these could be above average months for prices and volume. Now, as the Leo portion is activated from July through October, these are very weak months. You cannot expect too much in the way of prices or volume. If there is any weakness in the market it will more or less have a breakdown during these months. Not only are we in the six-month period after the birth

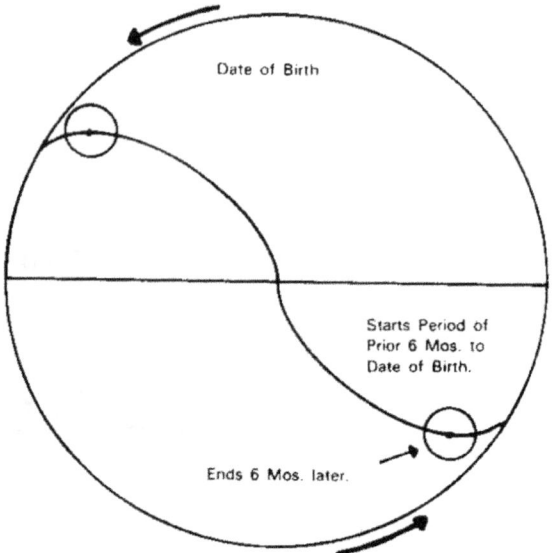

Example 1

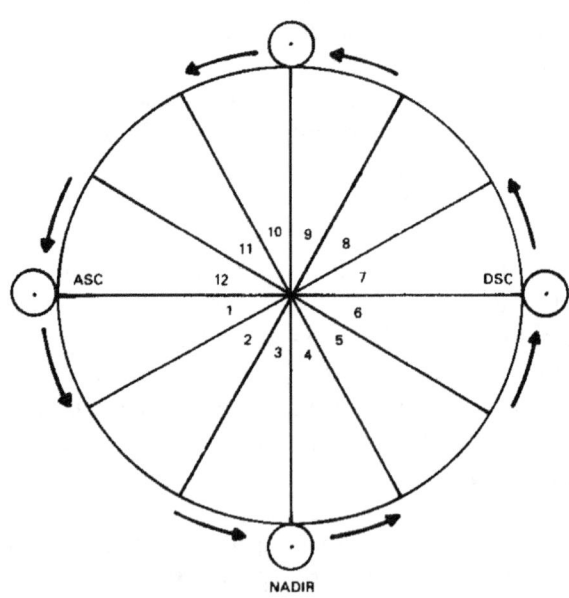

Example 2

date but we also have the effect in the Leo portion of the house when the Sun is moving downward towards the Nadir, which is the cusp of the fourth house. The Midheaven is always the cusp of the tenth house.

So the low points in this pattern would mainly be in February through Aquarius and in August when it drops down, with a peak at the Midheaven which would be in April under the sign of Aries.

The six-month cycle tends to extend from the Aquarius portion to the Leo portion and, again, from the Leo point to the February point prices tend to follow the volume curves from these aspects, with the weaknesses in the February-March, July-August and October-November periods. Therefore, in judging the stock market as to whether it will turn up or down, it is best to look at the Sun and the aspects pertaining to the Sun. If the Sun is under heavy affliction, these periods represent a bearish market. In good aspect, it will be bullish. In the good periods moving upward toward the Midheaven, it will be higher than normal. Moving toward the lower section, it will be lower than normal. This is why there will be so many depressions, recessions, panic and fear in the stock exchange in the latter part of the year as October approaches.

The Sun's aspect and influence on the market will also affect a lot of stocks because individual stocks are affected by the movement of the Dow-Jones Industrials. You have to relate a 50 percent mark-up on a bullish market and take away 50 percent of an individual stock if the market is bearish. You can only give a stock 25 percent on its own merit. This means if the market is bad and the stock shows an indication of moving up, the price ratio as far as at what price to sell should be at a 25 percent profit. There are other indications, though, at which you could go for a 50 percent profit if the earnings are extremely high. A lot of gold and silver stocks will generally do the opposite in a bad market, and go all the way up. But if the market is bad and the Sun cycle is moving into that low period, you want to go short, or short at 50 percent from its point at that degree at that time, when the market shows indications of falling backwards. The Sun is a minor influence in relation to the overall picture of the market; however, it affects the market every year and there will be a pattern to each period of the year as far as the Sun's transit through that sign. This will also relate to individual stocks, which will show the same pattern. So do your homework. Any time you select a stock, find the month in which to buy it and the month in which to sell . . . the month in which it is usually at its highest point. You can relate this to the Moon for its exact day for buying or selling.

The market is always influenced by the Sun pattern and it will happen year after year. From January to the last two weeks in July, market prices will trend upwards, and in the latter part of the year after the influence of Leo, the market will be down in price. This is the average trend that will always occur and it affects volume as well as prices. However, it is important to realize the influence of the Sun in the chart of the New York Stock Exchange, and the Sun's complete cycle. Also, any corporation will be affected by certain cycles of the Sun through these signs. It is important to backtrack about 12 years during the pattern of the Sun's cycle in order to see the pattern on which the company is being activated as far as the solar cycle.

The period of the Sun in Aries is usually from March 20 through April 19; Taurus, April 20 through May 20; Gemini, May 21 through June 20; Cancer, June 21 through July 22; Leo, July 23 through August 22; Virgo, August 23 through September 22; Libra, September 23 through October 22; Scorpio, October 23 through November 21; Sagittarius, November 22 through December 21; Capricorn, December 22 through January 19; Aquarius, January 20 through February 15; and Pisces, February 19 through March 20. These are the twelve signs with the transit of the Sun.

Again, let me stress the importance of the aspect of the Sun during these periods. If it involves a combination that relates to panic, crashes, recession or depression, then these months will be more intensified as far as the effect. If the transit is in a trine or a good aspect then the movement will be less severe than under normal conditions.

There is one more important point to the solar cycle which is really the result of another cycle. This is the 19-year cycle of the motion of the plane of the Moon's orbit. It is the solar eclipse cycle. Although there is partial or total eclipse each year, usually there will be an eclipse near the same degree of the zodiac once every 19 years. This is a major eclipse. This major eclipse does have an effect on changes within the stock market and these changes have been reflected year after year during these cycles. Since this eclipse involves the Moon, it represents changes in relation from a Moon-Sun characteristic.

In this cycle the Sun makes a complete circuit of the sky and reaches the same Node at the same place on the ecliptic as shown in diagram 3. This length of time is 6585.321 solar days, which is 18 years, 11.33 days. The shortest time required for the Sun to travel from and return to the same node is 346.6 solar days, an interval known as an eclipse year. It is listed on the calendar year because of the effect of the session which is known as a slow regression of the nodes around the ecliptic. Nineteen of the eclipse years contain 6585.4 days, which is precisely 223 synodic months. This is when the Nodes themselves become important in the predictions on the stock market.

The Moon affects changes and emotions. The daily influence on the stock market is related to changes of the Moon as it transits through each sign. Its effect on individual corporations would be the same.

The Moon works in association with the planet Saturn. The Moon's phase cycle is from 28 to 29.5 days. Saturn's cycle is 28 to 29.5 years. So, where it takes Saturn 2.5 years to transit one

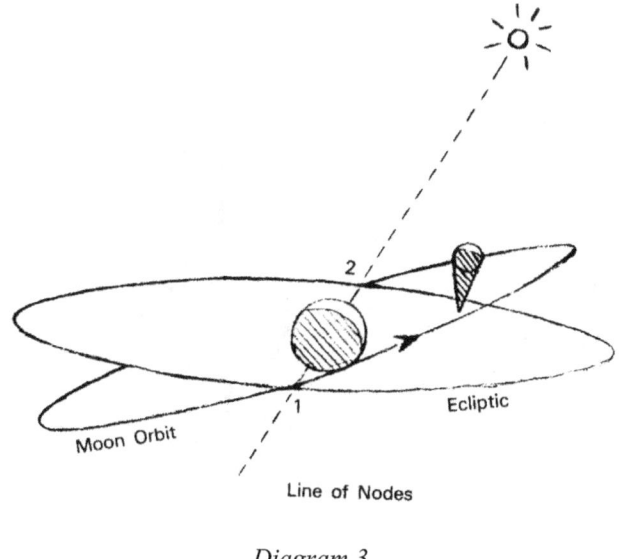

Diagram 3

sign, it takes the Moon 2.5 days. If the Moon shows weakness in one sign as to where a stock would drop rapidly during that time, then when Saturn is also in the sign this would cause a 2.5 year downtrend for the stock. For example, if the Moon goes into Taurus and the stock goes up or down, it will do the same when Saturn is in that sign. So even though a lot of aspects related to the Moon are minor, such as a stock might drop one-eighth to one-half, during its transit through any one sign, it does relate to a longer trend with the effects of Saturn.

In judging the daily influence of the Moon's dominance over a certain stock, bear in mind the influence of a transit of the Sun. If the Sun's movement shows a high point for the Dow-Jones averages, then the Moon as a negative factor on the Dow-Jones will not have that much influence. If they are both at a high point, then the stock would rise extremely high on that day. So use the Moon as a daily indicator together with the 30-day movement of the Sun in each sign.

There are three cycles related to the Moon. One is called a Moon return. This cycle occurs every four years, when the Moon returns to the same position. (Check the four-year cycles day by day of a stock.) Another cycle is 27.5 days by the sign itself and 28 or 29.5 days by phase. These are the cycles represented by the Moon. The pattern of the four-year cycle is more dominant in a long-term trend relating to the stock market. The Moon also has a period in which it is stagnant, or void of course. It is a period when the Moon is changing from one sign to another without being aspected. From research this is not a period to purchase stock as it represents changes indicating a complete reverse. It is an unstable period of the Moon.

You can also determine monthly trends by watching the Moon under each cycle. In a period of 28-29.5 days, if the Moon falls square, conjunction, or opposite to planets passing over the Midheaven, this will give you an indication of good or bad returns following the week in relation to the stock market itself. It generally relates to people's emotions. The Moon's Nodes are also prominent indicators as far as the movement around the zodiac. If an individual stock has the Moon's North Node going toward the Midheaven, this indicates it will have movement. If it

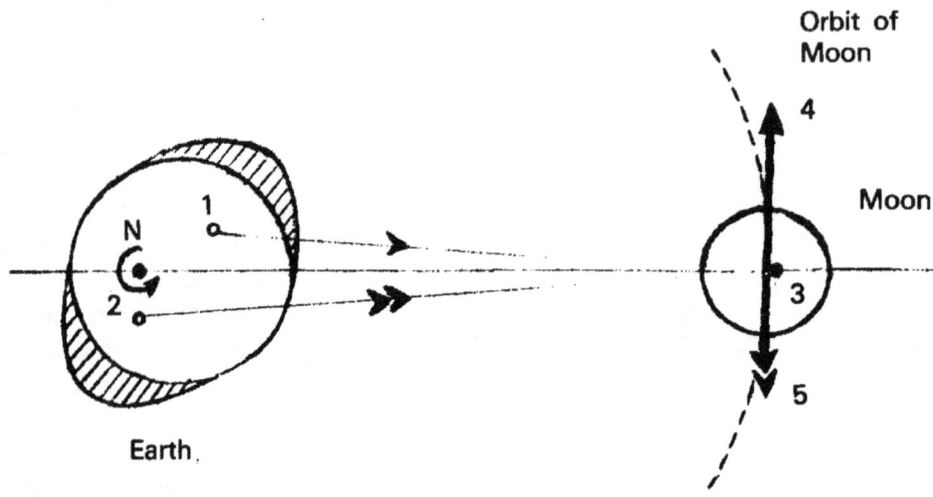

Plan View

Diagram 4

falls below the Ascendant, this generally causes it to move downwards. However, again, you have to use the other planetary movements to make a complete judgment. You cannot do it by the Nodes themselves, but the Nodes would reinforce any conditions shown as a downtrend in a certain stock.

The Moon and Sun in relation to each other show a type of speed that a certain cycle is indicated to move under because the effects of the Sun, the Moon and Earth are the prominent factors relating to the movement during the year. The other planets more or less determine long-term trends. The

The speed of the Moon is affected by the tidal deformation of the Earth which produces a gradual increase on the Moon's orbital speed which in turn makes the Moon slowly recede, causing a fast or a slow Moon which does reflect the aspects as far as movement of a cycle. If it's fast, there's a lot of action in the market, or if it's slow, then a change is predicted. In Diagram 4 we have a plain view of the Moon's orbit. We show that the Earth-Moon gravitational inter-reaction generates two bulges, more or less like a plastic bubble. The Earth has an axial rotation which is faster than the orbital rotation of the Moon, and the effect of this frictional drag is that the bulges are carried around the Earth's rotation until a balance is established between the drag and the tide generating force.

In diagram 4 we have equilibrium point 1. This is nearer to the Moon than point 2, and is therefore experiencing a stronger gravitational attraction than 2. Both 1 and 2 are displaced from the central line so that the forces along with 1 and 3 and 2 and 3 converge toward the center of the Moon. These two forces may be resolved at the Moon into components that act, in one case, along the central line toward the Earth; and in the other case at right angle into the direction of the Moon's orbit. The components acting toward the century add together, whereas the components in direction of the orbit are in opposition. Because the force along 1 and 3 is larger than along 2 and 3, this means a net unbalance force acting on the Moon in the orbital direction, which has the effect of accelerating its motion, moving it into an orbit of a larger radius; modern estimates indicate a recessional speed of about 3.2 cm. per year.

For accurate calculation, there are many Moon sign books and Moon calendars, that will give you the transit of the Moon each day, which you can relate to stock predictions.

In the speed of a stock, we have the one-half cycle, the one-fourth, and the three-fourths, all of which indicate changes in relation to the up and down cycle price of each stock.

Venus is a stabilizing planet. It means harmony and it maintains balance. It has no effect on the market going to extremes one way or another. It seems to ride along with the other planets. Now, things connected with cosmetics, beauty, etc. it does affect, especially if Venus is transiting the sign of Libra since Libra rules this type of product. One thing I've found is that when Venus crosses the Midheaven of the stock exchange, it gives favorable results.

Venus has a cycle of eight years. It relates to changes in stock prices relating to changes in hair styles, clothing, fashions, music and other things in this area, which is a more prominent aspect in individual stocks relating to these areas than the Dow-Jones average itself.

Mercury has a return cycle of 10 years. It affects the market as Mercury is a planet of the mind. It represents all things connected with communications. The effects of Mercury have been prominent through the ages with regard to the stock market itself. The Dow-Jones average was established in 1885 on the basis of 20 stocks then traded on the New York Stock Exchange. This began a trend in relation to the planet Mercury. Every 10 years a Mercury return influence would be represented. This would be positive, for the establishment of the Dow-Jones average this was a period which showed promise and growth, in a 10-year cycle from birth. The next 10-year period would be 1985, the next period after that would be 1995, and almost any year ending with a five would be affected by this motion. The Dow-Jones has never closed down in a year ending in a five. Every year it has been mixed, other than the 10-year cycle period from birth. In the area of the Dow-Jones rail performances, the same thing. In a year ending in five, it has never closed down; it has always closed up.

So as a trend from Mercury the 10-year cycle will always be prominent. Since the beginning there has been no trend as far as the breaking point.

In tracing the other influence of Mercury on the Dow-Jones or individual stocks you will see the same pattern at its 10-year return to the same position. The pattern is there for you in relation to the Sun, the Moon, Venus and Mercury. You have so far these four planets as combinations to give you trends of events of individual stocks as well as the Dow-Jones averages.

When Mercury is in retrograde motion it affects all forms of business being transacted during that period. It is usually an unfavorable period as far as buying stocks, signing papers, or involvement in anything of a business nature. Retrograde motion means that the movement of events will go backward. Therefore, when you purchase a stock at that time, it will not go the way you want it to; it will do the opposite. The planet Mercury does not actually move backward; it just appears that way because of the orbit. Let me stress that retrograde Mercury periods are not periods to purchase stock. They do represent changes on the stock market itself. Many times you can go back in history and check the pattern of a certain stock when Mercury was retrograde to see the full effect on that stock. Mercury retrograde periods are listed in astrological calendars and ephemerides of the planets.

When Mercury is retrograde it represents confusion, indecision. This does not mean that in these periods the stocks would fall. Sometimes you can have highs in these periods, but there will be nothing stable and it will be changeable. Even when th Moon, Sun and other favorable planets are transiting at this time, it still relates to pull-back. It is best to use caution during Mercury retrograde periods. And remember, in any year ending in five, you can almost be assured that Mercury's return will end the year on a high note. The following is a research report from the Foundation for the Study of Cycles.

Stock Prices, Mercury and Space

The late Edward Dewey of the Foundation for the Study of Cycles, reported in the December 1969 issue of Cycles his findings on stock prices and Mercury. The following is that report. Copyright 1969 by the Foundation for the Study of Cycles, Inc.

In a recent article I told you that since 1897 there has been a correspondence between stock price movements and the times of conjunctions and oppositions of certain planets (the ones nearest the Sun) *when these conjunctions and oppositions took place in a certain. direction in space.* I promised to give you the back-up to substantiate this statement. This article will provide this back-up (and some supplemental figures) for Mercury.

You will remember that we are talking about conjunctions and oppositions as seen from the earth. You will also remember that a conjunction of a planet and the Sun occurs when the planet and the Sun are in the same part of the sky (celestial longitude). As Mercury's orbit is smaller than the orbit of the earth, there are two conjunctions with the Sun for each orbit: one when Mercury passes between the earth and the Sun, the second when it passes beyond the Sun. The first kind is called *Inferior Conjunction* and is the time when Mercury changes from evening star to morning star. The second kind of conjunction is called a *Superior Conjunction* and is the time when Mercury changes from morning star to evening star.

Oppositions of a planet and the Sun occur when the planet is on the opposite side of the earth from the Sun. Obviously, as Mercury is always between us and the Sun, there are no oppositions of Mercury and the Sun.

In the former article I reported upon the comparison of stock prices and the superior and inferior conjunctions of Mercury from 1943 through 1961. Since that time we have carried the computations back to January 1, 1897, the beginning of the Dow-Jones index of daily industrial stock prices, and forward through June 30, 1968. These additional computations and tabulations give us nearly four times as many data points as we had previously. These in turn give us a greatly increased probability that the observed behavior cannot be the result of chance. Moreover, the continuation of a *particular predetermined* behavior over an additional 54 years is quite impossible (in the popular as against the scientific use of the term) as a matter of mere happenstance.

I should explain why the comparison ends in June of 1968.

Stock prices are available (at present writing) through September of 1969 and dates of conjunctions are available through 1970. However, the stock prices are adjusted for trend, and the trend for 1968-1969 cannot be known until we have stock prices for all of 1969. It is this fact that makes the stock price, planet, and space comparisons end at June 30, 1968.

During the entire 73 years Mercury and the Sun had 223 superior conjunctions, 224 inferior conjunctions—a total of 447 in all—for which we have stock price comparisons. Table 1 shows the distribution of all of these conjunctions among the twelve 30° segments of the ecliptic.

Table 1

The number of Conjunctions (Superior Conjunctions and Inferior Conjunctions Combined) of Mercury and the Sun, January 1, 1897-June 30, 1968 by Segments of the Ecliptic and by Celestial Longitude; Together with the Number of Associated Advances and Declines of Stock Prices (adjusted for trend) Compared to 30 days Previous; and the Percentages that the Advances are of the Total Number of Advances and Declines (excludes three conjunctions during 1914-15 for which no corresponding stock price figures are available).

Segment	Degrees of Longitude	Number of Advances of Stock Prices	Number of Declines of Stock Prices	Number of Advances and Declines	Total Percentages that Advances Are of Total
1	0- 29.9	15	23	38	39
2	30- 59.9	25	13	38	66
3	60- 89.9	21	17	38	55
4	90-119.9	21	18	39	54
5	120-149.9	26	14	40	65
6	150-179.9	19	18	37	51
7	180-209.9	21	17	118	55
8	210-239.9	15	20	35	43
9	240-269.9	13	22	35	37
10	270-299.9	29	6	35	83
11	300-329.9	14	21	35	40
12	330-359.9	18	21	39	46
Total	0-359.9	237	210	447	53

Table 2

The Number of Superior Conjunctions of Mercury and the Sun January 1, 1897 - June 30, 1968 by Segments of the Ecliptic and by Longitude; Together with the Number of Associated Advances and Declines of Stock Prices (adjusted for trend) Compared to 30 days Previous; and the Percentages that the Advances are of the Total Number of Advances and Declines (excludes 2 conjunctions during 1914-15 for which no corresponding stock pile figures are available).

Segment	Degrees of Longitude	Number of Advances of Stock Prices	Number of Declines of Stock Prices	Total Number of Advances and Declines	Percentages that Advances Are of Total
1	0- 29.9	8	11	19	42
2	30- 59.9	16	5	21	76
3	60- 89.9	13	9	22	59
4	90-119.9	14	8	22	64
5	120-149.9	14	6	20	70
6	150-179.9	8	10	18	44
7	180-209.9	12	7	19	63
8	210-239.9	4	12	16	25
9	240-269.9	5	9	14	36
10	270-299.9	13	2	15	87
11	300-329.9	4	13	17	24
12	330-359.9	13	7	20	65
Total	0-359.9	124	99	223	56

Table 3

The Number of Inferior Conjunctions of Mercury and the Sun January 1, 1897 - June 30, 1968 by Segments of the Ecliptic and by Longitude; Together with the Number of Associated Advances and Declines of Stock Prices (adjusted for trend) Compared to 30 days Previous; and the Percentages that the Advances are of the Total Number of Advances and Declines (excludes a conjunction during 1914 for which no corresponding stock price figures are available).

Segment	Degrees of Longitude	Number of Advances of Stock Prices	Number of Declines of Stock Prices	Total Number of Advances and Declines	Percentages that Advances Are of Total
1	0- 29.9	7	12	19	37
2	30- 59.9	9	8	17	53
3	60- 89.9	8	8	16	50
4	90-119.9	7	10	17	41
5	120-149.9	12	8	20	60
6	150-179.9	11	8	19	58
7	180-209.9	9	10	19	37
8	210-239.9	11	8	19	58
9	240-269.9	8	13	21	38
10	270-299.9	16	4	20	80
11	300-329.9	10	8	18	56
12	330-359.9	5	14	19	26
Total	0-359.9	113	111	224	50

Table 1 also shows, for each segment, the number of instances where there was a stock price advance compared to 30 days previous, the number of instances of similar decline, and the percentages that the advantages are of the total. Tables 2 and 3 give the same information for Superior conjunctions and inferior conjunctions separately.

The values given in Tables 1, 2 and 3 are charted in Figure 1. The peaks of all three curves at the tenth segment are visible by inspection.

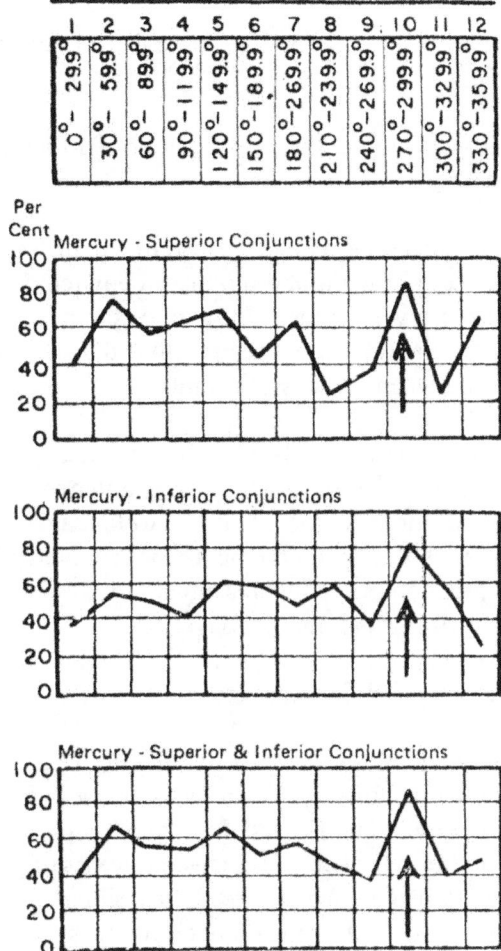

Figure 1. Percentages that stock price advances are of total stock price advances and declines from 30 days prior to each conjunction of Mercury and the Sun to the day of such conjunction by 30o segments of the ecliptic, February 1, 1897-June 30, 1968

Mercury is the smallest of the planets, being only half gain bigger (in diameter) than the Moon. It goes around the in a little less than 88 days (87.9686 days, relative to the stars).

The days. and hours when Mercury and the Sun are in superior conjunction and the corresponding stock prices on that day and 30 days previous are shown in Table 4. The same information for inferior conjunctions is given in Table 5. It is tables that provide the information from which Tables 1, 2 and 3 are constructed.

There seems to be no question but that the concentration of advances in the tenth segment cannot reasonably be the result of chance. This, however, is a far cry from proving a cause and effect relationship among the elements involved. I think that all we can say at this juncture is that the observations reported upon here should—nay MUST—be investigated further. This we propose to do.

Explanation of Tables 4 and 5

Referring now to Tables 4 and 5, these tables differ only in that Table 4 refers to superior conjunctions, Table 5 to inferior conjunctions.

In both tables the first columns called A, give year, the day, and the hour of all the various conjunctions of Mercury and the Sun, 1897-1970.

The next column, labeled B, gives the "stock market day." Because of the difference of time zones, the New York Stock exchange does not close until 8:00 p.m, Greenwich, England time. The nearest times to this are 8:00 a.m, of the given day to 8:00 a.m. of the next day. This, in terms of Greenwich Civil Time, is the stock market day and determines the stock prices to be used to compare with conjunctions falling between these two instants.

A slight complication enters the picture in that up through 1924 the hours of conjunctions were given in hours after Greenwich noon (12h). From 1925 forward they are given in hours after 0h, for Greenwich Civil time, which is of course 12 hours earlier. Thus, up to January 1, 1929 a conjunction on January 14, 22 hours, would be 10:00 a.m, on the next day or January 15, in stock market days. After January 1, 1925, a conjunction occurring at January 14, 22 hours would occur at 10:00 p.m. the same day, or January 14, in stock market days.

Column B thus shows the day for which stock price figures were recorded.

Column C gives the longitude in degrees, minutes and seconds of Mercury and the Sun when they are in conjunction. This value is obtained as follows: From the *American Ephemeris and Nautical Almanac* we read the time of the conjunction in years, days, and hours. From the same source we read the Sun's longitude at 0h for the day involved (mean equinox as of the beginning of the year during which the conjunction took place). We also read the seconds involved to the next ensuing day. These, divided by 24 and multiplied by the number of hours to the time of the conjunctions give a correction factor which is added to the Sun's longitude to give the correct longitude at time of conjunction.

Column D gives the segment (I to 12) in which the degrees listed in Column C fall.

Column E gives Dow-Jones closing prices on the day of the conjunction and on the day 30 days prior to the day of the conjunction and on the day of the conjunction. When these days fell on days when the stock exchange was closed, an interpolated value was Used. Such days are indicated by an asterisk (*).

Column F gives the price increase or decrease for the 30-day interval.

Column G gives the trend for the span of time involved between 30 days prior to the conjunction and the date of the conjunction itself.

Trend was determined as follows: Average prices were obtained for each year. The absolute changes up or down from one year to the next were then computed. and one-twelfth of these values were obtained. These values were considered as the monthly trend of stock prices from July I of one year through June 30 of the next year, except that stock movements ending in July of any year were treated as follows:

Let us suppose an adjustment for July of 1908. If the conjunction or opposition took place in the first quarter of July 1908, the 1907-1908 correction factor was used, because the bulk of the change from 30 days previous took place during the span of time mid-year 1907 to mid-year 1908. If the contact (conjunction or opposition) took place in the second or third quarter of July 1908, an average of the correction factors for 1907-08 and 1908-09 was used. If the contact took place in the fourth quarter of July 1908, the correction factor for 1908-09 was used.

Column H gives the detrended values.

Column I shows the percentages by which the detrended values advanced or declined in the 30-day period. That is, if this column has no sign, it means that prices went up more than trend went up, or did not go down as much as the trend went down; a "-" sign shows the reverse.

1. Dewey, E.R. "Stock Prices and Space," *Cycles,* Vol. XX, No. 10, October 1969.

Footnotes to Tables 4 and 5:
1897-1924, hours based on Greenwich noon
1925-1959, hours based on 0h Universal Time under various names (Greenwich Civil Time, etc.) 1960-1970, Hours based on 0h Ephemeris Time
* * Stock Market Day (see text for explanation)
* * * Longitude from mean equinox of 0.0o of the year indicated.
*Market Closed. Value interpolated

Table 4: Relationships Between Stock Price Movements and Superior Conjunctions of Mercury and the Sun

A			B	C			D	E		F	G	H	I
								Stock Prices				De-	Percent
Time of Superior			Stock	Longitude at						Advance		Trended	of In-
Conjunctions			Market	Time of Superior			Seg-	13	on	or	Trend	Advance	crease
			Day**	Conjunctions***			ment	Days	the	Decline		or	or De-
								Prior	Day			Decline	crease
Year	Day	Hour		°	′	″							
1897	Apr 1	10		12	26	18.6	1	41.88	39.77	-2.11	.17	-2.28	-5.44
	Jul 13	5		113	23	36.10	4	42.80	45.25	2.47	.28	2.19	5.12
	Nov 7	23		225	52	59.12	8	51.64*	45.99	-5.65	.39	-6.04	-11.70
1898	Mar 15	12	Mar 16	355	54	7.17	12	49.49	45.58	-3.91	.39	-4.30	-8.69
	Jun 19	14		98	15	56.82	4	52.54	52.79	.25	.39	-.14	-.27
	Oct 18	22	Oct 19	206	3	30.32	7	57.61	51.56	-6.05	1.12	-7.17	-12.45
1899	Feb 26	22	Feb 27	338	37	57.00	12	64.87	66.98	2.11	1.12	.99	1.53
	Jun 14	2		83	15	21.50	3	69.77	71.92	2.15	1.12	1.03	1.48
	Sep 30	12		187	35	37.98	7	75.66	*71.91	-3.75	-.59	-3.16	-4.18
1900	Feb 9	3		320	27	20.38	11	64.14	66.86	2.72	-.59	3.31	5.16
	May 29	14		68	11	45.54	3	*61.56	58.01	3.55	-.59	-2.96	-4.81
	Sep 13	0		170	13	17.6	6	58.77	58.20	-.57	.48	-1.05	1.79
1901	Jan 21	9		301	10	54.22	11	70.03	64.92	-5.11	.48	-5.59	-7.98
	May 14	0		52	58	49.3	2	*74.50	69.59	-4.91	.48	-5.39	-7.23
	Aug 27	4		153	39	33.76	6	*72.82	72.81	-.01	-.24	.23	.32
1902	Jan 1	13		280	43	16.03	10	*66.39	*67.21	.82	-.24	1.06	1.60
	Apr 28	7		37	32	41.84	2	*67.20	67.31	.11	-.24	.35	.52
	Aug 10	21	Aug 11	137	44	55.72	5	64.45	66.19	1.74	-.40	2.14	3.32
	Dec 11	19		259	20	16.93	9	60.96	59.97	-.99	-.56	-.43	-.71
1903	Apr 12	10		21	49	9.30	1	64.11	61.17	-2.94	-.56	-2.38	-3.71
	Jul 25	23	Jul 26	122	16	33.45	5	57.27	*49.59	-7.28	.10	-7.58	-13.24
	Nov 20	21	Nov 21	237	53	4.23	8	44.77	44.15	-.62	-.10	-.52	-1.16
1904	Mar 26	4		5	34	53.50	1	47.47	48.21	.74	-.10	.84	1.77
	Jul 9	6		107	3	2.80	4	48.66	50.84	2.18	.72	1.46	3.00
	Oct 30	17		217	21	20.14	8	57.59	*63.79	6.20	1.53	4.67	8.11
1905	Mar 9	11		348	43	27.99	12	72.63	77.36	4.73	1.53	3.20	4.41
	Jun 23	16		91	57	30.66	4	73.75	75.78	2.03	1.53	.50	.68
	Oct 11	15		198	7	23.25	7	79.06	80.83	1.77	.90	.87	1.10
1906	Feb 20	4		331	7	46.28	12	*102.55	97.07	-5.48	.90	-6.38	-6.22
	Jun 8	4		76	55	30.86	3	92.87	94.50	1.63	.90	.73	.70
	Sep 23	15		180	9	31.00	7	96.07	*95.71	-.36	-1.11	.75	.78
1907	Feb 2	0		312	30	50.0	11	94.35	90.48	-3.87	-1.11	-2.76	-2.93
	May 23	15		61	48	18.85	3	84.63	79.04	-5.59	-1.11	-4.48	-5.59
	Sep 6	11		163	10	58.50	6	74.91	73.89	-1.02	-.08	-.94	-1.25
1908	Jan 13	18		292	41	26.62	10	57.33	64.98	7.65	-.08	7.73	13.48
	May 7	1		46	33	7.88	2	67.48	70.91	3.43	-.08	3.51	5.20
	Aug 19	22	Aug 20	146	57	17.54	5	78.62	82.57	3.95	1.06	2.89	3.68
	Dec 23	11		271	45	56.39	10	86.17	85.48	-.69	1.06	-1.75	-2.03

A			B	C			D	E		F	G	H	I
Time of Superior Conjunctions			Stock Market Day**	Longitude at Time of Superior Conjunctions***			Seg-ment	Stock Prices		Advance or Decline	Trend	De-Trended Advance or Decline	Percent of In-crease or De-crease
								13 Days Prior	on the Day				
Year	Day	Hour		°	′	″							
1909	Apr 21	6		30	58	58.22	2	83.28	87.65	4.37	1.06	3.31	3.97
	Aug 3	19		146	36	10.76	5	*93.14	98.14	5.00	.42	5.42	5.82
	Dec 2	13		250	14	35.19	9	*99.84	96.66	-3.18	-.42	-2.76	-2.76
1910	Apr 5	6		15	4	18.9	1	*93.67	90.96	-2.71	-.42	-2.29	-2.44
	Jul 18	23	Jul 19	115	52	52.4	4	84.76	81.22	-3.54	-.30	-3.24	-3.82
	Nov 11	21	Nov 12	229	6	54.57	8	84.06	83.55	-.51	-.19	-.32	-.38
1911	Mar 19	20	Mar 20	358	36	11.30	12	85.30	84.13	-1.17	-.19	-.98	-1.15
	Jul 3	8		100	45	9.50	4	86.18	85.64	-.54	-.19	-.35	-.41
	Oct 23	4		209	8	4.74	7	73.62	77.77	4.15	.36	3.79	5.15
1912	Mar 1	21	Mar 2	341	26	41.60	12	80.19	81.96	1.77	.36	-.05	-.06
	Jun 16	19		85	41	58.15	3	89.35	*89.66	.31	.36	-.05	-.06
	Oct 3	13		190	26	9.01	7	90.62	94.12	3.50	-.54	4.04	4.46
1913	Feb 12	6		323	27	22.70	11	85.96	81.76	-4.20	-.54	-3.66	-4.26
	Jun 1	6		70	36	26.34	3	79.34	77.55	-1.79	-.54	-1.25	-1.58
	Sep 15	22	Sep 16	172	55	28.22	6	79.85	82.38	2.53	.00	2.53	3.17
1914	Jan 24	15		304	19	17.80	11	*78.60	82.18	3.58	.00	3.58	4.55
	May 16	17		55	26	55.44	2	79.90	80.82	.92	.00	.92	1.15
	Aug 30	1		156	18	13.05	6	War	War				
1915	Jan 4	23	Jan 5	284	2	34.18	10	War	55.44				
	May 1	1		40	4	41.30	2	61.05	71.51	10.46	1.36	9.10	14.91
	Aug 13	17		140	19	58.66	5	70.80	78.38	7.58	1.78	5.80	8.19
	Dec 15	7		262	44	31.90	9	95.05	98.18	3.13	1.78	1.35	.42
1916	Apr 14	9		24	34	33.31	1	95.76	91.63	-4.13	1.78	-5.91	-6.17
	Jul 27	22	Jul 28	124	58	7.42	5	88.29	88.35	.07	-.64	.71	.80
	Nov 23	14		241	28	56.50	9	105.15	107.48	2.33	-.64	2.97	2.82
1917	Mar 29	5		8	26	26.55	1	92.68	96.75	4.07	-.64	4.71	5.08
	Jul 12	4		109	41	57.54	4	97.52	93.64	-3.88	-.60	-3.28	-3.36
	Nov 3	6		220	45	27.38	8	80.62	72.32	-8.30	-.57	-7.73	-9.59
1918	Mar 12	14		351	41	41.90	12	78.92	78.67	-.25	-.57	.32	.41
	Jun 26	14		94	36	51.40	4	78.65	82.03	4.37	-.57	4.94	6.28
	Oct 15	0		201	19	45.2	7	81.49	86.21	4.72	1.56	3.16	3.88
1919	Feb 23	9		334	12	37.34	12	81.75	*84.48	2.73	1.56	1.17	1.43
	Jun 11	2		79	35	19.54	3	98.53	105.16	6.63	1.56	5.07	5.15
	Sep 26	20	Sep 27	183	10	5.90	7	103.01	110.06	7.05	-.81	7.86	7.63
1920	Feb 5	8		315	44	48.70	11	107.36	95.50	-11.86	-.81	-11.05	-10.29
	May 2S	14		64	30	52.60	3	96.48	90.24	-6.24	-.81	-5.43	-5.63
	Sep 8	14		166	12	16.92	6	94.43	87.13	-7.30	-1.39	-5.91	6.26
1921	Jan 16	7		296	9	.15	10	70.26	75.18	4.92	-1.39	6.31	8.98
	May 9	23	May 10	49	14	5.13	2	75.73	78.81	3.08	-1.39	4.47	5.90
	Aug 22	22	Aug 23	149	42	50.08	5	65.36	69.23	3.87	1.65	2.22	3.40
	Dec 27	4		275	23	35.08	10	77.93	80.69	2.76	1.65	1.11	1.42

18/THE KEY TO SPECULATION ON THE NEW YORK STOCK EXCHANGE

A			B	C			D	E Stock Prices		F	G	H	I
Time of Superior Conjunctions			Stock Market Day**	Longitude at Time of Superior Conjunctions***			Seg-ment	13 Days Prior	on the Day	Advance or Decline	Trend	De-Trended Advance or Decline	Percent of In-crease or De-crease
Year	Day	Hour		°	′	″							
1922	Apr 24	6		33	45	48.16	2	87.08	93.00	5.92	1.65	4.27	4.90
	Aug 6	18		133	56	32.94	5	94.63	*97.20	2.57	.15	2.42	2.56
	Dec 6	6		253	51	20.16	9	98.45	96.75	-1.70	.15	1.85	1.88
1923	Apr 8	6		17	52	58.24	1	104.48	*102.34	-2.14	.15	-2.29	-2.19
	Jul 21	22	Jul 22	118	34	23.14	4	93.55	*91.49	-2.06	.27	-2.33	-2.49
	Nov 15	12		232	36	32.40	8	86.91	90.87	3.96	.40	3.56	4.10
1924	Mar 21	22	Mar 22	1	31	15.80	1	97.40	95.72	-1.68	.40	-2.08	-2.14
	Jul 5	6		103	23	48;98	4	90.41	96.43	6.02	.40	5.62	6.22
	Oct 25	15		212	25	35.65	8	104.13	102.04	-2.09	2.90	-4.99	-4.79
1925	Mar 5	13		344	27	48.57	12	120.08	124.81	4.73	2.90	-1.83	1.52
	Jun 20	5	Jun 19	88	20	30.50	3	128.68	129.26	.58	2.90	-2.32	-1.80
	Oct 7	8		193	31	58.08	7	*141.01	145.60	4.59	1.55	3.04	2.16
1926	Feb 16	1	Feb 15	326	37	3.29	11	155.23	158.30	3.07	1.55	1.52	.98
	Jun 4	1		73	15	45.92	3	141.49	145.28	3.79	1.55	2.24	1.58
	Sep 19	14		175	52	20.54	6	162.06	*157.06	-5.00	1.91	-6.91	-4.26
1927	Jan 28	14		307	39	55.50	11	157.50	153.86	3.64	1.91	-5.55	-3.52
	May 20	3	May 19	58	7	.16	2	165.93	170.29	4.36	1.91	2.45	1.48
	Sep 2	15		159	8	35.25	6	183.56	192.83	9.27	4.19	5.08	2.77
1928	Jan 9	1	Jan 8	287	31	49.52	10	196.19	*200.80	4.61	4.91	.42	.21
	Aug 16	5	Aug 15	143	4	6.65	5	205.10	219.40	14.30	7.09	7.21	3.52
	Dec 18	13		266	23	45.99	9	*278.13	275.42	-2.71	7.09	-9.80	-3.52
1929	Apr 17	16		27	9	3.30	1	317.59	309.91	-8.68	7.09	-14.77	4.65
	Jul 31	4	Jul 30	127	27	20.44	5*	334.51	343.12	8.61	-6.24	14.85	4.44
	Nov 27	14		244	51	43.50	9	260.64	238.95	-21.69	-6.24	-15.45	-5.93
1930	Apr 1	13		11	4	44.88	1	*272.18	287.11	14.93	-6.24	21.17	7.78
	Jul 15	10		112	10	56.00	4	*237.15	233.79	-3.36	-7.19	3.83	1.62
	Nov 7	3	Nov 6	223	59	15.97	8	203.62	180.72	-22.90	-8.15	-14.75	-7.24
1931	Mar 16	0	Mar 15	354	26	45.10	12	180.99	*182.19	1.20	-8.15	9.35	5.17
	Jun 29	19		97	3	9.33	4	*137.11	152.67	15.56	-8.15	23.71	17.29
	Oct 18	16		204	18	7.88	7	115.08	*102.87	-12.21	-6.17	-6.04	-5.25
1932	Feb 26	21		337	4	7.87	12	77.82	82.09	4.27	-6.17	-10.44	13.42
	Jun 13	7	Jun 12	82	1	53.59	3	53.46	*48.19	-5.27	-6.17	.90	1.68
	Sep 29	9		185	59	37.26	7	74.30	71.53	-2.77	1.60	4.37	-5.88
1933	Feb 8	0	Feb 3	18	47	38.9	11	*62.53	58.38	4.15	1.60	-5.75	-9.20
	May 28	19		66	57	52.96	3	73.10	*89.82	16.72	1.60	15.12	20.68
	Sep 12	0	Sep 11	168	45	42.5	6	*97.16	103.59	6.43	1.21	5.22	5.37
1934	Jan 20	2	Jan 19	299	20	5.3	10	100.69	105.60	4.91	1.21	3.70	3.67
	May 13	5	May 12	51	44	38.10	2	104.80	92.22	-12.58	1.21	-13.79	-13.16
	Aug 26	6	Aug 25	152	18	4.38	6	85.51	95.71	10.20	1.81	8.39	9.81
	Dec 31	2	Dec 30	278	41	52.22	10	102.94	*104.39	1.45	1.81	-.36	.35

A			B	C			D	E		F	G	H	I
								Stock Prices				De-	Percent
Time of Superior Conjunctions			Stock Market Day**	Longitude at Time of Superior Conjunctions***			Seg-ment	13 Days Prior	on the Day	Advance or Decline	Trend	Trended Advance or Decline	of In-crease or De-crease
Year	Day	Hour		°	′	″							
1935	Apr 27	12		36	17	38.84	2	100.59	109.68	9.09	1.81	7.28	7.24
	Aug 10	1	Aug 9	136	28	41.74	5	122.69	127.27	4.58	3.52	1.06	.86
	Dec 10	7	Dec 9	257	17	2.40	9	144.36	144.10	-.26	3.52	-3.78	-2.62
1936	Apr 10	13		20	28	36.63	1	156.85	160.37	3.52	3.52	.00	.00
	Jul 24	3	Jul 23	121	0	55.34	5	158.94	164.61	5.67	1.93	3.74	2.35
	Nov 18	11		235	55	49.51	8	177.42	184.44	7.02	.34	6.68	3.77
1937	Mar 25	6	Mar 24	4	10	47.08	1	*187.46	184.32	-3.14	.34	-3.48	-1.86
	Jul 8	11		105	50	13.86	4	174.33	177.70	3.37	-1.28	4.65	2.67
	Oct 29	10		215	33	23.50	8	154.70	138.48	-16.22	-2.90	-13.32	-8.61
1938	Mar 8	12		347	16	4.96	12	122.14	125.33	3.19	-2.90	6.09	4.99
	Jun 22	21		90	44	52.21	4	112.35	123.99	11.64	-2.90	14.54	12.94
	Oct 10	11		196	28	19.24	7	138.29	149.55	11.26	.85	10.41	7.53
1939	Feb 19	2	Feb 18	329	31	51.80	11	149.47	145.51	-3.96	.85	4.81	-3.22
	Jun 7	9		75	43	10.35	3	131.67	138.71	7.04	.85	6.19	4.70
	Sep 22	14		178	39	15.52	6	*141.43	148.12	6.69	-.59	7.28	5.15
1940	Jan 31	19		310	46	6.42	11	*150.84	145.33	-5.51	-.59	-4.92	-3.26
	May 21	20		60	32	3.00	3	*147.84	114.13	-33.71	-.59	-33.12	-22.40
	Sep 4	12		161	46	48.90	6	126.44	132.16	5.72	-1.08	6.80	5.38
1941	Jan 11	10		290	49	4.20	10	132.14	133.49	1.35	-1.08	2.43	1.84
	May 6	5	May 5	45	16	35.85	2	124.32	115.84	-8.48	-1.08	-7.40	-5.95
	Aug 19	0	Aug 18	145	36	33.3	5	127.98	125.62	-2.36	-1.22	-1.14	-.89
	Dec 22	0	Dec 21	269	44	57.5	9	117.05	-107.20	-9.85	-1.22	-8.63	7.37
1942	Apr 20	10		29	41	30.40	1	100.82	97.25	-3.57	-1.22	-2.35	2.33
	Aug 2	22		129	56	57.26	5	104.49	105.99	1.50	2.30	-.80	.77
	Dec 1	2	Nov 30	248	14	18.72	9	115.07	114.50	.43	2.30	-1.87	1.64
1943	Apr 4	8		13	41	1.70	1	130.61	*136.02	5.41	2.30	3.11	2.38
	Jul 18	3	Jul 17	114	37	49.60	4	139.85	144.72	4.87	1.51	3.36	2.40
	Nov 10	12		227	13	13.12	8	136.61	132.68	-3.93	.71	-4.64	-3.40
1944	Mar 17	21		357	9	25.00	12	136.04	140.80	4.76	.71	4.05	2.98
	Jul 1	12		99	29	55.52	4	142.14	148.46	6.32	.71	5.61	3.95
	Oct 20	22		207	23	15.86	7	145.85	148.21	2.36	2.21	.15	.10
1945	Feb 28	21		339	55	43.31	12	154.06	160.40	6.34	2.21	4.13	2.68
	Jun 16	0	Jun 15	84	28	54.3	3	164.50	167.64	3.14	2.21	.93	.57
	Oct 2	11		188	52	59.58	7	*174.10	183.85	9.75	1.82	7.93	4.55
1946	Feb 11	2	Feb 10	321	45	27.02	11	200.04	*20 1.72	1.68	1.82	-.14	-.07
	May 31	11		69	23	2.52	3	205.67	212.28	6.61	1.82	4.79	2.33
	Sep 14	22		171	27	53.00	6	202.49	*173.92	-28.57	-1.17	-27.40	-13.53
1947	Jan 23	9		302	31	50.88	11	176.95	175.13	-1.82	-1.17	-.65	-.38
	May 15	22		54	13	10.40	2	166.82	167.88	1.06	-1.17	2.23	1.34
	Aug 29	3	Aug 28	154	56	20.90	6	182.05	177.70	-4.35	.21	-4.56	-2.50

A			B	C			D	E		F	G	H	I
								Stock Prices				De-	Percent
Time of Superior Conjunctions			Stock Market Day**	Longitude at Time of Superior Conjunctions***			Seg-ment	13 Days Prior	on the Day	Advance or Decline	Trend	Trended Advance or Decline	of In-crease or De-crease
Year	Day	Hour		°	′	″							
1948	Jan 3	13		282	4	39.40	10	178.79	*180.54	1.75	.21	1.54	.86
	Apr 29	5	Apr 28	38	43	13.30	2	173.65	181.01	7.36	.21	7.15	4.12
	Aug 11	20		139	1	8.90	5	191.48	179.27	-12.21	.08	-12.29	-6.42
	Dec 12	20		260	45	19.26	9	173.93	*177.41	3.48	-.08	3.56	2.05
1949	Apr 13	8		23	4	4.10	1	176.98	176.81	-.17	-.08	-.09	-.05
	Jul 26	21		123	30	17.46	5	*166.86	176.37	9.51	3.10	6.41	3.84
	Nov 21	22		239	16	.89	8	186.20	192.35	6.15	3.10	3.05	1.64
1950	Mar 28	2	Mar 27	6	50	3.31	1	204.15	209.10	4.95	3.10	1.85	.91
	Jul 11	4	Jul 10	108	17	13.46	4	227.37	208.10	-19.27	3.27	-22.54	-9.91
	Nov 1	17		218	41	49.88	8	228.94	225.69	-3.25	3.44	-6.69	-2.92
1951	Mar 11	10		350	1	33.22	12	254.24	*250.95	-3.29	3.44	-6.73	-2.65
	Jun 25	14		93	11	22.57	4	245.83	245.30	-.53	3.44	-3.97	-1.61
	Oct 13	15		199	27	29.93	7	276.37	275.13	-1.24	1.09	-2.33	-.84
1952	Feb 22	3	Feb 21	332	24	40.21	12	275.40	259.60	-15.80	1.09	-16.89	-6.13
	Jun 9	2	Jun 8	78	8	32.78	3	262.74	*268.78	6.04	1.09	4.95	1.88
	Sep 24	14		181	25	3.86	7	273.57	272.26	-1.31	.43	-1.74	-.64
1953	Feb 2	23		313	47	7.37	11	*292.69	290.03	-2.66	.43	-3.09	-1.06
	May 24	13		63	0	9.0S	3	271.26	*277.70	6.44	.43	6.01	2.22
	Sep 7	09		164	23	16.48	6	275.47	265.15	-10.32	4.83	-15.15	-5.50
1954	Jan 14 8			293	34	29.70	10	279.52	284.49	4.97	4.83	.14	.05
	May 8	23		47	44	14.81	2	307.79	*321.31	13.52	4.83	8.69	2.82
	Aug 21	20		148	8	40.18	5	342.97	*349.47	6.50	9.07	-2.57	-.75
	Dec 25	12		273	5	54.54	10	*386.21	*396.06	9.85	9.07	.78	.20
1955	Apr 23	4	Apr 22	32	9	52.78	2	410.87	425.52	14.65	9.07	5.58	1.36
	Aug 5	17		132	24	51.57	5	467.41	456.40	-11.01	4.19	-15.20	-3.25
	Dec 4	14		251	33	38.17	9	467.35	*485.68	18.33	4.19	14.14	3.03
1956	Apr 6	04	Apr 5	16	14	43.40	1	491.41	516.57	25.16	4.19	20.97	4.27
	Jul 19	21		117	1	58.35	4	484.52	513.86	29.34	1.38	27.96	5;77
	Nov 12	21		230	22	30.28	8*	489.93	487.05	-2.88	-1.44	-1.44	-.29
1957	Mar 20	18		359	45	54.61	12	467.40	473.93	6.53	-1.44	7.97	1.71
	Jul 4	05	Jul 3	101	50	46.38	4	503.76	513.25	9.49	-1.44	10.93	2.17
	Oct 24	3	Oct 24	210	20	.26	8	462.87	436.40	-26.47	1.33	-27.80	-6.01
1958	Mar 3	20		342	37	54.24	12	*451.34	443.38	-7.96	1.33	-9.29	-2.06
	Jun 18	17		86	48	26.89	3	455.98	476.65	20.67	1.33	19.34	4.24
	Oct 5	12		191	37	11.15	7	512.77	*535.44	22.67	11.71	10.96	2.14
1959	Feb 14	05	Feb 13	324	38	5.71	11	591.64	587.97	-3.67	11.71	-15.38	-2.60
	Jun 3	04	Jun 2	71	43	13.90	3	*625.06	637.45	12.39	11.71	.68	.11
	Sep 17	21		174	4	54.84	6	650.79	629.00	-21.79	-1.17	-20.62	-3.17
1960	Jan 26	15		305	40	39.52	11	*670.01	639.84	-30.17	-1.17	-29.00	-4.33
	May 17	15		56	41	24.41	2	*630.61	621.63	-8.98	-1.17	-7.81	-1.24
	Aug 31	00	Aug 30	156	36	44.10	6	*617.48	626.40	8.92	6.13	2.79	.45

A			B	C			D	E Stock Prices		F	G	H	I
Time of Superior Conjunctions			Stock Market Day**	Longitude at Time of Superior Conjunctions***			Segment	13 Days Prior	on the Day	Advance or Decline	Trend	De-Trended Advance or Decline	Percent of Increase or Decrease
Year	Day	Hour		°	′	″							
1961	Jan 5	18		285	11	19.24	10	597.11	622.67	25.56	6.13	19.43	3.25
	May 1	23		41	18	54.82	2	677.11	677.05	-.06	6.13	-6.91	-.91
	Aug 14	15		141	33	58.02	5	688.83	718.93	30.10	-4.32	34.42	5.00
	Dec 16	08		264	7	43.0	9	733.33	*728.84	-4.49	-4.32	-.17	-.02
1962	Apr 16	02	Apr 15	25	36	54.77	1	722.77	*685.34	-37.43	-4.32	-33.11	-4.58
	Jul 29	15		126	0	5.07	5	561.28	*589.30	28.02	6.25	21.77	3.88
	Nov 25	10		242	39	2.03	9	569.02	643.00	73.98	6.25	67.73	11.90
1963	Mar 30	22		9	29	16.34	1	662.94	*683.63	20.69	6.25	14.44	2.18
	Jul 13	22		110	46	34.14	4	721.43	*705.60	-15.83	8.10	-23.93	-3.32
	Nov 5	01	Nov 4	222	52	59.85	8	*744.66	749.22	4.56	9.94	-5.38	-.72
1964	Mar 13	08		352	47	0.03	12	792.16	816.22	24.06	9.94	14.12	1.78
	Jun 27	07	Jun 26	95	38	48.05	4	817.94	830.99	13.05	9.94	3.11	.38
	Oct 15	19		202	26	58.53	7	862.54	868.44	5.90	6.40	-.50	-.06
1965	Feb 24	03	Feb 23	335	18	10.11	12	*895.51	891.96	-3.55	6.40	-9.95	-1.11
	Jun 11	19		80	37	11.05	3	934.17	881.70	-52.47	6.40	-58.87	-6.30
	Sep 27	15		184	17	7.21	7	*895.85	937.88	42.03	-3.11	45.14	5.04
1966	Feb 6	03	Feb 5	316	52	50.66	11	985.46	*987.46	2.00	-3.11	5.11	.52
	May 27	07	May 26	65	32	55.66	3	947.21	891.75	-55.46	-3.11	-52.35	-5.5.3
	Sep 10	07	Sep 9	167	7	22.92	6	838.53	775.55	-62.98	.46	-63.44	-7.57
1967	Jan 18	02	Jan 17	297	17	15.72	10	*801.72	843.65	41.93	.46	41.47	5.17
	May 11	16		50	16	20.76	2	847.66	896.21	48.55	.46	48.09	5.67
	Aug 24	16		150	47	35.63	6	901.19	898.46	-2.83	2.24	-5.07	-.56
	Dec 28	12		276	31	12.98	10	884.88	897.93	12.95	2.24	10.71	1.21
1968	Apr 24	23		34	48	31.19	2	827.27	898.46	71.19	2.24	68.95	8.33
	Aug 7	11		134	58	45.29	5	912.60	*873.65	-38.95			
	Dec 7	03	Dec 6	254	4	17.41	9	949.47	978.24	28.77			
1969	Apr 8	23		18	55	27.23	1	*915.16	923.17	8.01			
	Jul 22	15		119	36	23.98	4						
	Nov 16	08		233	47	22.64	8						
1970	Mar 23	15		2	33	56.56							
	Jul 6	23		104	25	56.94							
	Oct 27	10		213	33	43.90							

Table 5: Relationships Between Stock Price Movements and Inferior Conjunctions of Mercury and the Sun

A			B	C			D	E		F	G	H	I
Time of Inferior Conjunctions			Stock Market Day**	Longitude at Time of Inferior Conjunctions***			Seg-ment	Stock Prices		Advance or Decline	Trend	De-Trended Advance or Decline	Percent of In-crease or De-crease
								13 Days Prior	on the Day				
Year	Day	Hour		°	′	″							
1897	Jan 21	22	Jan 22	302	42	46.98	11	42.42	.17				
	May 20	13		60	12	20.44	3	38.69	38.67	-.02	.17	-.19	-.49
	Sep 21	19		179	31	22.62	6	*52.12	52.63	.41	.39	.02	.03
	1898 Jan 5	23	Jan 28	6	13	12.19	10	49.46	50.18	.72	.39	.33	.67
	Apr 30	17		40	49	47.13	2	45.42	46.00	.58	.39	.19	.42
	Sep 5	0		162	54	56.90	6	*56.12	*60.22	4.10	1.12	2.98	5.31
	Dec 21	5		269	55	17.90	9	56.75	59.19	2.44	1.12	1.32	2.33
1899	Apr 11	15		21	59	52.75	I	*68.S3	74.49	5.96	1.12	4.84	7.06
	Aug 18	16		145	55	59.72	5	71.07	75.64	4.57	-.59	5.16	7.26
	Dec 5	12		253	41	24.14	9	75.03	73.57	-1.46	-.59	-.87	-1.16
1900	Mar 24	10		3	49	13.90	1	-65.06	64.26	-.80	-.59	-.21	-.32
	Jul 31	15		128	23	16.70	5	ҫ55.21	56.80	1.59	.48	1.11	2.01
	Nov 19	19		237	31	43.48	8	58.73	68.88	10.15	.48	9.67	16.47
1901	Mar 7	0		346	14	53.80	12	69.27	67.72	-1.55	.48	2.03	-2.93
	Jul 12	17		110	5	11.76	4	76.55	70.77	-5.78	.12	-5.90	-7.71
	Nov 4	1		221	25	35.02	8	63.48	64.48	1.00	-.24	1.24	1.95
1902	Feb 18	04		329	5	45.82	11	*63.50	64.81	1.31	-.24	1.55	2.44
	Jun 23	03		91	11	15.39	4	66.82	64.20	-2.62	-.24	-2.38	-3.56
	Oct 19	02		205	15	14.98	7	67.77	*66.54	-1.23	-.56	-.67	-.99
1903	Feb 1	20	Feb 2	312	19	17.00	11	64.65	65.53	.88	-.56	1.44	2.23
	Jun 2	22	Jun 3	71	39	6.76	3	64.06	59.90	-4.16	-.56	-3.60	-5.62
	Oct 2	22	Oct 3	189	1	9.68	7	51.85	47.53	-4.32	-.10	-4.22	-8.14
1904	Jan 16	19		295	45	51.38	10	46.70	48.08	1.38	-.10	1.48	3.17
	May 12	18		52	2	22.12	2	49.58	47.93	-1.65	-.10	-1.55	-3.13
	Sep 15	9		172	34	.80	6	53.54	56.66	3.12	1.53	1.59	2.97
	Dec 30	22	Dec 31	279	20	9.12	10	72.05	69.61	-2.44	1.53	-3.97	-5.51
1905	Apr 23	4		32	49	5.58	2	*76.24	81.31	5.07	1.53	3.54	4.64
	Aug 29	9		155	49	19.72	6	*81.17	82.79	1.62	.90	.72	.89
	Dec 15	5		263	5	15.90	9	82.77	96.05	13.28	.90	12.38	14.96
1906	Apr 4	11		14	15	46.35	I	92.90	97.48	4.58	.90	3.68	3.96
	Aug 11	19		138	38	53.74	5	85.70	92.03	6.33	-1.11	7.44	8.68
	Nov 29	13		246	56	31.92	9	93.68	-95.19	1.51	-1.11	2.62	2.80
1907	Mar 17	15		356	22	50.95	12	93.07	*82.91	-10.61	-1.1 I	-9.05	-9.72
	Jul 24	10		120	49	44.30	5	77.93	81.32	3.39	-.08	3.47	4.45
	Nov 13	19		230	45	50.30	8	62.14	55.37	-6.77	-.08	-6.69	-10.77
1908	Feb 28	11		338	58	47.76	12	62.08	61.07	-1.01	-.08	-.93	-1.50
	Jul 4	5		102	16	21.40	4	72.66	*73.58	.92	-.08	1.00	1.38
	Oct 27	23	Oct 28	214	38	18.55	8	79.58	82.72	3.14	1.06	2.08	2.61

THE PLANETS/23

A			B	C			D	E		F	G	H	I
Time of Inferior Conjunctions			Stock Market Day**	Longitude at Time of Inferior Conjunctions***			Seg-ment	Stock Prices		Advance or Decline	Trend	De-Trended Advance or Decline	Percent of In-crease or De-crease
								13 Days Prior	on the Day				
Year	Day	Hour		°	′	″							
1909	Feb 10	21	Feb 11	322	1	35.01	11	85.28	85.76	.48	1.06	-.58	-.68
	Jun 14	6		83	0	1.44	3	90.82	94.19	3.37	1.06	2.31	2.54
	Oct 11	22	Oct 12	198	26	18.88	7	96.19	96.95	.76	-.42	1.18	1.23
1910	Jan25	16		305	20	38.74	11	*98.39	90.66	-7.73	-.42	-7.31	-7.43
	May 25	0		63	23	14.5	3	88.73	88.67	-.06	-.42	.36	.41
	Sep 25	15		182	8	55.80	7	79.28	78.85	-.43	.19	-.24	-.30
1911	Jan 9	17		288	51	18.35	10	81.54	82.51	.97	-.19	1.16	1.42
	May 5	1		43	54	57.97	2	83.02	83.15	.13	-.19	.32	.39
	Sep 8	22	Sep 9	165	36	11.76	6	81.43	78.67	-2.76	.36	-3.12	-3.83
	Dec 24	22	Dec 25	272	30	56.96	10	81.53	*82.09	.56	.36	.20	.25
1912	Apr 14	19		24	56	53.24	1	85.15	*89.42	4.27	.36	3.91	4.59
	Aug 21	16		148	40	45.0	5	89.75	9.62	1.87	-.54	2.41	2.69
	Dec 8	6		256	19	9.54	9	91.31	*86.94	-4.37	-.54	-3.83	-4.19
1913	Mar 27	11		6	40	41.02	1	78.72	79.78	1.06	-.54	1.60	2.03
	Aug 3	18		131	14	27.56	5	*75.69	*78.51	2.72	.00	2.72	3.59
	Nov 22	13		240	8	57.32	9	78.40	76.14	-2.26	.00	-2.26	-2.88
1914	Mar 9	22	Mar 10	349	0	24.26	12	*82.48	81.94	-.54	-.00	-.54	-.65
	Jul 16	1		113	7	54.01	4	81.28	80.43	-.85	.68	-1.53	-1.88
	Nov 6	19		224	1	39.12		War	War				
1915	Feb 21	1		331	50	13.91	12	58.21	-55.26	-2.95	1.36	-4.31	-7.40
	Jun 26	12		94	16	35.46	4	64.95	70.71	5.76	1.78	3.98	6.13
	Oct 21	21	Oct 22	207	52	59.18	7	85.88	96.46	10.58	1.78	8.80	10.25
1916	Feb 4	20	Feb 5	315	12	25.20	11	96.44	93.39	-3.05	1.78	-4.83	-5.01
	Jun 5	13		74	59	18.28	3	90.51	92.19	1.68	1.78	-.10	-.11
	Oct 4	23	Oct 19	1	51	40.78	7	93.36	104.15	10.79	-.64	11.43	12.24
1917	Jan 18	18		298	37	18.66	10	97.76	97.50	-.26	-.64	.38	.39
	May 16	8		55	21	11.70	2	92.21	92.26	.05	-.64	.69	.75
	Sep 18	12		175	28	48.70	6	*91.35	81.63	-9.72	-.57	-9.15	-10.02
1918	Jan 2	21	Jan 3	282	11	58.87	10	71.72	76.18	5.46	-.57	6.03	8.53
	Apr 26	15		36	17	25.06	2	76.62	78.23	1.51	-.57	2.08	2.71
	Sep 1	13		158	45	23.72	6	80.76	*83.17	2.41	1.56	.85	1.05
	Dec 18	4		265	56	46.60	9	85.01	83.01	-2.00	1.56	-3.56	-4.19
1919	Apr 7	19		17	24	13.52		87.27	90.18	2.91	1.56	1.35	1.55
	Aug 15	1		141	38	35.41	5	111.47	102.25	-9.22	-.81	-8.41	-7.54
	Dec 2	11		249	44	9.70	9	*119.13	104.41	-14.72	-.81	-13.91	-11.68
1920	Mar 19	20	Mar 20	359	25	36.90	12	94.15	103.56	9.41	-.81	10.22	10.86
	Jul 26	19		123	55	21.09	5	90.88	87.66	-3.22	-1.39	-1.83	-2.01
1921	Mar 2	14		341	58	7.04	12	76.13	75.19	-.94	-1.39	.45	.59
	Jul 7	17		105	28	40.29	4	71.56	69.72	-1.84	-1.39	-.45	-.63
	Oct 30	22	Oct 31	217	27	11.44	8	71.68	73.21	1.53	1.65	-.12	-.17

24/The Key to Speculation on the New York Stock Exchange

A			B	C			D	E		F	G	H	I
								Stock Prices				De-	Percent
Time of Inferior Conjunctions			Stock Market Day**	Longitude at Time of Inferior Conjunctions***			Seg-ment	13 Days Prior	on the Day	Advance or Decline	Trend	Trended Advance or Decline	of In-crease or De-crease
Year	Day	Hour		°	'	"							
1922	Feb 13	22	Feb 14	324	56	59.24	11	*81.30	83.81	2.51	1.65	.86	1.06
	Jun 17	21	Jun 18	86	19	45.29	3	94.80	*91.70	-3.10	1.65	-4.75	-5.01
	Oct 14	23	Oct 15	201	18	30.54	7	100.99	*103.10	2.11	.15	1.96	1.94
1923	Jan 28	16		308	14	31.86	11	98.17	98.26	.09	.15	-.06	-.06
	May 28	15		66	44	10.65	3	100.63	97.25	-3.38	.15	-3.53	-3.51
	Sep 28	16		184	59	12.48	7	93.70	87.97	-5.73	.40	-6.13	-6.54
1924	Jan 12	16		291	42	46.26	10	94.70	97.25	2.55	.40	2.15	2.27
	May 7	14		47	12	21.78	2	93.03	92.47	-.56	.40	-.96	-1.03
	Sep 11	1		168	29	51.91	6	101.51	101.79	.28	2.90	-2.62	-2.58
	Dec 26	21	Dec 27	275	22	3.35	10	*110.63	119.18	8.55	2.90	5.65	5.11
1925	Apr 18	17		28	8	24.56	1	119.38	122.02	2.64	2.90	-.26	-.22
	Aug 25	9		151	37	52.56	6*	136.07	143.18	7.11	1.55	5.56	4.09
	Dec 11	16	259		7	7.88	9	154.18	154.21	.03	1.55	-1.52	-.99
1926	Mar 31	6	Mar 30	9	46	41.50	1*	152.68	135.20	-17.48	1.55	-19.03	-12.46
	Aug 7	14		134	17	47.36	5	155.66	1665.21	9.55	1.91	7.64	4.91
	Nov 26	0	Nov 25	242	58	38.20	9	149.35	*156.55	7.20	1.91	5.29	3.54
1927	Mar 13	15		352	2	54.20	12	156.05	*161.08	5.03	1.91	3.12	2.00
	Jul 20	0	Jul 19	116	17	41.80	4	*169.68	177.02	7.34	3.05	4.29	2.53
	Nov 10	6	Nov 9	226	50	55.34	8	189.03	189.31	.28	4.19	-3.91	-2.07
]928	Feb 24	15		334	46	39.40	12	198.58	193.15	-5.43	4.19	-9.62	-4.84
	Jun 29	13		97	30	38.81	4	219.81	210.55	-9.26	4.19	-13.45	-6.12
	Oct 24	8		210	40	24.06	8	240.13	257.03	16.90	7.09	9.81	4.09
1929	Feb 7 4 Feb 6			317	54	48.22	11	297.70	317.18	19.48	7.09	12.39	4.16
	Jun 9	11		77	56	29.19	3	325.70	-304.20	-21.50	7.09	-28.59	-8.78
	Oct 8	6	Oct 7	194	28	44.60	7	-376.25	345.72	-30.53	-6.24	-24.29	-6.46
1930	Jan 22	1	Jan 21	301	17	46.70	11	-234.04	259.58	15.54	-6.24	21.78	9.31
	May 20	5	May 19	58	27	15.20	2	*291.15	265.87	-25.28	-6.24	-19.04	-6.54
	Sep 21	20		178	6	13.90	6	232.63	*226.32	-6.31	-8.15	1.84	.79
1931	Jan 6	3	Jan 5	284	50	23.29	10	178.37	173.30	-5.07	-8.15	3.08	1.73
	Apr 30	10		39	6	.80	2	172.36	151.19	-21.17	-8.15	-13.02	-7.55
	Sep 5	0	Sep 4	161	27	59.59	6	134.10	132.62	-1.48	-6.17	4.69	3.50
	Dec 21	9		268	31	44.99	9	97.42	78.08	-19.34	-6.17	-13.17	-13.52
1932	Apr 10	11		20	21	34.44	1	83.61	-63.26	-20.35	-6.17	-14.18	-16.96
	Aug 17	14		144	24	52.70	5	44.07	67.50	23.43	1.60	21.83	49.53
	Dec 4	17		251	21	19.01	9	61.53	*56.18	-5.35	1.60	-6.95	-11.30
1933	Mar 23	8		2	14	41.72	1	53.99	58.06	4.07	1.60	2.47	4.57
	Jul 30	11		126	48	5.34	5	98.14	-92.03	-16.11	1.21	-7.32	-7.46
	Nov 19	0	Nov 18	236	12	22.1	8	84.38	98.67	14.29	1.21	13.08	15.50
1934	Mar 6	0	Mar 5	344	43	52.5	12	109.41	105.02	-4.39	1.21	-5.60	-5.12
	Jul 11	12		108	28	31.6	4	97.82	98.67	.85	1.81	-.96	-.98
	Nov 3	5	Nov 2	220	4	49.30	8	91.01	94.95	3.94	1.81	2.13	2.34

THE PLANETS/25

A			B	C			D	E		F	G	H	I
Time of Inferior Conjunctions			Stock Market Day**	Longitude at Time of Inferior Conjunctions***			Seg-ment	Stock Prices		Advance or Decline	Trend	De-Trended Advance or Decline	Percent of In-crease or De-crease
								13 Days Prior	on the Day				
Year	Day	Hour		°	′	″							
1935	Feb 17	6	Feb 16	327	39	7.20	11	102.36	104.54	2.18	1.81	.37	.36
	Jun 21	18		89	24	46.46	3	116.24	119.48	3.24	2.67	.57	.49
	Oct 18	5	Oct 17	203	52	35.69	7	133.11	135.57	2.46	3.52	-1.06	-.80
1936	Jan 31	23		310	55	16.31	11	*144.13	149.49	5.36	3.52	1.84	1.28
	May 31	12		69	49	47.55	3	147.07	*152.77	5.70	3.52	2.18	1.48
	Oct 18	0	Sep 30	187	37	3.6	7	166.35	168.26	1.91	.34	1.57	.94
1937	Jan 14	22		294	21	20.40	10	181.97	183.71	1.74	.34	1.40	.77
	May 11	10		50	16	52.97	2	179.00	172.55	-6.45	.34	-6.79	-3.17
	Sep 14	10		171	9	11.00	6	*189.68	162.90	-26.78	-2.90	-23.88	-12.59
	Dec 30	3	Dec 29	277	59	49.61	10	121.58	120.15	-1.43	-2.90	1.47	1.21
1938	Apr 21	22		31	7	31.20	2	117.11	115.40	-1.71	-2.90	1.19	1.02
	Aug 18	9		154	23	11.59	6	141.20	*139.51	-1.69	.85	-2.54	-1.80
	Dec 14	10		261	44	54.17	9	155.61	151.83	-3.78	.85	-4.63	-2.98
1939	Apr 3	8		12	40	34.56	1	149.49	132.25	-17.24	.85	-18.09	-12.10
	Aug 10	16		137	6	34.10	5	134.56	137.25	2.69	-.59	3.28	2.44
	Nov 28	17		245	33	16.97	9	*153.17	148.31	-4.86	-.59	-4.27	-2.79
1940	Mar 15	15		354	53	18.83	12	148.33	146.53	-1.80	-.59	-1.21	-.82
	Jul 22	5	Jul 21	119	13	4.03	4	122.61	-121.97	.64	-.83	.19	.15
	Nov 11	23		229	24	47.53	8	*130.94	*137.65	6.71	-1.08	7.79	5.95
1941	Feb 26	12		337	30	50.05	12	129.03	122.39	-6.64	-1.08	-5.56	-4.31
	Ju12	21		100	32	54.81	4	116.18	123.58	7.40	-1.08	8.48	7.30
	Oct 27	3	Oct 26	213	18	3.32	8	125.81	-120.08	-5.73	-1.22	-4.51	-3.58
1942	Feb 9	23		320	34	59.98	11	110.54	108.12	-2.42	-1.22	-1.20	-1.09
	Jun 12	21		81	14	9.94	3	97.21	103.77	6.56	-1.22	7.78	8.00
	Oct 11	1	Oct 10	197	4	59.43	7	106.38	114.93	8.55	2.30	6.25	5.88
1943	Jan 24	19		303	56	2.83	11	-119.46	-123.06	3.60	2.30	1.30	1.09
	May 23	15		61	36	12.04	3	*134.27	*138.81	4.54	2.30	2.24	1.67
	Sep 24	17		180	45	58.52	7	135.90	140.21	4.31	.71	3.60	2.65
1944	Jan 8	21		287	29	9.03	10	134.05	138.09	4.04	.71	3.33	2.48
	May 2	17		42	9	12.40	2	*138.42	137.15	-1.27	.71	-1.98	-1.43
	Sep 6	22		164	8	37.11	6	145.32	144.42	-.90	2.21	-3.11	-2.14
	Dec 23	3	Dec 22	271	10	27.19	10	147.03	150.43	3_40	2.21	1.19	.81
1945	Apr 13	14		23	16	42.9	1	157.83	159.75	1.92	2.21	-.29	-.18
	Aug 20	15		147	12	28.73	5	*162..22	163.11	.89	1.82	-.93	-.57
	Dec 7	10		254	56	58.41	9	192.04	194.08	2.04	1.82	.22	.11
1946	Mar 26	9		5	6	22.18	1*	-188.58	200.56	11.98	1.82	10.16	5.39
	Aug 2	15		129	41	56.85	5	207.06	202.82	4.24	-1.17	-3.07	-1.48
	Nov 21	17		238	47	9.49	8	171.25	164.12	-7.13	-1.17	-5.96	-3.48
1947	11.8	22		347	30	5.40	12	181.57	175.84	-5.73	-1.17	4.56	-2.51
	Jul 14	18		111	25	55.64	4	*175.60	185.60	10.00	-.48	10.48	5.97
	Nov 5	23		222	40	43.79	8	180.08	181.89	1.81	.21	1.60	.89

26/THE KEY TO SPECULATION ON THE NEW YORK STOCK EXCHANGE

A			B	C			D	E		F	G	H	I
								Stock Prices				De-	Percent
Time of Inferior Conjunctions			Stock Market Day**	Longitude at Time of Inferior Conjunctions***			Seg-ment	13 Days Prior	on the Day	Advance or Decline	Trend	Trended Advance or Decline	of In-crease or De-crease
Year	Day	Hour		°	′	″							
1948	Feb 20	3	Feb 19	330	24	3.55	12	175.27	167.86	-7.41	.21	-7.62	4.35
	Jun 24	3	Jun 23	92	29	52.01	4	180..84	171.97	-8.87	.21	-9.08	-5.02
	Oct 20	0	Oct 19	206	30	7.10	7	*178.72	186.18	7.46	-.08	7.54	4.22
1949	Feb 2	18		313	35	42.40	11	175.03	180.27	5.24	-.08	5.32	3.04
	Jun 3	22		12	57	47.45	I	176.63	167.24	-9.39	-.08	-9.31	-5.27
	Oct 3	20		190	15	50.08	7	*179.34	182.67	3.33	3.10	.23	.13
1950	Jan 17	17		297	2	6.55	10	*198.08	198.78	.70	3.10	-2.40	-1.21
	May 14	18		53	21	34.06	2	215.31	*217.91	2.60	3.10	-.50	-.23
	Sep 17	8		173	51	26.43	6	219.23	*226.47	7.24	3.44	3.80	1.73
1951	Jan 1	20		280	36	26.90	10	227.55	*238.42	10.87	3.44	7.43	3.27
	Apr 25	4	Apr 24	34	9	.10	2	*248.64	254.19	5.55	3.44	2.11	.85
	Aug 31	8		157	6	21.60	6	259..89	270.25	10.36	1.09	9.27	3.57
	Dec 17	3	Dec 16	264	20	53.18	9	260.39	*265.64	5.25	1.09	4.16	1.60
1952	Apr 5	10		15	32	6.35	1	265.44	261.54	-3.90	1.09	-4.99	-1.88
	Aug 12	18		139	54	0.32	5	*274.79	278.14	3.35	.43	2.92	1.06
	Nov 30	11		248	9	35.10	9	269.23	*283.69	14.46	.43	14.03	5.21
1953	Mar 18	13		357	35	45.63	12	282.18	290.32	8.14	.43	7.71	2.73
	Jul 25	9		122	3	54.17	5	268.93	*269.33	.40	4.83	-4.43	-1.65
	Nov 14	17		231	59	17.28	8	271.22	*277.00	5.78	4.83	.95	.35
1954	Mar 1	10		340	13	46.60	12	*292.21	296.55	4.34	4.83	-.49	-.17
	Jul 6	05	Jul 5	103	32	3.33	4	*327.74	*340.26	12.52	4.83	7.69	2.35
	Oct 29	21		215	50	29.15	8	361.73	352.14	-9.59	9.07	-18.66	-5.16
1955	Feb 12	19		323	13	31.15	11	398.34	*413.12	14.78	9.07	5.71	1.43
	Jun 16	6	Jun 15	84	15	14.57	3	415.01	441.93	26.92	9.07	17.85	4.30
	Oct 13	21		199	39	55.27	7	480.93	444.91	-36.02	4.19	-40.21	-8.36
1956	Jan 27	14		306	31	59.32	11	484.22	466.56	-17.66	4.19	-21.85	-4.51
	May 26	00	May 25	64	37	33.50	3	503.02	472.49	-30.53	4.19	-34.72	-6.90
	Sep 26	13		183	18	46.43	7	505.70	481.60	-24.10	-1.44	-22.66	4.48
1957	Jan 10	15		290	2	2.20	10	490.36	495.51	5.15	-1.44	6.59	1.34
	May 6	00	May 5	45	06	7.70	2	*440.30	461.12	20.82	-1.44	22.26	5.06
	Sep 9	00		166	44	51.10	6	*495.29	474.28	-21.01	1.33	-22.34	-4.51
	Dec 25	20		273	40	40.22	10	444.38	*431.64	-12.74	1.33	-14.07	-3.17
1958	Apr 16	19		26	9	46.50	1	448.23	444.35	-3.88	1.33	-5.21	-1.16
	Aug 23	15		149	51	5.25	5	497.12	*508.28	11.16	11.71	-.55	-.11
	Dec 10	03	Dec 9	257	25	37.42	9	*556.57	564.9	8.41	11.71	-3.30	.59
1959	Mar 29	10		7	50	37.27	1	603.50	*603.63	.13	11.71	-11.58	-1.92
	Aug 5	17		132	23	30.20	5	660.09	672.33	12.24	-1.17	13.41	2.03
	Nov 24	11		241	16	50.30	9	*636.10	649.69	13.59	-1.17	14.76	2.32
1960	Mar 10	21		350	18	32.78	12	628.45	602.31	-26.14	-1.17	-24.97	-3.97
	Jul 17	01	Jul 16	114	26	39.95	4	648.27	*628.23	-19.44	2.48	-21.92	-3.38
	Nov 7	17		225	17	11.65	8	*586.71	597.63	10.92	6.13	4.79	.82

A			B	C			D	E		F	G	H	I
Time of Inferior Conjunctions			Stock Market Day**	Longitude at Time of Inferior Conjunctions***.			Seg-ment	Stock Prices		Advance or Decline	Trend	De-Trended Advance or Decline	Percent of In-crease or De-crease
								13 Days Prior	on the Day				
Year	Day	Hour		°	′	″							
1961	Feb 22	00	Feb 21	333	08	34.5	12	*638.00	652.40	14.40	6.13	8.27	1.30
	Jun 27	12		95	34	59.54	4	*696.28	683.88	-12.40	6.13	-18.53	-2.66
	Oct 22	19		209	8	5.60	7	701.57	*696.77	-4.80	-4.32	-.48	-.07
1962	Feb 5	13		316	15	44.00	11	*712.89	706.14	-6.75	-4.32	-2.43	-.34
	Jun 7	08		76	5	55.36	3	663.90	602.20	-61.70	-4.32	-57.3.	-8.64
	Oct 6	16		192	54	59.99	7	600.81	*586.42	-14.39	6.25	-20.64	-3.44
1963	Jan 20	11		299	40	24.30	10	646.41	674.34	27.93	6.25	21.68	3.35
	May 18	03	May 17	56	28	32.66	2	710.25	724.81	14.56	6.25	8.31	1.17
	Sep 20	05	Sep 19	176	31	9.13	6	717.27	743.22	25.95	9.94	16.01	2.23
1964	Jan 4	14		283	15	9.77	10	763.86	*768.90	5.04	9.94	-4.90	.64
	Apr 27	10		37	10	12.29	2	*815.60	811.87	-3.73	9.94	-13..67	-1.68
	Sep 2	07	Sep 1	159	49	38.26	6	*840.10	844.00	3.90	6.40	-2.50	-.30
	Dec 18	21		266	59	32.37	9	891.71	868.73	-22.98	6.40	-29.38	-3.29
1965	Apr 8	13		18	29	8.03	1	894.07	897.90	3.83	6.40	-2.57	-.29
	Aug 15	19		142	42	47.50	5	880.43	*890.03	9.60	-3.11	12.71	1.44
	Dec 3	04	Dec 2	250	46	44.65	9	*960.04	944.59	-15.45	-3.11	-12.34	-1.29
1966	Mar 21	14		0	30	27.45	1	*972.30	929.17	-43.13	-3.11	-40.02	-4.12
	Jul 28	14		125	2	25.97	5	880.90	854.06	-26.84	.46	-27.30	-3.10
	Nov 17	11		234	38	42.43	8	791.87	816.03	24.16	.46	23.70	2.99
1967	Mar 4	08		343	3	21.16	12	853.12	*845.15	-7.99	.46	-8.45	-.99
	Jul 9	12		106	35	40.00	4	874.89	*873.47	-1.42	1.35	-2.77	-.32
	Nov 1	15		218	29	41.26	8	921.00	867.08	-53.92	2.24	-56.16	-6.10
1968	Feb 15	15		326	0	16.07	11	887.14	839.23	-47.91	2.24	-50.15	-5.65
	Jul 18	16		87	26	46.16	3	*897.39	900.20	2.81	2.24	.57	.06
	Oct 15	16		202	21	7.06		*919.99	955.31	35.32			
1969	Jan 29	09		309	17	52.30		945.11	938.09	-7.02			
	May 29	10		67	50	56.40		934.10	937.56	3.46			
	Sep 29	10		186	4	33.43							
1970	Jan 13	09		292	46	28.64							
	May 9	09		48	17	39.60							
	Sep 12	18		169	32	37.95							
	Dec 28	14		276	25	6.11							

Jupiter

Jupiter is a planet of expansion, of growth. The only time it represents weakness is in three-year periods from a corporation's birthday. This means that the third, sixth and ninth years of a corporation generally represent a few financial setbacks and complications. Jupiter has a return cycle of every twelve years. That means it takes 12 years to transit all 12 signs. Therefore it stays in one sign about 12 months. Its return is a beneficial aspect. It is very beneficial when the Sun transits the sign ruling that corporation. For example. if the corporation is born under the sign of Aries, and Jupiter moves into the sign of Aries, this is going to affect that corporation, as far as growth or expansion in one area. For this return to the 12-year periods of a stock and see what the stock did on these 12-year periods. Going back every 12 years will relate to its coming twelve years and its coming movement. On the other hand. Jupiter can make things too plentiful. This means it brings expansion—it gives. It can hit high prices, for example, as it goes through the sign of Leo. Leo is a sign that represents gold. Gold can hit an all-time high as to prices and then they can drop as Jupiter in Leo retrogrades. It means there is plenty of this product but there is also expansion and growth in relation to this product. It gives this growth pattern but it is moving strong for only 12 months. So with Jupiter you have to know when to get off the ride. as it ends when Jupiter leaves one sign and enters another.

It is advisable to watch stocks that move backwards or have a fast drop during the periods when Jupiter is retrograde. This means they can reverse just as fast when Jupiter goes direct. A lot of bargains can be found from this Jupiter retrograde influence. The periods during which Jupiter will be retrograde can be found in an astrological calendar or ephemeris.

What is pulled back at these times will expand when it is released. The products represented by the sign that Jupiter occupies at the time will also give you an idea of what is about to move.

Saturn has a return cycle of every 29 years, 167 days. It is known as the 30-year cycle of Saturn which comes into effect every 28 to 30 years. It also makes aspects every seven years. It is the planet that restricts, that holds back. When it goes through a certain sign of the zodiac it represents restrictions, shortages of things connected with that sign. And when involved in certain cluster patterns it represents a bearish market—panic. It is the planet of fear and all our recessions and depressions are related to this element of Saturn under affliction. When Saturn turns retrograde it can also lead the way for a bullish trend. But in direct motion it has its full power and brings limitations. In the past as Saturn has entered the sign of Sagittarius this has always represented a good market, a bullish trend, because of its favorable aspects to the New York Stock Exchange natal chart. If the market is under a bearish trend there can be some periods, due to Saturn's retrograde motion, when there will be relief for a few months or so. Saturn's retrograde periods can be found in an astrological calendar or ephemeris.

Mars

The planet Mars has a return cycle of one year and 322 days. It also has what is known as a 15-year return cycle. Its effect is impulsive, fiery and quick. The two worst planets affecting the stock market are Mars and Saturn. When they do come into conjunction or Mars goes retrograde it can bring the market down very, very fast. As Mars is somewhat of an impulsive planet, people react to it. With the feat of Saturn and the impulsiveness of Mars this does take its toll on the market itself. In 1899, the market fell 24.9 percent between September 5 and December 18, with Saturn conjunct Mars. In 1903, Mars went retrograde and between February 16 and November 9 the Dow-Jones plunged 37.7 percent. The next period of Mars retrograde was in February 1905, when the market took a sharp turnaround as, again, Mars is impulsive and it is fast. Between April 10 and November 15, 1907, again there was the Mars conjunction and the market dropped 37.5 percent. Between January 3, 1910 through February 8 the market dropped 13.5 percent and again throughout the year this was affected by Mars conjunct Saturn. As Saturn entered the sign of Taurus, the Dow-Jones went to its second leg of the bear market. Between March 8 and May 5 the market dropped 10.4 percent, and between May 21 and July 26 it dropped another 17.9 percent. Again, Mars was also an influence here.

In August 1911, the conjunction again affected the market between June 11 and September 25, when the market dropped 16.2 percent. During 1914 and 1915 the stock market closed down from August to November as Mars was very heavily affected with the Saturn influence during this cycle. Between December 27, 1915 and September 22, 1916, the market took a very, very heavy drop as Saturn was retrograde and the Dow-Jones stalled suddenly, at the decrease in the low point from this 1914-1915 cycle. During the period of June 9 through December 19, the Dow dropped 33.13 percent; Mars was still the influence. Between July 14 and August 20, 1919, the Dow-Jones dropped 11.04 percent. With Mars conjunct Saturn between November 3 and December 12, the market dropped another 13.04 percent. Mars went retrograde in March 1920, and when it was stationary the market dropped again. Between January 3 and February 25 it dropped 18.1 percent, and between April 8 and December 21 it dropped 36.9 percent as retrograde Mars was in motion.

The effect of Mars was very prominent during 1932 because the recession that came in the latter part of 1929 was also triggered by Saturn. Mars had a triggering effect on it but it was more of a Saturn influence. In 1932, between February 24, 1931 and July 8, 1932, with Mars conjunct Saturn, the market dropped 78.78 percent and kept on tumbling into the 1932 period another 18.6 percent into July 19 and 22. Mars dominated through 1934. Between February 5, 1934 and July 26, 1934, the Dow-Jones dropped 22.8 percent. In 1937 Mars went retrograde and the bull market ended. Between March 10 and June 14 the market dropped 14.9 percent, and between August 14 and November 24 it dropped 40.1 percent. The retrograde motion of Mars was very much in effect. In 1938, Mars was conjunct Saturn. Between January 1 and March 31 under the conjunction the market dropped 26.3 percent. In March 1940 when Saturn entered Taurus the market dropped under the conjunction in the month of May; between May 9 and June 10, the market dropped 24.5 percent. Mars went retrograde again in 1941. Its effect marked a seven-year low, and between January 10, 1941 and April 28, 1942 it dropped 30.4 percent.

In 1946, Mars was conjunct Saturn. The four-year bull market ended during this period and between December 11, 1945 and February 26, 1946 there was a five percent drop. The influence ran through 1946 between May 29 and October 9, and a 23.2 percent drop was registered. In June 1967, Mars was conjunct Uranus; between July 12 and October 22, a 19.4 percent drop was registered. In 1958, there was no affliction of Mars, and there was only one bad month, February. In 1966, Mars was conjunct Saturn, and between February 9 and March 15, there was an 8.4 percent drop. In May 1959, Mars was retrograde again, and between May 14 and July 29, a 17.2 percent drop was registered. As Mars was conjunct Saturn in 1970 between April 9 and May 26, there was a 20.4 percent drop. So Mars retrograde does affect a market. It can be a stationary influence, and when it is connected with Saturn it is not at all a good influence. There is a relationship with a standstill or change of direction, and mostly for the bad as fast drops are indicated by Mars. Where Saturn represents a long-term drop in the market, Mars represents a fast drop; there can be an extreme drop during just those couple of months from the effects of Mars. So again it is not wise to sell or hold anything into a Mars retrograde period. The time to sell stock is just prior to it. Mars retrograde periods are available in astrological calendar or ephemeris.

Outer Planets

Our next planet is Uranus, which has a seven-year cycle. It affects the events that take place as far as the nature of the products of the sign that it enters because Uranus is the planet of invention. It is the tomorrow; it is explosive and changes fast. It changes technology. It changes things related to inventions. And whatever sign Uranus is in you can be sure we will have research and new technology in related areas. The planet Neptune is more connected with unusual influences in relation to our thoughts and energy, but has no real deep bearing on the market except for its long trends over 45 periods. And the planet Pluto has no connection at all with the market. So we are relating mostly to the seven major heavenly influences. They all have cycles within cycles, so as the market moves it is motivated by these monocycles that have an effect on cycles of a longer term, and one cycle is reacting against the other and this is where we get the ups and downs and wavelengths as far as the influence of the market moving at different speeds and different angles. When the market is not bearish then it has to be bullish and the main factor is knowing when the market is going to turn around because you can make money on the market most any time if it is going up or it is going down. There's a time to buy and there is a time to sell and this is the whole key factor with the market. The signs and retrograde periods of the outer planets can be found in an astrological calendar or ephemeris

Lengths of Various Fractions of the Orbital Periods of the Five Outer Planets

Copyright 1978 by the Foundation for the Study of Cycles, Inc.

Before his passing Edward R. Dewey set another example of his research of cycles in relation to the orbital periods of the five other planets. This is what astrologers have been saying for years. The following is his report, and as you read, notice these cycles in stock prices.

To begin, let me review some of the known facts about cycles, and restate some of the questions about them. Although cycles come in all lengths (periods), from a fraction of a second to millions of years, interdisciplinary cycles, in which we are primarily interest, have been noted mostly in lengths measured in days, months, and years. For example, 40 months, 5.9 years, 12.6 years, etc.

Some 3,000 cycle periods are listed in our master catalogue of cycles. Some time ago we made a study from these listings that shows there is a tendency for cycles to bunch at certain periods and also for all cycles of the same period to crest roughly at the same calendar time regardless of phenomena. That is, there is a tendency for all four-year cycles to crest more or less together, Whether found in U.S.A. cheese consumption, sunspots (alternate cycles reversed, arctic fox abundance, pork prices in Germany or whatever).

Similarly, there is a tendency for all six-year cycles to crest at about the same calendar time, whether they occur in the levels of Lakes Michigan and Huron, or steel production in the U.S.A., or wholesale sugar prices, or in some 34 other phenomena.

An observation of this sort is possible only when the time of crest has been determined—when the cycle has been "timed." When the study was made, this fact limited us to those cycles for which the phase had been computed. (This study on the synchronicity of timing was published in the August 1970 issue of *Cycles*). To hold the study to workable proportions, it was decided to limit it to all cycles four years long or longer. Therefore we do not yet know if cycles under four years in length also behave this way.

Every example in the literature known to me was included regardless of the span of time over which it was observed, regardless of its statistical significance, and regardless of the competence of the investigator. However, the selection was limited to cycles of which we have three or more examples to provide a rough screening of cycles that might be "real." It was assumed that there is no significance to any identity of crest timing in a mere couple of cycles, and so unless there were at least three cases of a particular period that has been timed, no record was made of this coincidence.

At that time, out of the total catalogue, there were only 309 cycles known to me that (1) were four years long or longer, (2) that had been timed, and (3) of which there were, regardless of phenomena, three or more examples of the same period, or almost the same period. I want to emphasize that no selection was made—every cycle that met the criteria was included.

I also want to emphasize that this study was our first attempt to bring order out of the chaos of our collection of cycles, that it should be considered preliminary, that it should be repeated with up-to-date information, and that it should be steadily expanded.

Several interesting clues about the nature of cycles emerged from this grouping, and this article is intended to increase the information necessary to pursue one of these clues. It turned out that all 309 cases grouped themselves into what have been called "master cycles." There are 19 of these lengths. All of the 309 cycles can be grouped into 19 master lengths as follows:

16 examples of 4-year periods
10 examples of 5.9-year periods (5.89 to 5.92)
37 examples of 6.0-year periods (5.98 to 6.01)
87 examples of 8.0-year periods (7.96 to 8.02)
31 examples of 9.0-year periods (8.95 to 9.14)
28 examples of 9.2-year periods (9.17 to 9.34)
7 examples of 9.5-year periods (9.41 to 9.54)
24 examples of 9.6-year periods (9.58 to 9.7)
16 examples of 9.9-year periods (9.75 to 9.94)
6 examples of 11.2-year periods (11.19 to 11.3)
3 examples of 12.0-year periods (12.0 to 12.05)
11 examples of 12.6-year periods (12.4 to 12.84)
5 examples 16 2/3-year periods
6 examples of 17 1/3-year periods
9 examples of 17.7-year periods
14 examples of 18.2-year periods
10 examples of 22-year periods
35 examples of 54-year periods
4 examples of 164-year periods

In all but three of these "master lengths" there is a tendency for all the cases noted to synchronize. That is, all 6-year cycles (for example) tended to turn at about the same time, all the 9.2-year cycles tended to turn at their own time—a different time, and so on.

The fact that the cycles when listed tend to bunch into various "master periods" is quite remarkable and cannot reasonably be chance. If not chance, there must be some cause, or more accurately, 19 causes. Of course this figure is not final. If we time another 300 cycles there would doubtless be other lengths at which three or more cycles clustered. But this result is good enough for present purposes.

A consideration of the cycles tabulated, for example, of the 37 examples of the 6-year cycle that range from 5.98 to 6.01 years, directs attention to one of the general questions that exist about cycle analysis. Why is it that this variation occurs in the measured length to the cycle? It seems reasonable to assume that the analysts were all dealing with the same behavior, yet the measurement of the average period varies slightly from case to case.

Furthermore, we know that if any one of these examples is considered individually, we will find some wobble in the cycle. That is, the time from crest to crest will vary from wave to wave, and the period that is definitized is an *average* value. No matter how regular a cycle, the crests will always come unpredictably a little early or late. Why?

This problem itself, together with other facts, suggest a possible solution. In one case at least, the wobble itself suggests a possible cause. There is a cycle in cotton prices that has an average length of 5.9 years. But, it is not precisely 5.9 years from crest to crest, wave after wave. The 5.9~year figure is an average. However, the variation that occurs itself is cyclic. An exact wave length repeats itself every five cycles. Now, five times 5.9 is 29.5 years, which happens to be, almost exactly, the sidereal period of the planet Saturn.

It happens that all but three of the 19 "master" periods are multiples of the orbital period of Earth or are unit fractions of one or another of the five outer planets. As early as 1931 unit fractions of the orbital periods of Neptune were recorded in the thought that they might be useful in comparative cycle analysis. Although correspondences have been noted from time to time, there has been no systematic study made of this clue about possible cycle cause.

But, increasingly we are subject to suggestions that the orbital periods of the planets of the fractions of the orbital periods are in some way related to terrestrial cycles. As I mentioned above, this memorandum is being prepared just to clear the way for further study. An investigation of the possibility of identity between the average period of various cycles on the earth and the fractions of the various orbital periods of the planets is not as straightforward as one might hope because of the elliptical orbits of the planets, and the variation in speed Over the course of an orbit.

The orbital periods of the five outer planets are well-known. They are given in Table I. However, the fractional orbital periods are not easy to come by. Therefore, I asked George W. Jones of our staff to make the necessary computations. Table II gives the fractional orbital periods of the five outer planets. The segments are measured .in two ways. First, from perihelion to perihelion, and second, from one-half a segment prior to perihelion. Rough schematic drawings are included to show the divisions. Table III gives certain facts useful in building the computations and programs from which Table II is derived.

Table I: The Orbital Periods of the Planets as Seen from the Sun, and the Location in Longitude of Perihelion

Planet Name and Number	Orbital Period Time required to go once around the Sun (in tropical years)	Mean Longitude at Perihelion
Mercury 1	0.24085	76.67750
Venus 2	0.61521	130.86750
Earth 3	1.00004	102.08055
Mars 4	1.88089	335.13861
Jupiter 5	11.86223	13.51722
Saturn 6	29.45770	92.06833
Uranus 7	84.01300	169.85166
Neptune 8	164.79300	44.15861
Pluto 9	248.43000	223.19277

Table II: Selected Fractional Orbital Periods Measured (1) from Perihelion and (2) One Half Segment Prior to Perihelion and Diagrams

Orbit Undivided:

Jupiter	Saturn	Uranus	Neptune	Pluto
11.86223	29.4577	84.03100	164.79300	248.4300

Orbit Divided into Two Segments:
Starting at Perihelion:

	Jupiter	Saturn	Uranus	Neptune	Pluto
Segment 1	5.93111	14.72885	42.00650	82.39650	124.21500
Segment 2	5.93111	14.72885	42.00650	82.39650	124.21500

Starting at ½ Segment Prior to Perihelion:

	Jupiter	Saturn	Uranus	Neptune	Pluto
Segment 1	5.67877	13.67921	39.49366	81.45232	85.24510
Segment 2	6.29346	15.77849	44.51934	83.34068	163.18490

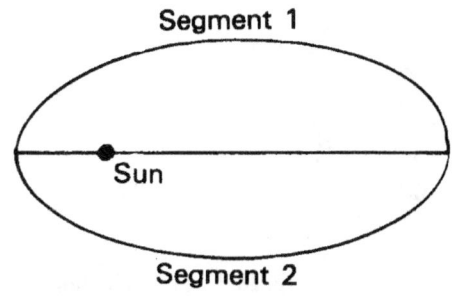

Measured from Perihelion

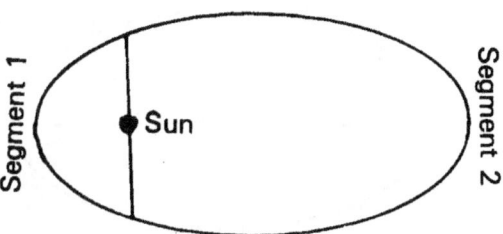

Measured from One Half
Segment prior to Perihelion

Orbit Divided into Three Segments:
Starting at Perihelion:
Segment 1	3.79429	9.35494	26.89666	54.52077	64.17245
Segment 2	4.27365	10.74782	30.21968	555.57145	120.08509
Segment 3	3.79429	9.35494	26.89666	54.52077	64.17245

Starting at ½ Segment Prior to Perihelion:
Segment 1	3.64581	8.92884	25.86572	54.11606	51.88592
Segment 2	4.10821	10.26443	29.07364	55.33847	98.27204
Segment 3	4.10821	10.26443	29.07364	55.33847	98.27204

36/The Key to Speculation on the New York Stock Exchange

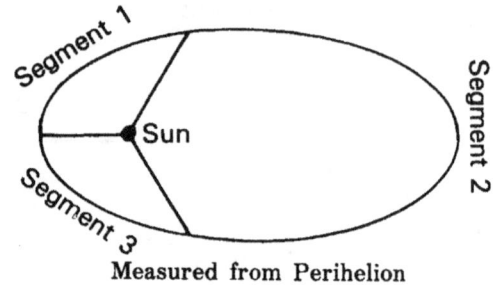

Measured from Perihelion

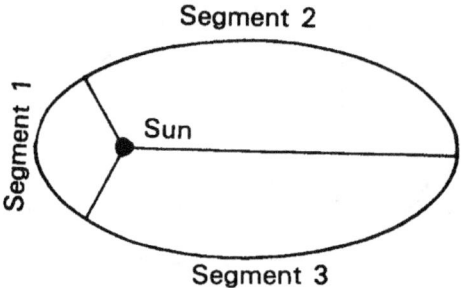

Measured from one half segment prior to Perihelion

Orbit Divided into Four Segments

Starting at Perihelion:

Segment 1	2.78439	6.83961	19.74683	40.72616	42.62255
Segment 2	3.14673	7.88924	22.25967	41.67034	81.59245
Segment 3	3.14673	7.88924	22.25967	41.67034	81.59245
Segment 4	2.78439	6.83961	19.74683	40.72616	42.62255

Starting at ½ Segment Prior to Perihelion:

Segment 1	2.71567	6.64351	19.26942	40.53378	37.68612
Segment 2	2.95903	7.34236	20.95893	41.19506	58.39215
Segment 3	3.22850	8.12947	22.82573	41.86909	93.95957
Segment 4	2.95903	7.34236	20.95893	41.19506	58.39215

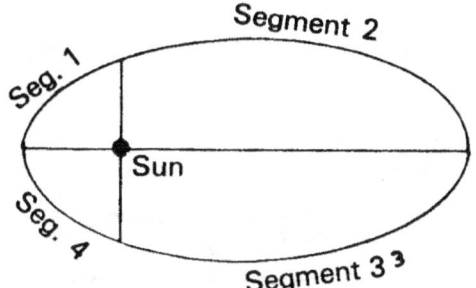
Measured from Perihelion

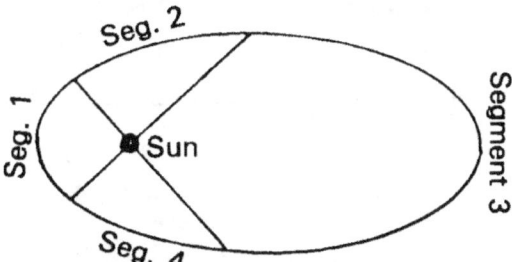
Measured from One Half
Segment Prior to Perihelion

Orbit Divided into Five Segments:

Starting at Perihelion:

Segment 1	2.20203	5.39879	15.62052	32.51055	32.15082
Segment 2	2.43316	6.06489	17.22438	33.12764	53.66799
Segment 3	2.59185	6.53034	18.32320	33.51663	76.79238
Segment 4	2.43316	6.06489	17.22438	33.12764	53.66799
Segment 5	2.20203	5.39879	15.62052	32.51055	32.15082

Starting at ½ Segment Prior to Perihelion:

Segment 1	2.16546	5.29473	15.36633	32.40664	29.70514
Segment 2	2.30169	5.68424	16.31263	32.78466	40.00322
Segment 3	2.54669	6.39725	18.01071	33.40852	69.35921
Segment 4	2.54669	6.39725	18.01071	33.40853	69.35921
Segment 5	2.30169	5.68424	16.31263	32.78466	40.00322

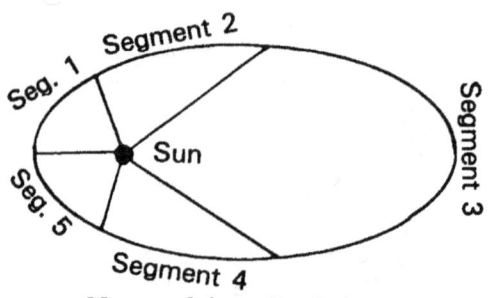

Measured from Perihelion

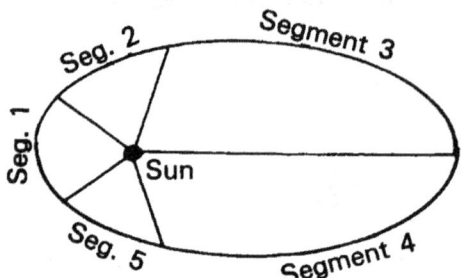

Measured from One Half
Segment Prior to Perihelion

Orbit Divided into Six Segments:

Starting at Perihelion:

Segment 1	1.82290	4.46442	12.93286	27.05803	25.94296
Segment 2	1.97139	4.89052	13.96380	27.46274	38.22950
Segment 3	2.13682	5.37391	15.10984	27.87573	60.04255
Segment 4	2.13682	5.37391	15.10984	27.87573	60.04255
Segment 5	1.97139	4.89052	13.96380	27.46274	38.22950
Segment 6	1.82290	4.46442	12.93286	27.05803	25.94296

Starting at ½ Segment Prior to Perihelion:

Segment 1	1.80131	4.40309	12.78276	26.99615	24.55593
Segment 2	1.88373	4.63806	13.35545	27.22808	30.34458
Segment 3	2.06469	5.16205	14.61048	27.70016	49.20448
Segment 4	2.16407	5.45438	15.29838	27.94037	64.77594
Segment 5	2.06469	5.16205	14.61048	27.70016	49.20448
Segment 6	1.88373	4.63806	13.35545	27.22808	30.34459

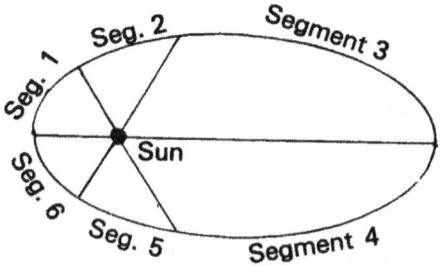
Measured from Perihelion

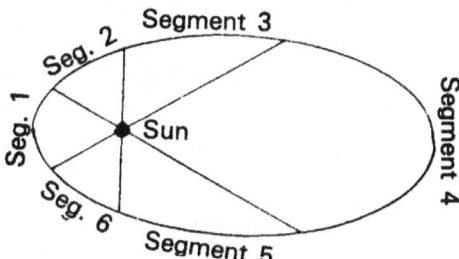
Measured from One Half
Segment prior to Perihelion

Orbit Divided into Seven Segments

	Planets				
Fraction	5	6	7	8	9
1	1.55605	3.80834	11.04059	23.17431	21.80845
2	1.65510	4.09165	11.72851	23.44846	29.34923
3	1.79140	4.48801	12.67334	23.79672	45.08664
4	1.85712	4.68170	13.12811	23.95403	55.94135
5	1.79140	4.48801	12.67334	23.79672	45.08664
6	1.65510	4.09165	11.72851	23.44846	29.34924
7	1.55605	3.80834	11.04059	23.17431	21.80845

	Planets				
Fraction	5	6	7	8	9
1	1.54230	3.76931	10.94494	23.13467	20.94618
2	1.59553	3.92077	11.31491	23.28589	24.51407
3	1.72492	4.29377	12.21279	23.63077	36.45534
4	1.83952	4.62965	13.00633	23.91251	52.77249
5	1.83952	4.62965	13.00633	23.91251	52.77249

6	1.72492	4.29377	12.21279	23.63077	36.45534
7	1.59553	3.92077	11.31491	23.28589	24.51408

Orbit Divided into Eight Segments

			Planets		
Fraction	5	6	7	8	9
1	1.35784	3.32175	9.63471	20.26689	10.84306
2	1.42655	3.51785	10.11212	20.45927	23.77949
3	1.53248	3.82451	10.84681	20.73580	34.61266
4	1.61425	4.06474	11.41286	20.93454	46.97979
5	1.61425	4.06474	11.41286	20.93454	46.97979
6	1.53248	3.82451	10.84681	20.73580	34.61266
7	1.42655	3.51785	10.11212	20.45927	23.77949
8	1.35784	3.32175	9.63471	20.26689	18.84306

			Planets		
Fraction	5	6	7	8	9
1	1.34855	3.29543	9.57015	20.24004	18.27038
2	1.38478	3.39838	9.82199	20.34364	20.62418
3	1.47817	3.66662	10.47031	20.59687	28.47490
4	1.58077	3.96602	11.18122	20.85461	41.38464
5	1.62624	4.10023	11.49582	20.96272	49.19217
6	1.58077	3.96602	11.18122	20.85461	41.38465
7	1.47817	3.66662	10.47031	20.59687	28.47490
8	1.38478	3.39838	9.82199	20.34364	20.62418

Orbit Divided into Nine Segments

			Planets		
Fraction	5	6	7	8	9
1	1.20468	2.94618	8.54850	18.00844	16.60518
2	1.25406	3.08686	8.89145	18.14785	20.00875
3	1.33555	3.32190	9.45692	18.36448	27.55853
4	1.41366	3.55044	9.99792	18.55806	38.10403
5	1.44632	3.64694	10.22385	18.63532	43.87704
6	1.41366	3.55044	9.99792	18.55807	38.10405
7	1.33555	3.32189	9.45692	18.36448	27.55852
8	1.25406	3.08686	8.89145	18.14785	20.00875
9	1.20468	2.94618	8.54830	18.00844	16.60518

| | | *Planets* | | | |
Fraction	5	6	7	8	9
1	1.19813	2.92701	8.50273	17.98944	16.20539
2	1.22384	3.00061	8.68149	18.06331	17.84026
3	1.29262	3.19763	9.15913	18.25234	23.23275
4	1.37779	3.44510	9.74960	18.47077	32.76195
5	1.43780	3.62171	10.16491	18.61537	42.27735
6	1.43780	3.62171	10.16491	18.61537	42.27735
7	1.37779	3.44510	9.74960	18.47077	32.76195
8	1.29262	3.19763	9.15913	18.25234	23.23275
9	1.22384	3.00061	8.68149	18.06331	17.84026

Orbit Divided into 10 Segments

| | | *Planets* | | | |
Fraction	5	6	7	8	9
1	1.08273	2.64736	7.68316	16.20332	14.85257
2	1.11930	2.75142	7.93736	16.30723	17.29825
3	1.18239	2.93281	8.37527	16.47743	22.70497
4	1.25077	3.13208	8.84911	16.65021	30.96302
5	1.29593	3.26517	9.16160	16.75831	38.39619
6	1.29593	3.26517	9.16160	16.75831	38.39619
7	1.25077	3.13208	8.84911	16.65021	30.96302
8	1.18239	2.93281	8.37527	16.47745	22.70497
9	1.11930	2.75142	7.93736	16.30723	17.29825
10	1.08273	2.64736	7.68316	16.20332	14.85257

| | | *Planets* | | | |
Fraction	5	6	7	8	9
1	1.07794	2.63378	7.64983	16.18939	14.56240
2	1.09682	2.68736	7.78113	16.24385	15.74446
3	1.14860	2.83536	8.14079	16.38763	19.59690
4	1.21764	3.03521	8.61967	16.56794	26.58432
5	1.27799	3.21218	9.03754	16.71592	35.21444
6	1.30219	3.28372	9.20492	16.77295	39.58738
7	1.27799	3.21218	9.03754	16.71592	35.21444
8	1.21764	3.03521	8.61967	16.56794	26.58432
9	1.14860	2.83536	8.14079	16.38763	19.59690
10	1.09682	2.68736	7.78113	16.24383	15.74446

Orbit Divided into 11 Segments

Fraction	\multicolumn{5}{c}{Planets}
	5	6	7	8	9
1	0.98330	2.40385	6.97773	14.72739	13.44076
2	1.01109	2.48286	7.17093	14.80675	15.25762
3	1.06051	2.62460	7.51407	14.94168	19.24220
4	1.11840	2.79267	7.91538	15.09055	25.57486
5	1.16575	2.93176	8.24317	15.20568	32.67206
6	1.18414	2.98620	8.37044	15.24892	36.05499
7	1.16575	2.93176	8.24317	15.20568	32.67206
8	1.11840	2.79267	7.91538	15.09055	25.57486
9	1.06051	2.48286	7.17093	14.80675	15.25762
10	1.01109	2.48286	7.717093	14.80675	15.25762
11	0.98330	2.40385	6.97773	14.72739	13.44077

Fraction	\multicolumn{5}{c}{Planets}
	5	6	7	8	9
1	0.97969	2.39363	6.95262	14.71688	13.22347
2	0.99395	2.43408	7.05180	14.75812	14.10605
3	1.03375	2.54765	7.32832	14.86956	16.95134
4	1.08949	2.70847	7.71507	15.01738	22.14609
5	1.14467	2.86967	8.09731	15.15513	29.25413
6	1.17941	2.97217	8.33769	15.23787	35.14566
7	1.17941	2.97217	8.33769	15.23787	35.14566
8	1.14467	2.86967	8.09731	15.15513	29.25413
9	1.08949	2.70847	7.71507	15.01738	22.14608
10	1.03375	2.54765	7.32832	14.86956	16.95134
11	0.99395	2.43408	7.05180	14.75812	14.10605

Orbit Divided into 12 Segments

Fraction	\multicolumn{5}{c}{Planets}
	5	6	7	8	9
1	0.90066	2.20155	6.39138	13.49807	12.27797
2	0.92225	2.26287	6.54146	13.55996	13.66499
3	0.96148	2.37519	6.81397	13.66813	16.67959
4	1.00991	2.51533	7.14983	13.79461	21.54990
5	1.05479	2.64672	7.46065	13.90554	27.65458
6	1.08204	2.72719	7.64919	13.97018	32.38797
7	1.08204	2.72719	7.64919	13.97019	32.38797

8	1.05479	2.64672	7.46065	13.90554	27.65458
9	1.00991	2.51534	7.14983	13.79461	21.54990
10	0.96148	2.37519	6.81397	13.66813	16.67959
11	0.92225	2.26287	6.54148	13.55996	13.66499
12	0.90066	2.20155	6.39138	13.19807	12.27796

Planets

Fraction	5	6	7	8	9
1	0.89787	2.19366	6.37200	13.48996	12.11101
2	0.90890	2.22493	6.44871	13.52191	12.78756
3	0.94008	2.31377	6.66534	13.60977	14.94833
4	0.98526	2.44379	6.97894	13.73116	18.88646
5	1.03370	2.58480	7.31464	13.85413	24.55736
6	1.07140	2.69571	7.57560	13.94518	30.43128
7	1.08570	2.73805	7.67453	13.97873	33.09701
8	1.07140	2.69571	7.57560	13.94518	30.43128
9	1.03370	2.58480	7.31464	13.85413	24.55736
10	0.98526	2.44379	6.97894	13.73116	18.88646
11	0.94008	2.31377	6.66534	13.60977	14.94833
12	0.90890	2.22493	6.44871	13.52191	12.78756

Table III

Planet Name & Number	(Degrees/day)			(km/sec)			(Years)				
	W	Wa	Wp	V	Va	Vp	P	Pa			
Mercury 1	4.09239	2.75888	6.85215	47.874	38.845	59.002	0.2408	0.8580	0.1552	48.68	85.57
Venus 2	1.60214	1.57991	1.62477	85.021	84.777	85.267	0.6152	0.6289	0.6066	1.41	1.89
Earth 8	0.98561	0.95875	1.01882	29.785	29.298	80.281	1.0000	1.0885	0.9674	8.84	8.26
Mars 4	0.52404	0.48675	0.68425	24.180	21.981	26.489	1.8809	2.2568	1.5540	19.98	17.88
Jupiter 5	0.08809	0.07557	0.09158	18.064	12.452	18.707	11.8622	18.0484	10.7682	9.96	9.27
Saturn 6	0.08846	0.02996	0.08749	9.645	9.119	10.201	29.4577	82.9010	26.2921	11.69	10.75
Uranus 7	0.01178	0.01069	0.01290	6.801	6.488	7.128	84.0180	92.1977	76.8858	9.74	9.08
Neptune 8	0.00598	0.00587	0.00609	5.488	5.884	5.482	164.7980	167.7794	167.7794	1.81	1.79
Pluto 9	0.00897	0.00246	0.00681	4.788	8.674	6.110	248.4800	400.1545	400.1545	61.07	41.77

W = Mean daily angular motion of planet as seen from the Sun (heliocentric) in degrees
Wa = Daily angular motion at apogee in degrees
Wp = Daily angular motion at perigee in degrees
V = Mean (or circular) Velocity in km/sec.
VA = Velocity at apogee in Km/sec.
Vp = Velocity at perigee in km/sec.
P = Period in years (sidereal years)
Pa = Period if planet moved at constant angular velocity of Wa
Pp = Period if planet moved at a constant angular velocity of Wp
$\% A = \frac{(Pa - P)}{P} 100\%$

Table 2 shows the limits within which any terrestrial cycle affiliated with any fractional orbital period will fall. For example, the successive fifths of the Saturn orbit into which the average 5.9-year cycle might fall cannot, when measured from perihelion to perihelion, be less than 5.39 or more than 6.53 years.

I suppose the most dramatic fact revealed by Table II is the changing length of the fractional orbital periods of Pluto due to the eccentricity of Pluto's orbit. For example, if the orbit is divided into six sections, the sections vary in length from 25.94 to 60.04 years (as measured from perihelion).

Although there is no magic about the various divisions that were selected, the matter has to be checked point by point against the facts as they occur. If cycles on Earth are related in some way to the planets, we may have the answer to the old problem of why cycles first crest early, then late, when compared to a rigid model.

There is another mystery that may be cleared up by this new concept. Why do we have so many slightly different measurements of what seems to be the same cycle? If the unit fractions of the orbital periods of the planets do have some relationship to cycles on the earth, it is now possible (1) to determine the period of cycles much more accurately by taking this factor into account, and (2) to see if the irregularities of the terrestrial cycle lengths correspond to the irregularities of the planetary orbital periods.

For example, suppose your data show cycles that average 5.9 years in length, and that your data cover a time span of 29.5 years (the period of Saturn). We now know that successive fifths of the orbital period of Saturn, from perihelion, are 5;29, 5.68, 6.397, and 5.68 years. This information is needed for a comparison of any variation of the actual cycle from the ideal over the 29.5-year span of time.

But, suppose the data cover a complete orbit plus another one-fifth of an orbit. If this extra span of time is a time when Saturn is going fastest, the total elapsed time will be 29.4577 years plus 6.397 years, or an average of 5.97 years rather than 5.89, the average period based on one complete orbit. (Of course this error will become less and less as we use more and more data.)

If there is no relationship between the planetary orbital periods and cycles on the earth, then the dismissal of the idea as nonsense should be based on valid comparisons which are now Possible. The variation in the orbital fractions are only one of the complexities of comparisons of this sort. But one thing at a time.

Chapter II

Planetary Aspects

The aspects related to the planets show the conditions of the changes. If we are talking about conjunctions, this means that all the planets are in one sign. If the influences in one sign are all negative then it's going to be a turning point of negativity which would relate to a bear market. If the planets in conjunction are positive planets then this relates to a bullish market. Venus, Jupiter and the Sun are all positive. Saturn and Mars can be very negative. Uranus is neutral, but also explosive in whatever aspect it's involved in. If it's being aspected by a positive planet, then it is positive. If it's hit by a negative planet, then it's negative. Venus and Jupiter are the two most positive and Mars and Saturn are the two negative points. A conjunction is an indication of a new pattern, that the pattern that has been present before is now going to end. New potentials are released, a new cycle is beginning, a cycle that is in relation to the conjunction at the time.

The semisextile is an aspect of 30 degrees that reacts as a vocal center. The novile is a 40-degree aspect that relates to subjective growth. A septile is a 51-degree aspect that relates to an unexpected move. A semi-square is a 45-degree aspect which is interfused with a high degree of intensity causing activity. The sextile is a 60-degree aspect and is productive; it brings spontaneous growth. The quintile is a 72-degree aspect that relates to creative transformation. The square is a 90-degree aspect that points to a crisis point bringing confrontation with obstacles. The biseptile is 102 degrees. It is the enforcer of the square aspect. The trine, a 120-degree aspect, is harmonious, and brings growth and expansion. The sesquiquadrate is a 135-degree aspect and is an interfunctional aspect that relates to activity; it activates a stock's volume. The biquintile is 144 degrees and it is rational aspect which relates to the movement in relation to a stock. The quincunx is a 150-degree aspect which indicates a demand for externalization, a situation that is near maturity and one that is activated by the aspects from the sign that relate to the stock hitting a potential high or potential growth or a product that comes in demand under this aspect. The triseptile, a 154-degree aspect, is a cooperation aspect that leads in from the 150-degree aspect. An opposition is a 180-degree aspect and relates to the opposite part of a cycle, the apex of the cycle. The energies involved are negative and generally indicate conflicting situations, a falling apart. Under the opposition the stock market often will be confronted with conditions that tear it apart because the opposition is more of a bearish aspect and relates to a change from bullish to bearish. Using an aspect orb of ten degrees sometimes causes two aspects to be activated at the same time. The nature of the planet involving the aspects determines the motion in relation to the speed of a certain stock or the Dow-Jones averages.

To help you understand each aspect, the following illustrations use the Sun in a fixed position and the transiting Moon to show how each aspect is formed between two planets.

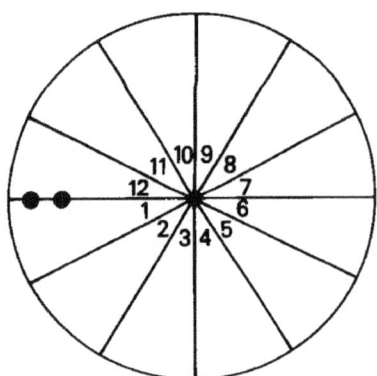

1, Conjunction 0° Apart

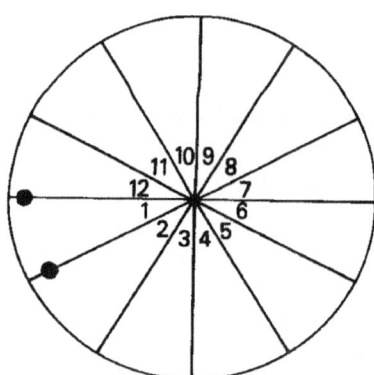

2, Semi-sextile 30° Apart

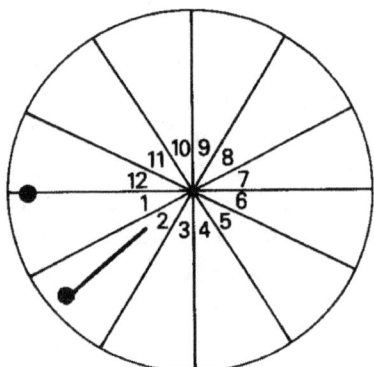

3, Novile 40° Apart

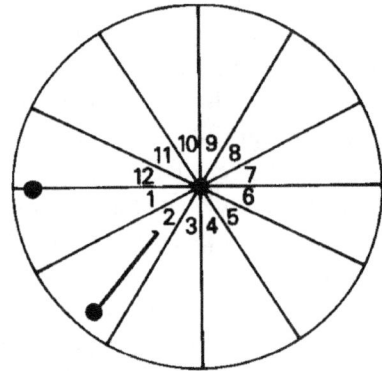

4, Semi-square 45° Apart

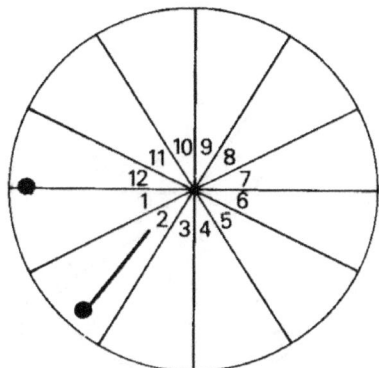

5, Septile 51° Apart

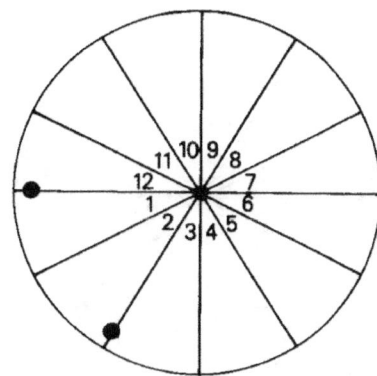

6, Sextile 60° Apart

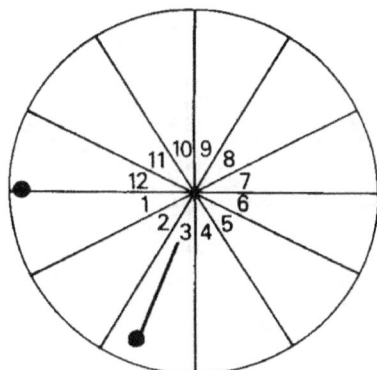

7, Quintile 72° Apart

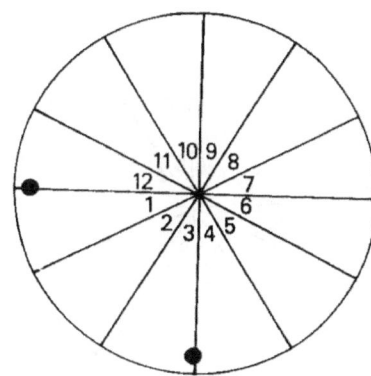

8, Square 90° Apart

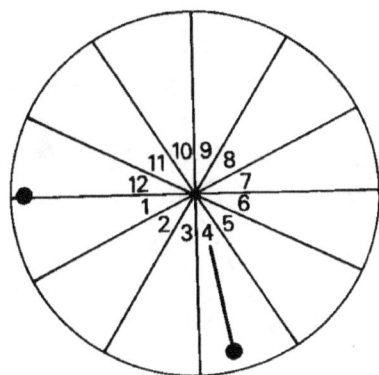

9, Biseptile 102° Apart

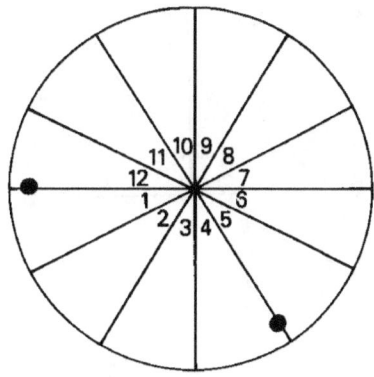

10, Trine 120° Apart

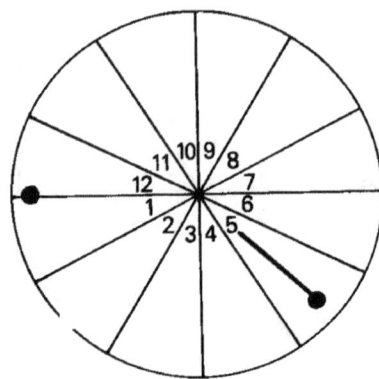

11, Sesquiquadrate 135° Apart

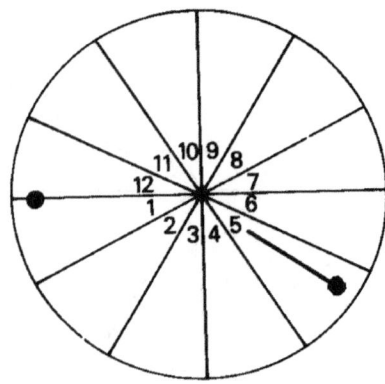

12, Trine 120° Apart

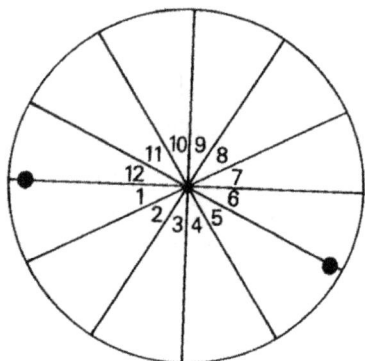

13, Quincunx 15° Apart

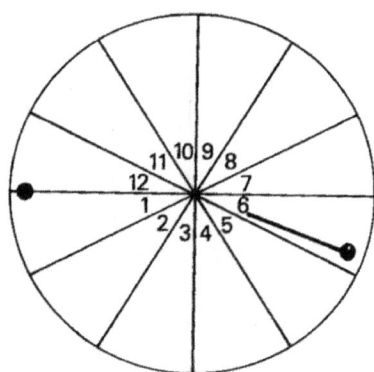

14, Triseptile 154° Apart

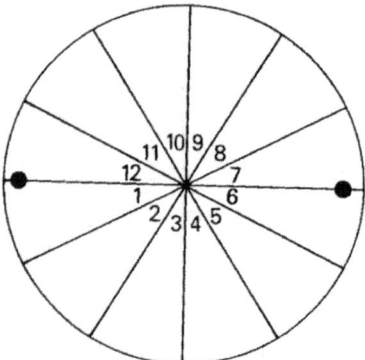

15, Opposition 180° Apart

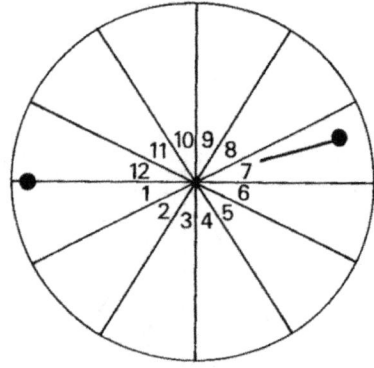

16, Triseptile 154° Apart

THE PLANETARY ASPECTS/51

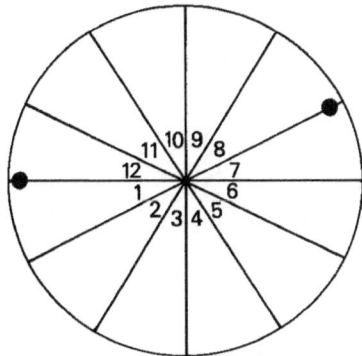

17, Quincunx 150° Apart

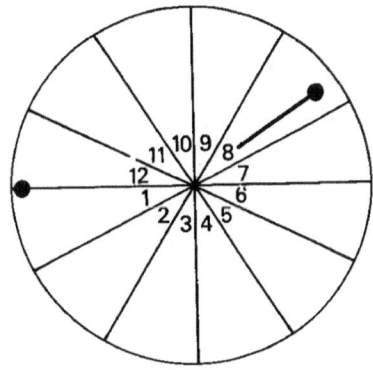

18, Biquintile 144° Apart

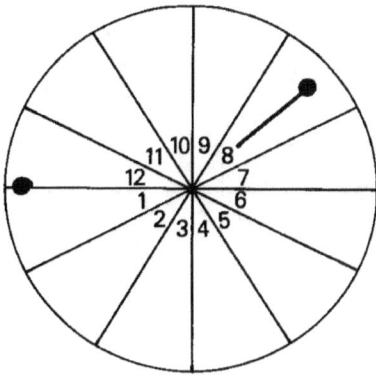

19, Sesquiquadrate 136° Apart

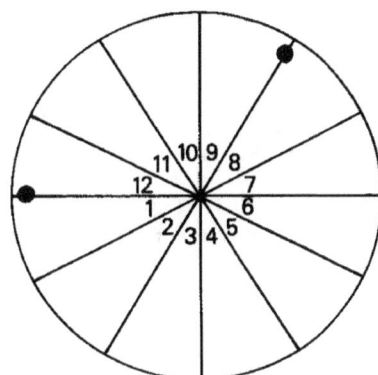

20, Trine 120° Apart

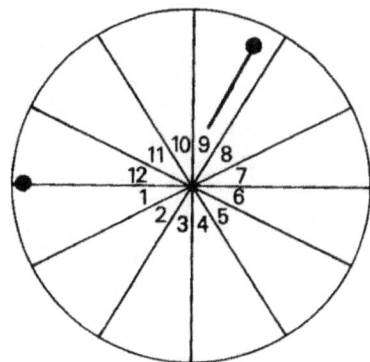

21, Biseptile 102o Apart

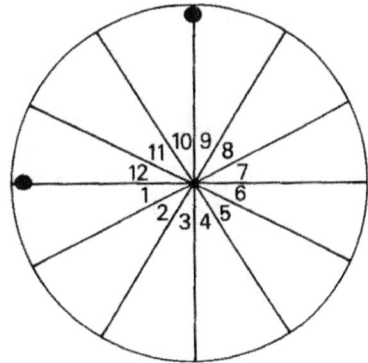

22, Square 90o Apart

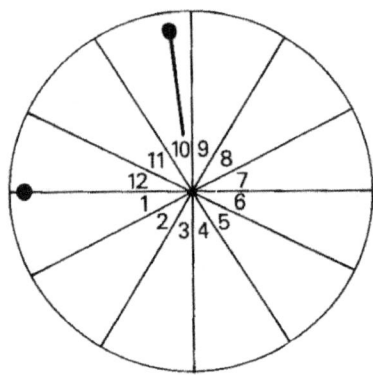

23, Quintile 72° Apart

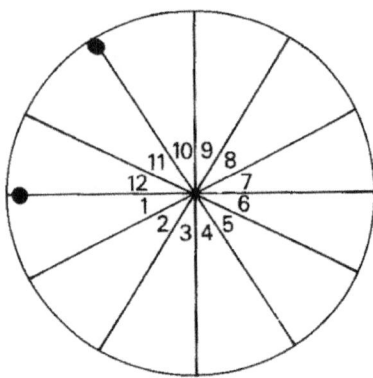

24, Sextile 60° Apart

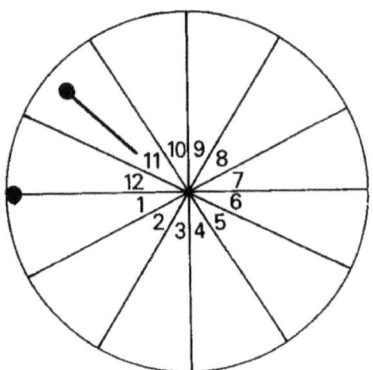

25, Septile 51° Apart

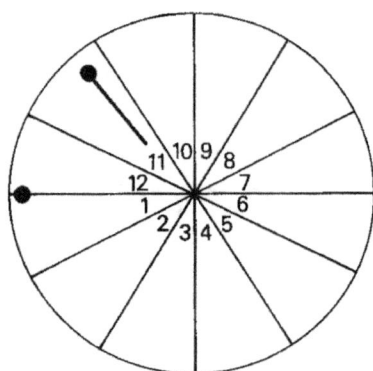

26, Semi-square 45° Apart

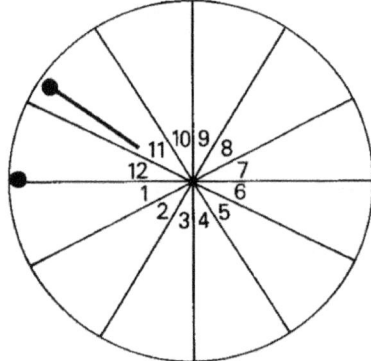

27, Novile 40° Apart

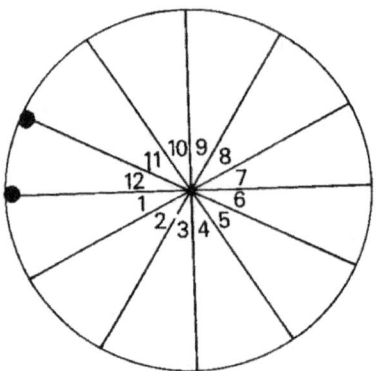

28, Semi-sextile 30° Apart

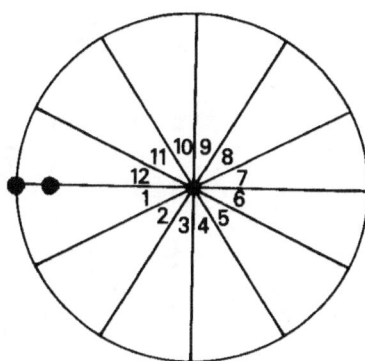

29, Back to Conjunction 0°

Chapter III

Planetary Signs

Each sign represents a category of certain products or things concerning different items that a certain stock might produce or might be involved in. As the planets transit these signs, the products ruled by them are subject to the transit's influence. For example, if Saturn were transiting the sign of Cancer then all products related to Cancer would come under restriction, especially building materials and home products. Problems related to these areas would result in sky-high prices. With Jupiter there would be expansion of these products and there would be many of them. Because Jupiter is superficial, it can indicate over-valued products. For example, if Jupiter is transiting the sign of Leo, ruler of gold, it would boost the price of gold, but it would fall as soon as Jupiter's influence ended, and return to a realistic price. Jupiter always indicates prices higher than the product is worth. Saturn is the planet that restricts and other planets associated with it show a trend of thinking; Mars, for example, could represent a fast upswing without stability.

Aries rules diamonds, diamond mines and energy projects (whether laser technology or solar energy) and is connected indirectly with fireplaces, garage manufacturers, hardware dealers, heat systems, any instruments used for cutting, iron, steel, anything connected with the military, machine tools or the machinery itself.

Taurus rules financial institutions, such as banks and loan companies, carpet manufacturers, cash register manufacturers, the cattle industry, copper, emeralds, wheat, hogs, jewelry, anything related to the music industry, sodium sulfate, building materials, meat packing, forest products, toys, and moving and storage.

Gemini rules such things as advertising, advertising houses, billboards, publishing, book stores, broadcasting, communications, crystal, private or public education, highways, telegraph, typesetting machinery, telephone industry, weather machinery, quicksilver, office and business machine equipment, pollution control devices, transportation such as trucks and anything connected with fast movement.

Cancer rules bakery goods, the boat industry, fishing industry, inns, motels, hotels, milk and milk-related products, not necessarily dairy but products that are associated with milk such as chocolate milk or things made from milk other than cheese, butter, etc. It also rules pearls, areas connected with real estate, restaurants, swimming pools, sheep, silver, aluminum, canned foods or processed foods, home furnishings and mobile homes.

Leo rules almonds, citrus fruit, gold and the entertainment area. This relates to movies, all types of entertainment stock, anything connected with casinos, golf courses, government buildings, olive groves, trees, showboats, solariums, sports arenas, stadiums, stock brokers, sunflowers and walnuts.

Virgo rules the products of animals in general but it is more or less related to chickens and things connected with exotic foods. It also rules bees, honey, any stocks that deal with craftsmanship, farmers, areas related to the medical field, grain elevators, oats, paper products, quicksilver, refrigerators, turkeys, any form of container, tobacco and retail stores.

Libra rules things connected with the fine arts, beauty parlors, chinaware, cosmetics. dressmakers, luxury furniture, luxurious jewelry, musical instruments, weights, women's apparel and soap. It also rules strawberries, strawberry products and copper products.

Scorpio rules chemical laboratories, dentistry related stocks, sewage, iron, steel and products related to the dead such as funeral homes.

Sagittarius rules stocks involved with imports, exports, mass-market publications, race tracks, insurance, and the metal tin.

Capricorn rules air conditioning systems, clockmakers, products dealing with watches and clocks, ice dealers, lumber, pine trees, lead, dairy products, oil, offshore drilling, railroads and shoes.

Aquarius rules aerospace products and anything involved with aeronautics. It rules airports, aircraft, automobiles, batteries, electronic components or devices, lighting products such as lamps and lights made for industry, photographic supplies, radio, TV, x-ray equipment, computers and everything connected with the computer system and laser beam products. It also rules air transport, auto parts, and the metal lead.

Pisces rules alcoholic beverages, brewers, distillers, soft drink products, the metal platinum, gas systems and plants and anything connected with oil and oil drilling. It rules drugs, fishing canneries and anything connected with products from the sea.

These are only some products related to each sign. As these signs are affected by transits, these products will come into demand or there will be shortages.

On our chart we see where aerospace and air transport in 1967 started moving up to an all-time high as the planet Venus transited the sign of Aquarius on January 7, 1967. It affected the movement of these products as it conjoined the Sun, also in the sign of Aquarius. In March 1973 both Mars and Jupiter went into the sign of Aquarius. If you look at the pattern in 1973 as it started, both air transport and aerospace started to fall to a new low. It hit the new low in the first market during 1974, but what happened was that Mars brought on the action as far as changing things and the expansion of Jupiter resulted in too much of the product. When too much of something exists, prices have a tendency to drop, especially if connected with Mars. But as Saturn moved into the sign of Leo, the sign opposite Aquarius, the aspects that were applying to this started to move up to a new high in the period of 1978.

Many products fell during the period of 1974 and 1975 because of the aspects that were applying to a depressed market. As the transit from Cancer was the dominant factor, it caused a wide drop. Entertainment stocks were hurt by it as well as cosmetics stocks. But gold mining stocks, as an example, ruled by the sign of Leo, hit new highs as Saturn was transiting Leo. Look at the gold mining stocks as they project through the 1974-1975-1976-1977 period. As they hit highs during 1974-1975, Saturn was in Leo. This brought restrictions to gold. The market was depressed, gold was needed because there wasn't enough of it, and thus the planetary movement caused this product to be in need. Even though everything else was down, gold went up. And what made it so different this time was that when the market is depressed gold usually has a tendency to move up, but during this period the effect of it was more dominant and gold mining stocks reached new highs. Notice that machinery, oil well equipment and services were not hurt by this influence as they kept moving up from 1974 to 1975, again not being affected by this cycle. We know that the sign of Cancer also affects restaurants. Again, for some unusual reason, that restaurant period from the 1973 factor was also at a high because of the restrictions of the Saturn influence. Steel products also rose during this period, as did trucking stocks. You can see the same influence in the 1970 cycle. So this will help you to determine what stocks will hold out during a depressed market. Whatever sign Saturn is in, that's a stock or stock-related product that will do the opposite.

CHAPTER IV

PANICS AND CRASHES

Panics are the product of Saturn as it relates to the human emotions. Saturn represents fear, depression and produces many types of phobias which start out slow and cover a wide path where everyone follows, dashing in the wrong direction and fearing everything in sight. Instead of trying to develop a sound and original way to deal with the crises which are aspected ahead, most people try to escape by running and, from this, we have panics, crashes, depressions and recessions.

It takes Saturn 28 to 30 years to make a full cycle through the 12 signs. It takes Jupiter around 12 years to transit all the signs. It takes Saturn about 60 years to return in conjunction with Jupiter, which means that a period of about 58 to 60 years is needed for Jupiter and Saturn to come back together in the same sign.

As we look at the chart of the New York Stock Exchange, May 17, 1792 at 8:52 a.m., we look at the sensitive zones to indicate what areas of the chart are sensitive points that can lead to a crash, recession or panic. With this chart we also take the chart of the United States, July 4, 1776, to see the difference between a panic, recession and depression. (See charts on pages x and xi.)

Recessions and depressions often relate to the chart of the United States, but as we look at the chart of the New York Stock Exchange we can see the Ascendant is in the sign of Cancer, Descendant in the sign of Capricorn, Midheaven in the sign of Aries, Nadir in the sign of Libra. The United States has similar sensitive points. Libra is on the Ascendant, Aries on the Descendant, Cancer on the Midheaven and Capricorn on the Nadir. What this is telling us between both charts is that when Saturn is in the sign of Cancer, Capricorn or Libra, these hit the negative zones.

Aries is a fire sign, so it would be a trine aspect and would have no effect as far as the United States because of the fire element. So we know that our worst cycles would be when Saturn is in Cancer, Capricorn or Libra.

To check any other sensitive points, we know that the New York Stock Exchange, being under the sign of Taurus, would be affected by transiting Saturn in Taurus, causing the market to be somewhat low but not actually a depression. With Mars in Virgo, this would be an affected sign, as would the United States with Neptune in Virgo; these are sensitive points. So we would have to consider Virgo as a negative area. We would also have to include Mars as the New York Stock Exchange has Mars in Virgo.

In the United States chart, Saturn in Gemini would also represent a low point but not what would be called a critical point. It does represent a division. And the other mutable aspect involving Pisces would react the same way.

So we have three cardinal points—Cancer, Capricorn and Libra—and we have the three mutable points—Gemini, Virgo and Pisces. So we know we have these major points that are affected and can lead to panics and crashes.

But there is always a combination. Don't forget we have the 58 to 60 cycle of the complete return with Jupiter and Saturn together, and we have the 28 to 30 cycles of the spin-offs with just Saturn returning with Mars. The spin-offs are not as dangerous as the 58 to 60 year cycles.

So these six points are our major points. However, there is one other before we get into predicting the trends and changes related to these aspects. The New York Stock Exchange has three planets in Taurus which would be affected by the transit of Saturn in Taurus. That would be a more severe affliction than the opposition of Saturn transiting Scorpio. So let's put these combinations together and I will explain each point and each effect as we go through the zodiac.

We will begin with the Gemini point, Saturn in Gemini. This point is very sensitive in the chart of the United States, dealing with eighth and ninth house matters. The home of the United States, the ninth house, is also Cancer; so this would be the prominent point of Jupiter. And going from this point the other sensitive point would be the tenth house, Leo. So the combination of Saturn in Gemini, Jupiter in Cancer, Mars in Leo is the affected part. The transits of Saturn in Gemini, Mars in Leo are spin-offs and not quite as bad.

Gemini affects communication. It deals with railroads, rumors, publishers, communication of all sorts by air, rail, car, telephone. All of these areas are associated with the Gemini-Saturn influence, whereas Jupiter in Cancer affects the home. But to go to the beginning of this combination, let's go to 1884.

In 1884 we had this combination, but the effect of it was not that of a long duration. It was more concerned with a scandal, a variation, more or less a Gemini characteristic. Hetty Green, a female Wall Street speculator, suddenly called for $25 million in securities and $475,000 in cash from the firm J.J. Cisco and Company, which forced the bankers to close their doors. Again, there was a connection with the banks. All the influence of Saturn was prominent.

This was a shock to the security market in which one thing led to another as a chain reaction. This panic caused the closing of Wall Street due to the irregularities of its cashiers. So it was strictly a panic that arose from the vast money manipulation of this one woman that related to a financial disturbance.

The next return of a 60-year cycle was a little short, as Saturn in Gemini, Jupiter in Cancer, Mars in Leo came in the year 1942. It was during this period that the United States was involved in World War II. Now, on the lesser cycles of the 30-year duration of just Saturn in Gemini, Mars in Leo, around 30 years from 1884 to 1912 and again to 1942. But as I mentioned, this is still a minor aspect as related to panics. The influence was in effect from 1912 and through May 1914 (the combination came back due to a retrograde), and in the middle came the Panic of 1913.

Again the Gemini influence affected things, this time on rumors of war. And due to the rumors of war it affected the commodity market. Unemployment and company failures started to spread and, when war was declared in August 1914 (and war was declared right when this aspect came in), businesses were paralyzed and the stock market went into complete chaos. Again the Gemini influence, with Saturn, led to these problems. The New York Stock exchange, and the other exchanges as well, closed from August to November, the whole duration of this aspect. And, again with Gemini, the crisis was short-lived in relation to stock prices.

The other 30-year spinoff with Saturn in Gemini and Mars in Leo was 30 years from 1942, which affected the United States in 1972. Again the stock market took a dive and there was loss due to this period of Saturn in Gemini. As of May 1917 the bull market ended and the Dow tumbled all the way through the cycle.

The attack on Pearl Harbor was December 7, 1941. Jupiter was in Gemini, but Saturn was three degrees away and did not enter Gemini until May 9, 1942. This dragged us into World War II. On the return of this cycle, we were concerned about another war, with Saturn again in Gemini, under the 60-year cycle. On September 11, 2001, this cycle returned with the attack on the World Trade Center. The United States invaded Afghanistan on October 7, 2001.

What about the Hetty Green of 1884. On December 2, 2001, Enron filed Chapter 11 Bankruptcy and became the largest bankruptcy in U.S. history. This was topped with the cycle of Saturn in Gemini, when WorldCom filed for Chapter 11 on June 21, 2002. Again we look to the 60-year cycle, this time the one that will take place during 2060-62. Will the U.S. be faced with another surprise attack, and will another corporation swindle millions of dollars from its stockholders?

Our next sign with Saturn is Cancer. We take Cancer ruling the birth of the United States which is under the sign of Cancer in conjunction with its natal Sun, Venus and Jupiter. Remember, Jupiter rules finances, money. The combination where the money will be affected is Taurus; Mars in Taurus rules this combination. So the cycle with Saturn in Cancer, Jupiter in Taurus, and Mars in Taurus again relates to panics and crashes.

Cancer rules homes. It affects what comes into a home, the weather, agriculture, energy, land interests, shortages, taxation and living conditions, and is also the aspect of people versus government. The combination of Saturn in Cancer alone can be devastating, but what's bad about this combination of Taurus with Jupiter especially is that it steals from the home to bring wealth to large corporations. The combination is bad for schemes—shortages where there are no shortages, deception. It is also an aspect that seems to bring out the precious metals, gold, silver. The minor cycles of Saturn as far as the 30-year duration are not that severe.

Let's take the first negative point of Saturn and see how it was affected and the duration of it. In 1857 we had Saturn in Cancer, Jupiter in Taurus, and Mars in Taurus. This was known as the period of the California Gold Rush, which led to the panic of 1857. As the discovery of gold encouraged people to move west, everybody was speculating on railroads, transport, building of new homes. There was a period of prosperity.

Business boomed, bankers were ready to loan anybody money—on paper. It was said back then that brokers with only $1500 on deposit could write checks for a hundred thousand or more. Mining schemes came into it and swindles went in every direction. It was a very speculative and deceptive time. Extra shares were being issued and floated with little or nothing to back them.

And the worst of these stocks was the New Haven Railroad where $2 million of stock had been forged. Credit was the main danger here as this is the aspect of the home conditions. Credit is a big part of the aspect of Saturn in Cancer. From this, many brokers were suspended, the market collapsed and the bankers called loans. There were panics in Cincinnati and other cities.

And even with all the gold that was produced in California within a period of 10 years, all that wealth had become a commodity for export only. Export of what was taken from our home into another home. Trusted heads of corporations had swindled investors in their own securities. Clerks had stolen what their superiors swindled. The failure of the Ohio Life Insurance and Trust Company in August 1857 was the last straw, the act that started the panic. There were runs on other banks all over the country. The paper inflation of the country was estimated at $2 billion. Bank after bank extended payments until, finally, the Bank of New York, the strongest and oldest bank, failed. As the Saturn influence of Cancer moved in, destruction was done. The Chemical Bank and Loan was the only bank to continue to pay out in gold.

This whole thing was caused by human nature and the greed from the discovery of gold which stimulated speculation because all everybody could see was "I know he's getting rich." Yet the whole country was being deceived by these elements of prosperity. Sixty years later, in May 1917, we again had Saturn in Cancer, Jupiter in Taurus and Mars in Taurus. And once again through deception, war for the United States.

In December 1973, Saturn in Cancer with Mars in Taurus would be making its way; the exact conjunction with Jupiter in Taurus would be somewhat delayed. But all evidence indicated the United States would fall into a recession and the stock market would fall between five and seven hundred points. Devious tactics would be used to create shortages, again with the effect on what is ruled by Saturn in Cancer.

The year 1974 will go down in history as one with an energy crisis. But when Saturn moved out of the sign of Cancer, its effects on housing and energy-related products would be over. Of course, prices would go sky-high on home products, energy products and things we need to live day-by-day. Phenomenal income from high prices would be made by businesses throughout the country, but there would be a panic that would cause the stock market to drop to new lows.

Again we have the deception point from man's own greed. Everybody would try to cash in on the run. But the American home would suffer from this aspect of Saturn in Cancer in December 1973. And 1974 will be known as a year of recession with the aspect of Saturn into the sign of Cancer and Mars in Taurus with the impulsive spending (see article on page 64).

As Saturn left Gemini, going into Cancer on March 20, 2003, we had the invasion of Iraq directed by a president whose Sun-sign is Cancer. This is the cycle that created the housing bubble, and everything from this cycle had remnants of the past.

The next sensitive sign is Virgo. Looking at the United States and New York Stock Exchange charts, we find that Virgo is its second house influence, affecting money, along with third-house matters of transportation, banking, loans, and things associated with Virgo such as public health, the working class, strikes, servants, civil matters, labor organizations, transportation, paper products. What we are looking for now is all combinations of Virgo. We have no other points that are in this point of Saturn, so we are looking for Saturn in Virgo, Jupiter in Virgo, Mars in Virgo.

In 1861 we had a conjunction of these three planets: Saturn in Virgo, Jupiter in Virgo, Mars in Virgo. It became known as the depression of 1861. It was the first economic effect of the Civil

D   THE MIAMI NEWS   Wed., Sept. 19, 1973

HERB RAU

'74 predictions: mostly bad news

TODAY'S HEARTBURN
Bumper strip on rear of Volkswagen trapped in Palmetto Expressway traffic jam: "I'd Rather Be Sailing!"

MIAMI CONFIDENTIAL: What's the prospects for 1974? Jack Gillen of Miami and Orlando, who has racked up a surprising number of accurate predictions during past few years, comes up now with his forecasts for the coming year. And very little of it is good. Here they are: "The new year will bring restrictions and turmoil throughout the world. The U.S. will be in a Saturn return recycle and will go into a recession. New government controls and spending will be initiated, with the possibility of the railroads falling under government control . . . In the stock market, the **Dow Jones** averages will fall between 500 and 700. President Nixon will be under a death aspect on July 4 . . . A European war will break out during 1974.

"**DAMAGE TO FOOD** crops, floods, droughts, earthquakes, epidemics, energy crisis, poison gasses, changeable weather and unemployment will be part of the world's problems . . . There will be many mine disasters all over the world. An earthquake from Canada to Virginia is aspected . . . With Uranus going into Scorpio, the U.S. will have it's highest divorce rate in history. New marriage views, sexual freedom, underworld crime and sexual-type murders will only be some of the problems under this cycle . . . The U.S. and England will have backouts. Japan will have tidal waves. Florida and California will have problems with off-shore drilling . . . Auto sales in the U.S. will be down. The Country Music field will produce many of the hits this year . . . France, South America, India and Israel will be hit hard with unrest and terrors."

War, throwing the North and the South into severe panic. There were nearly 6,000 failures of northern companies. Northern banks were able to maintain payments until the latter part of 1861, in the month of December, as this combination of Saturn, Mars and Jupiter in Virgo came into effect in August 1861. In Illinois, 89 out of 110 banks failed; 39 in Wisconsin and 27 in Indiana all went under. The effect of the third house and the second house dealing with banks and money related to this depression.

The South was not so fortunate. The war meant destruction and chaos, and the currency had no value at all and was known as "Confederate Money." And during the four years of the Civil War, government expenditures in the North were greater than in the whole previous history of the nation. One way the government chose to raise money was by issuing for the first time non-interest bearing notes which were called "greenbacks." This created an inflationary condition that took decades to overcome.

Again the matter of the depression of 1861 was through government inflationary methods that related to a combination that failed and led to depression.

In September of 1921, the 60-year combination of Saturn, Jupiter and Mars in Virgo again occurred; this became known as the Panic of 1921. It was the same problem again—we never learn from our mistakes! We were buying products from Europe with our *own money that we were loaning*. The import balance of the United States in 1920 was completely abnormal, based on the fact that we were selling goods abroad with our own money. This meant the Americans not only lost goods, but gold too, and the loss of goods further raised prices and brought about inflation which again encouraged speculation.

In the two years following the war, the United States government spent almost as much money as it had spent during the war years. Again, it was this strange combination of all these planets in Virgo. Like before, the government was involved, and it was the issuing of money and government programs that lead to inflation, that add up to depression or panic.

During 1921, it was difficult to get a dollar's worth of work for a dollar's pay. It was a very, very hard period as conditions became worse and worse due to the government program, resulting in a cut in the market for the American manufacturers and a disaster to many American farmers. By the 1920s, the post-war boom had attained unhealthy proportions. And the main thing was that credit expansion had reached the legal limit, and the banks again were forced to retreat. Manufacturers became convinced that they had to produce more than could be sold. So again all these elements with this combination brought the Panic of 1921.

The next appearance of the 60-year cycle will be in May 1980. But we are in store for two rounds of this aspect, as Saturn, Jupiter, and Mars are also in Virgo around December 1979.

What we're going to have in 1980 is promises that once again will be affected by strikes, people wanting more money, expansion of credit, people making more money than ever before because of the strikes, interest rates going up and the country going deeper in debt as inflation gets out of hand. Speculation will again be a prominent factor, with the stock market rising to all-time highs; it would not be surprising to see the stock market at the 1,000 mark at the midpoint of 1979, leading to the Panic of 1980. This will be a period of tension and scandal in labor areas and, just like the two following cycles, this one will be no different.

Saturn and Mars were also in Virgo in 1861, another 30-year period, and thus this combination occurred again in 1891. This was not a very drastic period as it was strictly only a spin-off point which was not a dominant factor. During this period it affected England and Germany more than any other countries.

The year 2008 began with the Saturn in Virgo. As in the previous cycles, banks started to fail because of sub-prime mortgages. With Virgo ruling the workplace, unemployment would climb to double digits. The stock market crashed, leaving millions of people heartbroken and broke. We also had fraud under this cycle, as before. On December 11, 2008, Bernard Madoff was arrested for the biggest swindle of its kind in history. The global economy would experience the 80-year cycle from 1929.

The question at this time: Could this be avoided by the time Saturn leaves Virgo, or will the federal cash supply be wiped out like it was under the Harrison administration and by the McKinley tariffs of the 1890s.

Our next point is the sign of Libra. Let's take Jupiter in Taurus back again to its sensitive point and use the combination with Mars: Saturn in Libra, Mars in Gemini, and Jupiter in Taurus. We use the Mars retrograde on each point because with the United States we have Saturn in the sign of Libra. Its only sensitive point here is that it affects personal matters.

The first aspect of this in 1893 became known as the Panic of 1893. It was actually to some extent the result of the presidential election of 1892, which brought modification in the government tariff policy. Also, there was apprehension that the gold standard could not be maintained.

Grover Cleveland was elected that year on a Democratic platform. He came in more or less committed to a reduction of the tariff, which many manufacturers did not like; but Cleveland believed in the gold standard. However, inflationary flat money segments prevailed and, to complicate the difficulties of this aspect, the federal cash surplus of the 1880s had been wiped out by the extravagance of the Harrison administration and by the McKinley tariff of the 1890s. This was a political aspect: Saturn.

The Act of 1892 authorized the Secretary of the Treasury to suspend the issue of gold certificates whenever the amount of the gold coin or bullion in the Treasury reserve for redemption of United States notes fell below a hundred million dollars. Added to this problem came the Sherman Silver Act of 1890, which compelled purchasers of various amounts of silver to be paid for by Treasury Notes redeemable in gold. All this was building up to another panic.

In the early months of 1893 Wall Street was more or less drained. Tension resulted there which also affected other areas such as buying land in Florida, ventures on new towns, disturbing life all over Florida as it was a prominent area during this period. And that's where the trouble started; in 1893, the Philadelphia and Reading Railroad failed.

It was more or less a signal for a downturn. Projects began to fail. A lot of prosperity hoped for in Florida was delayed. Money values shrank. Inflation was again getting out of control. Depositors crowded the rooms of banks and a lot of withdrawals were made. Again the panic was aspected under this influence of Saturn. Also, 74 railroad corporations owning more than 30,000 miles of track passed into the hands of receivers. By June 1894 at least 194 railroads operating over 40,000 miles had failed, not counting more than 15,000 commercial failures recorded in 1893.

President Cleveland was determined to maintain the gold standard even when gold stocks fell below the danger level. In 1896, an unexpected upturn in wheat prices led to the election of McKinley. Then business and the stock market picked up sharply. Two years later, successful termination of the Spanish-American War stimulated the industrial activity of the country. So the Panic of 1893 was short-lived; but, again, it was all these combinations that led to it. The entire situation lasted only about four years.

Sixty years later we fall into the period of 1953, with Saturn in Libra, Jupiter in Taurus, and Mars in Gemini. This became known as the recession of 1953-1954. The main reason was due to the policy of the United States regarding war-torn Europe—again, the United States loaned or gave money. It's almost like a repeat cycle that we have to go each time with these Saturn points from which Americans, or the American government, never learn. The United States sold war goods to its Allies during two world wars and as a result, skimmed off most of its gold which was the only true measure of its wealth.

We will have this aspect again in 2013: retrograde Saturn in Libra, Jupiter in Taurus, Mars in Gemini. Again we will be affected by the panic and recession of this aspect. By looking at the 30-year trend aspects (the spin-off aspects) for the period of 1923, we had Saturn in Libra and Mars in Gemini, but again it was a spin-off that did not affect the United States, but only areas of Europe. The same thing will apply in 1986. We will have the combination return, the 30-year spin-off, which will only affect the European countries as far as complications there.

The next combination is the sign of Scorpio, the opposition to the New York Stock Exchange's natal Sun in Taurus. We know the New York Stock Exchange is under the sign of Taurus, so the transits of Saturn in Taurus and Scorpio will affect it. The 180-degree aspect, when Saturn is in Scorpio, is the greatest danger as far as the fluctuation of prices that can lead to a panic or a recession.

The sign of Scorpio rules the area of government. It affects the financial relationships with other countries. It is more or less a sign that is secretive, things that are done without knowledge that can affect the market. But there are many elements of this aspect of Saturn in Scorpio.

The other affliction that we would have from the New York Stock Exchange's chart is Jupiter. To relate to Scorpio it would have to be in Leo, affecting the second house of the Stock Exchange, with Saturn affecting the fifth house, speculation. In return this would set Mars into the eighth house, Pisces, dealing with other people's money. The combination is thus Saturn in Scorpio, Jupiter in Leo, and Mars in Pisces. We had this combination in 1837, and it became known as the Panic of 1837, when a man named Nicholas Biddle, who was known as one of the greatest bankers in American history, actually ruled the money world and dazzled men of his time with his abilities and personality.

He became president of the Second Bank of the United States. President Jackson at the time feared the bank because money is power and that much financial power in hands other than government was a threat. Jackson decided to wage war on the bank. His official excuse was that the bank had failed to establish a sound currency throughout the 1830s when speculation was more or less out of hand. But his real desire was to close the bank at any price, and under any pretext. This was a period of underhandedness, things that are unseen.

Jackson vetoed the renewal of the bank's charter. But Biddle, not to be overcome, obtained a charter from the Commonwealth of Pennsylvania where there would be no federal restraining hand. Biddle was now able to expand the Bank's activities.

But the aspect of Saturn in Scorpio, Jupiter in Leo, and Mars in Pisces was still present. He embarked on speculation and encouraged the marketers to do the same. He also had principal interests in land and other speculative areas. Real estate became a vehicle of speculation, not an investment, during that period. But, as everything else goes, hunger leads to hunger for money, and greed sets in.

There were 634 banks in the country with loans of $525 million at that time. However, the backing of these loans was about $38 million, a position that continued to weaken. The battle between Biddle and Jackson continued during this period and split the bankers of Wall Street into two groups. In 1836, Jackson openly condemned the rush for public land and issued circulars demanding that payment for land should be made only in notes with 100 percent backing. But none of this worked. There were complications caused by bankruptcies of several important businesses in England toward the end of 1836. This reduced the demand for American cotton and depressed the United States cotton industry.

The panic itself came unexpectedly. Again we have this combination of Saturn in Scorpio with the Jupiter in Leo. On March 17, 1837, a Friday, everything broke loose under the combination of extended credit and cutbacks in the demand for cotton, with staggering losses to many people and the indebtedness and liabilities of the cotton factories. So the New Orleans banks stopped payment because of the failure of the cotton houses. This in turn caused a fall on Wall Street that had never been seen before. There was a fearful crisis on the money market. Bank failures mounted and silver more or less disappeared from circulation, causing widespread alarm and financial chaos. Riots were also feared in this period.

The next cycle came in the late part of 1956. At that time Saturn was in Scorpio and retrograde, Jupiter was in Leo, and Mars was in Pisces. Complications resulted. New orders were placed with equipment manufacturers and there was a decline at the end of 1956; again, there was more than was needed. There was a fall in exports which affected the markets in England, Canada, and Japan. In October 1957 the Federal Reserve adopted a geared money policy, the main effect being to delay the revival of housing starts. So the recession of 1957-1958 came from this 1956 aspect.

The next 60-year period will be in 2016, when again money will be affected. Our currency will be changed under this aspect as panic, recession and depression result from dealings with other countries. The aspect of Saturn in Scorpio and Jupiter in Leo seems to affect other countries more than it does the United States economy. The spin-off aspects are not that powerful with the influence of just Saturn in Scorpio and Mars in Pisces. But the 60-year cycles when Saturn in Scorpio and Jupiter in Leo come together do relate to this type of panic. Therefore, in the year 2016, the same pattern will emerge and another cycle will begin just like the 1956-57 period and the 1837 period. From 1956 to the 60-year cycle in 2017, this will result in a complete change in currency itself as we know it today.

The next is the most deadly influence of all because it affects the New York market and the United States natal chart: Saturn in Capricorn. This is in opposition to the natal chart of the United States. These are the periods of the worst depressions known to man.

The United States chart is influenced by the sign of Cancer and Capricorn is Cancer's opposite sign. Saturn is the ruler of Capricorn and any time that Saturn enters Capricorn, it is bad. Not only do the 60-year cycles affect this, but the 30-year cycles of the Saturn return can be devastating. Jupiter has no effect whatsoever because any sign that Saturn hits has the malefic Mars going from Sagittarius into Capricorn with these conjunctions every 30; this relates to panics, depressions and recessions.

It is generally a period of negative thinking and it brings scandal in high places and affects government and credit. But the main influence is in the negative aspect of government conditions. In 1873, Saturn was in Capricorn, retrograde, with Mars in Sagittarius. This brought on what was known as the Panic of 1873, which resulted from unrestrained speculation in railroad construction and wildcat investment in business schemes.

From 1869 to 1873, business showed abundant prosperity until the effect of Saturn took hold. The main cause of the failure was that the federal government failed to check inflation during the boom years. In 1868, an act was passed by Congress by a large majority restricting any further contraction of the currency. Railroads were overbuilt and the Government was at fault for the Panic of 1873.

In 28 to 30 years, the next time with Saturn in Capricorn and Mars in Sagittarius, was in 1901. Without warning, it became the Panic of 1901. This was related to the Northern Pacific Railroad as complications related to the stock market affected it almost overnight.

The next period of Saturn in Capricorn and Mars in Sagittarius came in 1929. As this aspect hit near the end of the year, it became the Panic of 1929 and created a stock market crash in October of that year (when the Sun also was in bad aspect to Saturn) and marked the beginning of the worst depression the United States had ever experienced. It was a build-up from prosperity and inflation Between January 25 and October 1929, the number of shares listed on the stock market more than doubled. The easy money to be made in speculation as stock prices mounted stimulated increased interest until everyone wanted to ride. But then, in October 1929, the negative influence of Saturn in Capricorn and Mars in Sagittarius came in. Also, the whole duration of Saturn in Capricorn affected the depression, which lasted worldwide for about eight years.

The next period, during 1960-1961, we had a combination of Saturn in Capricorn and Mars in Sagittarius. In 1961, and into the period of 1962, this became known as the Panic of 1962. Again this was a recession period.

We will experience the Saturn in Capricorn-Mars in Sagittarius combination again in 2020. Again we can relate to problems associated with government. In the period of 2020 the aspects indicate that the President and Vice President of the United States will be assassinated, creating chaos in the stock market. This will be a very negative period for the United States.

But one thing for sure is that the market and market prices will never be able to withstand the influence of Saturn in Capricorn. It will be the period to go to the top and sell short.

Our last influence is retrograde Saturn in the sign of Pisces in combination with Mars in Aquarius and Jupiter in Leo, affecting the New York Stock Exchange.

The 60-year period was 1907, which became known as the Panic of 1907. Crime, forgery, scandal and things that are unexpected that arise through the Pisces influence. Leo is gold, and gold played a prominent part in this 1907 cycle. The next period that would have retrograde Saturn in Pisces and Jupiter in Leo was 1966, the period in which the Dow-Jones hit an all-time peak and then dropped 25 percent within 10 months. Again, the element of gold. This same cycle will be back in 2026.

In the year 2026, a panic caused by a drop in the stock market is expected. However, as we look at the 28- or 30-year cycle spin-offs from 1907, look at 1937, which was known as the Panic of 1937. It involved almost the full government's responsibilities. Again the Pisces influence related to this crash period. The Panic of 1937 was very easily foreseeable as the government aspect applies to this Saturn in Pisces.

The next 30-year spin-off came in 1966, to be followed by one in 1996. Again, government involvement, but during this period the aspects are long because during the first taste of the Saturn in Pisces-Mars in Aquarius combination will hit us during the period of 1994 and will return during the period of 1996 as a retrograde. So, 1994 through 1996 will relate to a shaky market.

Remember that the market is playable at all times. When the crisis periods shown here come up, it is a period to sell short. After the market crashes, it is a time to buy and go long. The effect of Saturn relates to things that cause the market to go into a frenzy and affects the people in their involvement with it, causing them to panic. In almost everything, someone will win and someone will lose. Saturn does affect time (it rules timing), so the key factor involving panics is from the timing point of Saturn as it relates to these combinations.

First, banks offer increasingly attractive terms in interest rates, which attracts people. The merchant increases his stock because it is cheap to do it, and he sees a killing in the making. This produces larger orders than required. Increased output leads to increased consumer spending as money circulates. This leads to the inflationary prices of the manufacturer which in turn increases consumer spending. And, again, this influence causes a rise in the price of the stock.

When everything goes in an upturn, everything rises to the tap. But remember that whatever goes up has to come down. Credit expansion is a key factor to watch as far as things that lead to crises because Saturn does represent the credit factor. Then the panic itself because people who buy at the top want to get away from it, and they fall into a panic and start the stock market down. Watch government programs because Saturn ruling the government affects government decisions that relate to crises: spending money that it does not have.

These facts and combinations will lead to panics. However, when all of these combinations return, be aware of these factors and stay one step ahead of panics and crashes.

Chapter V

Accidents and Their Effect on the Dow-Jones Industrial Average

Certain events during any year can affect the stock market. Accidents and disasters can cause a one-day drop or fall. Such events are indicated by the twelfth house, which deals with sadness, disasters and enemies. The twelfth house is ruled by the sign of Pisces. The house related to accidents is the sixth house, the opposite sign of Pisces, which is Virgo. So, more or less, you will find the Moon to be in the area of Pisces or Virgo on the definite disasters that do affect the stock market.

There haven't been too many aspects that have affected the market. March 1888, with the Sun in Pisces, the Moon in Pisces and Mercury in Pisces, is remembered for the Blizzard of '88. Only 32 stock brokers operated on the New York Stock Exchange trading floor, and volume dropped to 15,800 shares.

On September 8, 1900, we had the Sun in Virgo and the Moon in Pisces. Mercury was also in Virgo. Galveston, Texas had a hurricane and a flood on this day. The Dow-Jones Industrial averages closed at 57.88, a week later at 56.56 and the following week at 53.43 prior to reaching a low of 52.96 on the 24th. The next period was the spring of 1904; with the Moon in Pisces, we had the Baltimore fire, and the market did not fully overcome this aspect until the new bull uptrend got under way from the low of 47.43 reached in May.

The next period began April 18-19, 1906. We had the San Francisco earthquake and fire. The Moon again was in Pisces, as was Saturn. The Dow-Jones Industrial average fell 2.61 in two days on the way to an April 28 low of 88.70. The next aspect was April 15, 1912. Again the Moon was in Pisces, and the Titanic sank. There was no apparent market influence, although prices eroded slowly to 88.72 on April 22 from 89.71 on the 15th. So. although it was not a major change, the disaster still had a little effect.

The next period came September 16, 1920. Although the Moon was not in Pisces, the Sun, Mercury, Jupiter and Saturn were in Virgo, and there was an explosion in Wall Street outside J.P. Morgan and Company. But this did not seem to have a very serious influence on the market and the Dow-Jones Industrial average closed at the month's high of 89.95 the following day.

The next aspect came September 21, 1938, with the Sun, Moon and Mars in Virgo. This was the New England hurricane, and the Dow-Jones fell 1.94 to 137.35 the following day.

The next aspect came January 15-16, 1958, as the Moon was approaching the sign of Pisces from Aquarius. A blizzard hit the Northeast which occurred over the weekend, and the Dow-Jones fell 2.17 to 442.27 in Monday's session. The next aspect, March 27,1964, had the Moon in Virgo, Saturn and Mars in Pisces and Uranus in Virgo. This was the day we had the Alaskan earthquake, but the market was closed for the Good Friday holiday. So this disaster had no major effect on the market.

These are the only disasters that had an effect on the Dow-Jones Industrial averages. However, you will notice that the Moon was either in Pisces or Virgo when they occurred.

CHAPTER VI

Death and Illness of World Leaders

As we mentioned earlier, Pisces and Virgo are responsible for natural disasters which affect the stock market. As a rule, most disasters happen in these periods. But what about world leaders, people in prominent places, death and illness? The same signs are responsible for this; Pisces and Virgo will dominate, especially with Mars, Saturn and Uranus in these signs. This influence is extremely negative and has taken its toll on the market. Let's trip back to the past and see the aspects that were applicable and their effects on the market at the time.

On April 14, 1865, President Lincoln was shot; he died April 15. The New York Stock Board adjourned at 10:30 a.m. It was a national day for mourning. On July 2, 1881, President Garfield was shot. He died September 19, but on July 2, 1881, the market dropped abruptly. Panic was averted only by the intervention of a Sunday and the July 4 holiday. On that day the Moon was and Mercury were in Virgo—the disaster points mentioned earlier.

On September 6, 1901, the Sun and Mercury were in Virgo. President McKinley was shot, and died September 14. The following day the Dow-Jones Industrial average fell 3.22 to 69.03 and it did not regain ground lost from the September 6 level until November 28, 1904.

All three presidents were shot under the influence of Pisces, with the last two shot also under the influence of Virgo, both of whom died in the month ruled by the sign of Virgo.

The next aspect was June 28, 1914, when the Moon and Mars were in Virgo. On June 28, 1914, Archduke Ferdinand was assassinated, which led to World War I. The Dow-Jones Industrial average closed off fractionally at the 80.00 mark. The following session rallied to a high of 81.79 on July 8, a level not duplicated for fourteen months.

The next period came with Uranus in Pisces on August 2, 1923. President Harding died in office. The Dow-Jones Industrial average dropped one point to a month's low of 87.20 the next day. The year's closing low was 85.76, a bottom not broken until December 9, 1931.

The next period was February 15, 1933, with Mercury in Pisces, Jupiter in Virgo and Mars in Virgo. President-elect Roosevelt escaped as Chicago Mayor Cermak was assassinated. The Dow-Jones Industrial average declined 1.26 to 55.49 on the 16th and to 50.16 on the 27th, a low for February and for 1933. Ten years from that date on the return aspect, with the Sun in Pisces. on February 24, 1943, Churchill became ill with pneumonia. The Dow-Jones was not affected by this, as it rose just a little to 129.58. So Churchill's illness had no great effect on the market at that time even though it was critical. But also in the same period, under the influence of Pisces, on March 12, 1943, with the Moon and Mercury in Pisces, Hitler had a nervous breakdown. The Dow-Jones closed at 130.73 and continued moving forward to a high of 136.82 in March. This aspect with Hitler was favorable; it had no effect on the Dow-Jones.

On April 12, 1945, with the critical factor of Mars in Pisces and Jupiter in Virgo, President Roosevelt died in office. The Dow-Jones continued to rise, with a closing of 195.80 by December 11. On January 30, 1948, with Mars in Virgo and Venus in Pisces, Gandhi was assassinated. Again no apparent influence on the market as the Dow-Jones declined into February and March where it was affected only slightly, but advanced to a year's high of 196.16 on June 15.

On November 1, 1950, dominated by Saturn in Virgo but not to a critical degree, Truman escaped assassination. The Dow-Jones Industrial average rose slightly, .68, to 225.69. On March 5, 1953, with the Sun in Pisces, Stalin died. Again, there was only a very slight effect on the stock market, but on September 24, 1955, with the Sun approaching Virgo and Mars in Virgo in conjunction, this critical aspect related to a heart attack for President Eisenhower. The Dow-Jones dropped 31.89 from a 1955 closing high of 487.45 reached on the 23rd to 455.56, which rallied in two sessions to 472.61. The initial setback represented a one-day loss of 6.5 percent.

The next period is June 9, 1956, with Mars in Pisces, when Eisenhower had surgery. The Dow-Jones declined 7.70 to a month's low of 475.29 on the day preceding the operation. But announcements of its success boosted confidence and sparked a recovery to June's closing peak of 488.26.

On May 30, 1961, when Trujillo was assassinated, the market was closed for Memorial Day. In 1963, on November 22, Uranus approached Virgo, which would represent a series of setbacks for people in high places. It began with President Kennedy's assassination, and the Dow Jones Industrial average was affected. It dropped to 710.83 and closed at 711.49, down 21.16. The Exchanges halted trading to prevent panic and the public's confidence was restored over the weekend, including the day of national mourning. On Monday, the 25th, the Dow-Jones Industrial average rose 32.03 to 723.52 in the first session following the assassination, and the year's high was posted at 767.21 on December 18. But Uranus, still in Virgo, contacted Mars in Virgo and Saturn in Pisces on June 9, 1965. This brought rumors of President Johnson's stroke or heart attack. The Dow-Jones dropped 25.66 to 876.49 in three days between June 8 and 10, and reached a month's low of 840.59 on the 28th. This was just a rumor so the market did recover at the close of the year at 969.26. On October 6, 1965, again with the Moon and Saturn in Pisces and Uranus in Virgo, President Johnson was operated upon and the Dow-Jones fell 4.28 to 934.42 in two days.

On November 4, 1966, with Saturn in Pisces and Mars and Uranus in Virgo, President Johnson's surgery was taken in stride. The Dow-Jones was no longer shaken by this. On April 4, 1968, with Venus, Mercury and Pisces in opposition to Uranus in Virgo, we had the assassination of Martin Luther King. The Dow-Jones Industrial average fell 6.71 due mainly to worry about race riots, but rallied 18.61 the following session and continued uptrading to an April 30 high of 912.22. But Uranus was still prominent in Virgo and this time we had the Moon in Virgo on June 5, 1968. On that date Robert F. Kennedy was assassinated; he died June 6. The market's reaction to this second assassination of a leading figure in two months was negative. On August 8, 1968, as Uranus began to leave Virgo, with Jupiter in Virgo, it had its final influence when President Johnson became ill August 8, 1968. The Dow-Jones Industrial average fell 6.66 to 870.37 and posted a low for the month the next day of 869.65.

On September 3, 1969, with the Sun in Virgo, Ho Chi Minh died. This did not seriously affect the market, but there was a low of 811.64. However, it recovered.

On September 28, 1970, with the Moon, Mars and Mercury in Virgo, Nasser died. The Dow-Jones Industrial average dropped 2.80 to 758.97. But the death of Egypt's leader had little market influence.

Major events involving national leaders, either through illness, natural death or assassination, have had only a temporary effect on the market. However, generally, when the Moon is in either Pisces or Virgo, a disturbance at the national or international level causes the market to drop suddenly, either in fear or, as the Moon goes, changeable moods. It's a good idea to watch these transits that affect Virgo and Pisces, looking for periods during which you can pick up stocks at a lower price as these periods generally represent sudden drops that are unusual, but which recover just as fast.

Chapter VII

Sensitive Degrees of the Sun and Moon

The Moon has the greatest control as far as daily activity on the stock market. The 28-day cycle of the Moon in conjunction, square or opposition to the planets passing over the Midheaven will affect a cycle. Each 28-day cycle of the Moon begins with the New Moon, which is when the Sun and the Moon are in the same sign. If the New Moon were in Pisces with Saturn in Sagittarius on the Midheaven, for example, this would represent a bearish trend in the Dow-Jones Industrial average. On the individual stocks it would represent a change, a bearish trend, but if it were a positive aspect it would represent a bullish trend, upwards.

The Moon's Nodes are very important, and it takes the Nodes 19 years to transit all 12 signs. When the Node is in Leo, the trend seems to be upward, but the Node reflects a lot of the daily activity from month to month according to the aspects it makes.

Jupiter in good aspect to the Node brings an upswing to the market; a bad aspect brings it down. But Jupiter with the Node is the best combination. Saturn conjunct, square or opposition the Node is bad, as is the case if the Sun and the Moon are both on the Nadir.

Any time Mars affects the Moon or the Moon's Node look for activity in the market. If Mars is in good aspect, the activity will be high volume; in bad aspect, it will be high volume but it will be selling volume. The Moon trine the Sun is one of your best combinations as far as an uptrend. The Moon square or in bad aspect to Saturn brings a downtrend each day. So a day can be mixed with certain combinations. There are also certain degrees from the Moon that affect the market, and also the Sun. As far as looking at the Moon's degrees in aspect to the New York Stock Exchange's chart, a powerful degree for the Moon is nine degrees of Aries. This affects the descending aspect of the United States chart and the Midheaven of the New York Stock Exchange chart as far as its relationship to a 20-degree Moon.

Now every sign of the Zodiac that the Moon goes through has at least two major points where it becomes very sensitive. This means that when it goes through a certain sign at a certain degree, that degree will activate an event that day. It might be a minor upward trend, it might move only a few points, but something is going to happen. A lot of the major trends as far as daily activities are related to these aspects. And the aspects that are negative from the Moon, especially when the Moon is in certain degrees of a sign, can bring the market down, causing a fast decline. The degrees are 9 and 20 of Aries; 2 and 16 degrees of Taurus; 18 and 29 degrees of Gemini; 4 and 28 degrees of Cancer; 9 and 22 degrees of Leo; 11 and 21 degrees of Virgo; 17 and 29 degrees of Libra; 4, 15 and 21 degrees of Scorpio; 12 and 26 degrees of Sagittarius; 2, 5, and 25 degrees of Capricorn; 5 and 25 degrees of Aquarius; 9 and 28 degrees of Pisces. When the Moon hits these points it becomes sensitive, and the reason is because when the Moon hits 16 degrees of Taurus, this is the eleventh house cusp of the NYSE. When the Moon is 9 degrees of Aries, it contacts the United States chart. When the Moon is 4 degrees of Cancer, it relates to the natal United States chart with a cluster in Cancer; with the Moon in 25 degrees Capricorn, this is the descending of the NYSE chart; and the Moon 9 degrees in Pisces is the ninth cusp of the NYSE chart. Now looking at the positive factors of the Moon in each degree: in Aries, 7 and 16 degrees; in Taurus, 23 and 27; Gemini 20 and 27; Cancer 7 and 25; in Leo 6 and 15; in Virgo 24 and 28; in Libra 14 and 27; in Scorpio. 20 and 12; in Sagittarius 4 and 18; in Capricorn, 19 and 26; in Aquarius, 9 and 24; and in Pisces 15 and 25.

Now when the Moon is in these signs at these degrees, this causes the market to be bullish. In relation to the chart of the NYSE, the 23-degree Moon aspected in Taurus hits natal Mercury at 23 degrees in the NYSE chart. The Moon at 27 and 28 degrees of Taurus hits the Sun at 27 degrees of Taurus in the NYSE chart. The Moon at 27 degrees in Gemini is trine the natal Neptune in Libra in NYSE chart. The Moon at 25 degrees in Cancer hits the Ascendant of the NYSE chart. The Moon at 15 degrees in Leo hits the Uranus 15 degrees of Leo in the NYSE chart; and the Moon 27 degrees of Libra hits the 27 degree of Neptune in Libra in the NYSE chart.

In the United States chart the Moon at 25 degrees of Cancer hits Mercury at 25 degrees of Cancer; the Moon 6 degrees of Leo hits the node of the United States Chart at 7 degrees of Leo; the Moon 24 degrees of Virgo hits Neptune 24 degrees of Virgo; the Moon 14 degrees of Libra affects the earlier ascendant of 14 degrees of the United States; and the Moon 24 degrees of Aquarius hits the United States Moon 24 degrees of Aquarius. So all these aspects related from the Moon as to the sensitive points as far as making the stock market move up are related to both charts of the United States and the NYSE. Also by the midpoints and the sensitive points that relate to the stock market.

We will prove this by going back over data on the NYSE as far as taking the highest day of the year, the day that had the most activity, and the day that had the least activity, as far as price, and see how many of these days will correlate with these degrees.

Now the Sun as far as relating to the positive factors are the Sun at 4 or 11 degrees of Aries; 12 or 19 of Taurus; 18 or 16 of Gemini; 8 and 16 degrees of Cancer; 6 and 18 degrees of Leo; 12 and 28 degrees of Virgo; 21 and 29 degrees of Libra; 11 and 29 degrees of Scorpio; 3 and 24 degrees of Sagittarius; 6 and 11 degrees of Capricorn; 10 and 14 degrees of Aquarius; 13 and 24 degrees of Pisces. These represent days where there could be activity and high movement. The positive aspects of the Sun relate well with the United State chart as far as the 8 and 16 degrees of Cancer affects the cluster of the United States.

The 8 degrees of Gemini hits Uranus at 8 degrees in the United States chart; the Moon 6 degrees of Leo hits the north node 7 degrees of Leo in the US chart; the Sun 11 degrees of Scorpio hits the second house cusp of the United States. So the effects of the Sun are related here.

The negative degrees of the Sun are at 18 and 24 degrees of Aries; 6 and 18 degrees of Taurus; 5 and 17 degrees of Gemini; 13 and 28 degrees of Cancer; 2 and 17 degrees of Leo; 10 and 13 degrees of Virgo; 2 and 14 degrees of Libra; 2 and 4 degrees of Scorpio; 16 and 20 degrees of Sagittarius; 16 and 29 degrees of Capricorn; 17 and 29 degrees of Aquarius; 4 and 5 degrees of Pisces.

Now from the negative points the Sun at 18 degrees of Aries conjuncts the natal Moon of the NYSE; the Sun at 6 degrees of Taurus conjuncts with Venus at 5 degrees of Taurus; the Sun at 32 degrees of Leo squares the Venus of the NYSE; and the 10 degrees Virgo the third house cusp aspect.

On the United States chart, 24 degrees Aries squares Mercury at 24 degrees Cancer; 13 degrees Cancer hits the natal 13 degrees Cancer of the US chart; 17 degrees Leo is opposition to Pluto at 16 degrees Aquarius; 14 degrees Libra is conjunct Saturn at 14 degrees Libra; 20 degrees Sagittarius is opposition Mars at 21 degrees Gemini; the Sun at 16 degrees Capricorn hits the Nadir at 16 degrees Capricorn; and the Sun at 17 degrees Aquarius is conjunct Pluto at 16 degrees Aquarius.

So these are some of the sensitive points and important degrees regarding daily cycles on the NYSE. The Moon sign changes rapidly, but the degrees of the Sun are almost the same on the same date every year, so research will show you that in a lot of years, the stock market is bullish on about the same days. This of course depends upon leap year. As an example, let's take the negative days first, such as 18 and 24 degrees Aries, which fall generally around the 8th and 15th of April; 4 and 11 degrees Aries, which are good points, fall around the March 25 and April

1; 6 and 18 degrees Taurus, which are negative, fall around on April 27 and May 9; 5 and 17 degrees Gemini fall on the May 27 and June 8; 13 and 28 degrees Cancer fall around July 6 and 21; and 2 and 17 degrees Leo hit around July 26 and August 10.

These are the positions relating to the Sun's degrees as they fall each year, and you should keep an eye on these dates each year to see the activity. A lot of the activity depends upon the aspects that are applying to the degree, where the Node is and the transiting aspects. The more positive reinforcement the Node gets and when the Moon is in good aspect with the Sun, then the higher it can go; the more negative the effect, then the lower it goes. As an example let's go back and start with the year 1900 and look at the biggest advance of the year and the biggest decline in any one day of each year. Remember, the Moon square Saturn, or a bad aspect of Saturn, is very bad to begin with, but trine the Sun is good. But, again, you have to remember that with daily activity, there is a full 28-day cycle of the Moon as it goes from New Moon to New Moon that is used to determine the trend of the stock itself.

Let's begin with 1900 to determine the largest one-day advances and the largest one-day declines in the Dow-Jones Industrials average.

On January 2, 1900, the stock market rose 2.5 points for a percentage of 3.1. On that date the Moon was at 26 degrees Capricorn and the Sun was at 11 degrees Capricorn. The Moon and the Sun were in conjunction which relates to a good aspect as you will notice the Sun and the Moon were in. exact sensitive points that trigger this big advance. The low for the year came on April 16 when the Dow-Jones Industrials dropped 2.85 points, or a 4.4°Al drop. On April 16 the Sun was at 26 degrees of Aries and the Moon was at 15 degrees of Scorpio ... Scorpio is the sensitive point of the drop ... the sensitive point for the Sun to be was at 24 degrees but it was a 2-degree difference, so it was relating to the Moon at this sensitive degree. In the year 1901, on May 10, the Dow-Jones Industrials rose 4.29 points at a percentage rate of 6.4. On May 10, 1901, the Sun was at 19 degrees Taurus, which again represents a highly sensitive degree for the Sun. The Moon was at 9 degrees Aquarius, which represents, again, a high factor point for the stock market. The low for the year was just one day prior, on May 9. The Sun was at 18 degrees Taurus. When it is at this degree of Taurus it is the lowest cycle for the Sun. The Moon was at 25 degrees Capricorn, which again is a low factor relating to the Moon.

So even though both these dates were one day apart, both critical aspects were applying on the 9th, and both positive aspects were applying on the 10th. On the 9th, the stock market dropped 4.34 points, or 6.1 percent, and that was the lowest drop of the year. On September 30, 1902, the biggest one-day advance on the Dow-Jones, there were similar aspects, and the stock market rose 3.2 percent. On September 30, the Moon at 24 degrees Virgo, which indicates an uptrend; the Sun at 6 degrees Libra is a neutral aspect, so has no major effects. So, again, the sensitive point of the Moon caused this rise that was the year's biggest advance.

On September 29 of the same year the stock market had its lowest drop when it fell 2.21 points, or a decline of 3.3 percent. Here again is the one day difference between these two aspects. On the 29th the Moon was at 11 degrees Virgo, which is a critical point, and the Sun was at 5 degrees Libra, which was not a major factor.

On October 16, 1903, the Dow-Jones Industrials advanced 2.16 points, or 5.1 percent. On this date the Sun was at 21 degrees Libra and the Moon at 1 degree Virgo, the Sun being the sensitive point. The Sun was also conjunct the Moon's Node and Mercury in Libra. The low of the year came August 19, when the Dow-Jones dropped 2.18 points, or a percentage of 4.1. The Sun on August 19 was at 25 degrees Leo and the Moon at 13 degrees Cancer, a sensitive point. In 1904 the high for the year came on December 16, with an advance of 2.11 points for a percentage gain of 3.2; the Sun was at 24 degrees Sagittarius and the Moon was at 16 degrees Aries, both sensitive points. The low for the year came on December 12 when the market dropped 4.2 points, or a 6.1 percent drop; the Sun was at 20 degrees Sagittarius, a sensitive point, and the Moon was at 26 degrees Aquarius, not really a sensitive point. The North Node of the Moon was in Virgo square the Moon, and Saturn was conjunct the Moon in Aquarius. In 1905 the high for the year came on November 27, when the Sun was at about 4 degrees Sagittarius, close to the three-degree sensitive point of the Sun, and the Moon was at 18 degrees Sagittarius, which is a sensitive point. Mercury was at 26 degrees Sagittarius and trine the Moon's Node at 26 degrees Leo. The low for the year came on April 27, when the Sun was at 6 degrees Taurus, a sensitive point, and the Moon was at 17 degrees Aquarius, not a sensitive point. In 1906, the high for the year came on May 4, with the Sun at 13 degrees (sensitive point of the Sun is 12 degrees) and the Moon in Virgo at 24 degrees, which is a sensitive point. The Moon was in trine aspect to the Sun, and Mercury was in 16 degrees Aries, trine the Moon's Node in 18 degrees Leo.

The low for the year repeated its same cycle as it did the year before. It came on April 27, when there was a 2.52 point drop (2.7 percent), compared with the high advance of the year of 2.63, or 3 percent up. On April 27, 1906, the Sun was at 6 degrees Taurus, the same sensitive point, the Moon was at 18 degrees Gemini, another sensitive point, and also in bad aspect with Saturn.

In 1907, the high for the year came on March 26 when the Dow-Jones Industrials moved up 2.39 points, or a percentage of 3.2 percent. On March 26, 1907, the Sun was 4 degrees Aries, a sensitive point; the Moon was at 26 degrees Leo, which had no effect; Mercury was 20 degrees Pisces trine the North Node at 29 degrees Cancer; and Jupiter was also in Cancer on the North Node. The low for the year came on March 14 and the Dow-Jones Industrials declined 6.89 points, or 8.3 percent; the Sun was at 22 degrees Pisces, which had no effect, and the Moon was at 28 degrees Pisces, which was a sensitive aspect. The Moon also was conjunct Saturn.

In 1908, the high for the year came on November 4. The Dow Jones Industrials rose 1.97 points, or 2.4 percent; the Sun was at 11 degrees Scorpio and the Moon at 25 degrees Pisces, both representing sensitive points. Mercury at 28 degrees Libra was trine the Moon's North Node at 28 degrees Gemini. The low for the year came December 17 when the market declined 1.89 points, or 2.2 percent. The Sun was at 25 degrees Sagittarius, which was not a sensitive point; the Moon was at 17 degrees Libra, a sensitive point, and opposition Saturn; and Mercury in Sagittarius and Jupiter in Virgo were square the Moon's Node in Gemini.

The biggest advance day in 1909 was January 7, when the market rose 1.81 points, or 2.1 percent. The Sun was at 16 degrees Capricorn, not a sensitive point, but the Moon was at 6 degrees Leo, which was a sensitive point. The low for the year came on February 23, when the market dropped 2.91 points, or 3.5 percent. The Sun was at 4 degrees Pisces, which was a sensitive point, and the Moon was at 18 degrees Aries, also a sensitive point; Jupiter in Virgo was square the North Node.

In 1910, the biggest advance of the year came on June 7, when the Dow-Jones advanced 2.45 points, or 3 percent. On that day the Sun was at 16 degrees Gemini, a sensitive point, and the Moon was at 20 degrees Gemini, also a sensitive point; the Moon was conjunct with the Sun. The low for the year came on February 7, for a decline of 3.4 points, or 3.4 percent. On February 7, the Sun was at 17 degrees Aquarius, a sensitive point, and the Moon was at 5 degrees Capricorn, another sensitive point. The Moon was square Saturn in Aries.

In 1911, the high for the year came on November 9 when the Dow-Jones advanced 2.28, or 2.9 percent. On that day the Sun was 15 degrees Scorpio with no major effect as far as a sensitive point but the Moon was 27 degrees Gemini which was a sensitive point for the rise. The low for the year came on October 27 when the Dow-Jones average dropped 2.32 points, or 30 percent. On that day the Sun 2 degrees Scorpio a sensitive point, and the Moon 5 degrees Capricorn, another sensitive point relating to the drop.

In 1912, the high point of the year came on November 6, only three days difference from the previous year. The Sun on that day was 13 degrees Scorpio, a little off from the sensitive point of 11 degrees; the Moon was 14 degrees Libra, which is a sensitive point for a high; the Dow-Jones advanced 1.65 points for a percentage of 1.89percent. The low for the year came on July 5 and the Dow-Jones dropped 2.01 points for a percentage drop of 2.2. On July 5 the Sun was at 13 degrees Cancer, a very sensitive point for a drop, and the Moon at 21 degrees Pisces, which had no effect.

In 1913 the high point of the year came on June 12. The Sun at 20 degrees of Gemini, which is not a sensitive point; the Moon was at 4 degrees of Libra, which is not an important effect within itself; Mercury was trine the north node and the only correlation we had on this day as far as representing a high is that the Sun factor of the Moon 13 degrees of Scorpio the sensitive point was 11 ... this is the only factor could relate to this high but this is the first year that the high was not related to the exact sensitive point that we are looking for. The high point of the year rose 2.17 points for a percentage advance of 3 percent, and the low point of the year came on January when the market declined 4.20 points, or 4.9 percent. On that day the Sun was at 29 degrees Capricorn, which is a sensitive point, and the Moon was at 4 degrees Cancer, which is also a negative point.

In 1914, the high point of the year came on December 14 when the Dow-Jones Industrials rose 2.04 points, or 3.7 percent. The Sun was at 21 degrees Sagittarius, which was not a sensitive point, and the Moon was at 20 degrees Scorpio, which was a sensitive point for movement upwards. The low for the year came only a couple of days earlier, on December 12, when the stock market dropped 16.70 points, or 23.24 percent. This was the heaviest drop to date. On this day the Sun was at 20 degrees Sagittarius (a low point), the Moon was at 17 degrees Libra, (a low point) and Mercury at 6 degrees was square the North Node at 6 degrees Pisces.

In 1915, the high point of the year was May 11, when the stock market rose 2.58 points, or 4.2 percent. On that day the Sun was at 19 degrees Taurus, a sensitive point; and the Moon was at 21 degrees Aries, not a sensitive point. The low for the year came just a few days earlier, on May 7, when the stock market dropped 3.1 points, or 4.5 percent. On that day the Sun was at 15 degrees Taurus, not a sensitive point, but the Moon was at 9 degrees Pisces, a sensitive point, and square Saturn; Jupiter was square Saturn.

In 1916, the high for the year came on December 22, when the Dow-Jones jumped 4.93 points, or 5.5 percent. On that day the Sun was at 0 degrees Capricorn, not a sensitive point, but the Moon was at 4 degrees Sagittarius, which is a sensitive point as far as the stock moving up. The low point of the year came on December 21, when the market dropped 5.1 points, or 5.4 percent. This was a one day difference between the high and the low of the year. On the 21st, the Sun was at 29 degrees Sagittarius, which is not a sensitive point, but the Moon was at 21 degrees Scorpio, a sensitive point for the industrials to decline.

In 1917, the high for the year was February 3, when the market soared 3.3 points, or 3.2 percent. On this day the Sun was at 14 degrees Aquarius, a positive zone, and the Moon was at 7 degrees Cancer, another positive zone. But the low for the year came a couple of days prior to this advance. On February 1, the Dow-Jones plunged 6.91 points, or 7.2 percent. We had the Sun at 12 degrees Aquarius, which was a neutral point, but the Moon was at a critical zone at 14 degrees Gemini, approaching the 18-degree mark which encouraged the down trend.

In 1918, the high point of the year came on January 31, with a rise of 2.82 points, or 3.7 percent. On January 31, the Sun was at 10 degrees Aquarius, a positive zone, and the Moon was at 28 degrees Virgo, again a positive zone. The low point of the year came on May 27, with a decline of 2.51 points, or 3.1 percent. The Sun was at 5 degrees Gemini, a critical zone, and the Moon was at 26 degrees Sagittarius, another critical zone, both in opposition, with the north node at the same degree in Sagittarius.

In 1919, the year's high was June 17, with the market up 3.72 points, or 3.7 percent. On that day the Sun was at 25 degrees Gemini, a degree that was not that important, but the Moon was at 9 degrees, which affected the movement upwards as 9 degrees is a positive zone; the Moon was also trine the Sun. The low for the year occurred August 4, with a drop of 5.17 points, or 4.8 percent. The Sun was at 11 degrees Leo, which was not a factor in the drop, but the Moon was at 21 degrees Scorpio, which represented a critical zone for a drop. The Moon also was square Saturn.

In 1920, the high for the year occurred November 22, with a 3.12 point advance of 4.3 percent. On that day the Sun was at 29 degrees Scorpio, which was not a factor in its movement, and the Moon was at 16 degrees Aries, which was a factor for the rise. Mercury was also in Scorpio, conjunct the North Node. The low for the year, on May 19, was a 3.85 point drop (4.2 percent). On May 19 the Sun was at 28 degrees Taurus, which is not a factor, but the Moon was at 18 degrees Gemini, which was a critical factor for the downfall. The Moon was also square Saturn in Virgo. Mercury in Taurus was opposition the North Node in Scorpio.

In 1921, the high occurred May 2, with the Sun at almost 12 degrees Taurus, a positive point, and the Moon at 7 degrees Pisces, a neutral point. The market rose 3.93 points (5 percent). The low for 1921 was June 20, when the market declined 2.35 (3.5 percent). The Sun on that day was 28 degrees Gemini, which is not a factor, but the Moon at 2 degrees Capricorn was at a critical point for this drop. The Moon was also in bad aspect to the North Node of Mercury.

In 1922, the day of the greatest advance was November 2, when the market rose 2.27 points (2.4 percent). On that day the Sun was at 9 degrees Scorpio, which is not a factor for this movement; but the Moon at 16 degrees Aries was the factor in this rise. Jupiter was conjunct the North Node. The low for the year came on June 12, with a decline of 2.47 points (2.6percent). On that date the Sun was at 20 degrees Gemini and the Moon was at 25 degrees Capricorn, which was the factor in the drop; the Moon was also square Saturn, Jupiter and the North Node.

In 1923, the high was October 31, with a gain of 2.62 (3 percent). The Sun was in 7 degrees Scorpio, which was not a main factor in its upward movement; but the Moon in 25 degrees Cancer was at a sensitive point for the rise. The Sun and the Moon were also trine. The low, on July 27, brought a drop of 2.62 points (3 percent). The Sun was at 3 degrees Leo, shy by one degree from its sensitive down point. The Moon was at 29 degrees Capricorn, from which there was no strong effect, but it was square Saturn.

In 1924, the high was December 31, when the market rose 2.49 points, or 2.1 percent. The Sun was 9 degrees Capricorn and the Moon was at 25 degrees Pisces, the sensitive point which triggered the rise. At the low on February 15, the market dropped 3.42 points (3.4 percent). The Sun was at 25 degrees Aquarius, which was not a critical point for the Sun, but the Moon was at 4 degrees Cancer, which was a critical point.

In 1925, the high was November 26, rising 2.86 points, or 1.9 percent. The Sun was at 3 degrees Sagittarius, which was a sensitive point for growth, and the Moon was at 7 degrees Aries, another point for growth. At the low on November 10, the market dropped 5.83 points, or 3.7 percent. The Sun was at 17 degrees Scorpio, which is not a factor for the downfall, but the Moon was at 11 degrees of Virgo, which was the sensitive point leading to the downfall.

In 1926, the high occurred March 4, with a rise of 6.32 points, or 4.4 percent). The Sun was at 13 degrees Pisces, a very good sensitive positive point. The Moon was at 12 degrees Scorpio, a very positive point, and Mercury was trine the North Node in Cancer. The Moon was trine the Sun. That made this the largest gain for one day advance to this date in 1926. The low occurred October 15, with a drop of 4.15 points, or 2.7 percent. The Sun was at 22 degrees Libra, which has no effect, but the Moon was the sensitive point here relating to the downfall at 5 degrees Aquarius.

In 1927, the market rose 5.65 points (3.3 percent) on September 6. The Sun was at 12 degrees Virgo, a positive sensitive point, and the Moon was at 6 degrees Capricorn. But the Moon's influence wasn't that prominent. The positive effect was from the Sun because the Sun and Moon were in trine aspect. The low, which occurred October 8, saw the market fall 7.21 points (3.7 percent). The Sun was at 14 degrees Libra, a negative zone. and the Moon was at 12 degrees Pisces, which was not a factor; but the Moon was in poor aspect to Saturn and Saturn was in square aspect to the Moon's North Node.

In 1928, the high was on November 22, when the market rose 9.81 points (3.5 percent); it also was a new high for the Dow-Jones. The Sun was at 29 degrees Scorpio, which is not really a factor; the Moon at 25 degrees Pisces was a factor in the upward movement. Jupiter was also conjunct the North Node. The low, which occurred December 8, saw the market drop 13.72 points (5.1 percent). The Sun was at 16 degrees Sagittarius, a critical zone; the Moon at 9 degrees Scorpio was not a factor in the downtrend. The Sun, however, was also conjunct Saturn, and the Moon was opposition the North Node.

The high of 1929, set on October 30, which was a new record, saw the market rise 28.40 points (12.3percent). The Sun was at 6 degrees Scorpio, which is not a major factor, and the Moon at 18 degrees Virgo, also not a factor; but the Moon was trine the North Node. This is one year where we had a high advance without the regular signals that indicate this from the sensitive zones. But the low for the year came a couple of days earlier, on October 28, when the Dow-Jones Industrials declined 38.33 points (12.8 percent). On that date the Sun was at 4 degrees Scorpio, a critical zone, and the Moon at 21 degrees Virgo, also a critical zone. With the Moon square Saturn, the effect was a new one-day low.

In 1930, the high was on June 19, when the market rose 10.13 points (4.6 percent). The Sun was at 27 degrees Gemini, which is not a factor, and the Moon was at 29 degrees Pisces, but also not a factor. This was another period where the sensitive zones did not trigger the high. The only thing that was unusual that day was an exact Sun-Mercury-Jupiter conjunction. So this could apply to the unusual pattern that was presented. A few days earlier the low of the year occurred on June 16, when the market dropped 14.21 points (5.8 percent). The Sun was at 24 degrees Gemini, which is not a factor, but the Moon was at 25 degrees Aquarius, which did represent a factor of a decline. The Moon was also square the Moon's North Node.

In 1931, the high occurred October 6, with a rise of 12.86 points (14.9 percent), the biggest percentage on record to this date. The Sun at 12 degrees Libra was not a contributing factor, but the Moon at 6 degrees Leo, was the factor. Also, the Moon was in Leo and trine the Moon's North Node in Aries. At the low on September 24, the market dropped 8.2 points (7.1 percent). The Sun was at 0 degrees Libra, approaching the 2-degree point, but the Moon at 9 degrees Pisces was a sensitive point relating to a decline.

1932 brought a high on September 21, with the market rising 7.67 points (11.4 percent). The Sun was at 28 degrees Virgo, which was a sensitive point for an upswing, and the Moon was at 20 degrees Gemini, once again representing a positive point. The low on August 12 dropped the market 5.79 points (8.4 percent). The Sun was at 19 degrees Leo, which was not a factor, but the Moon at 5 degrees Capricorn did represent the downfall.

In 1933, the high was on March 15, when the market rose 8.26 points (15.3 percent). To date this was a new high, percentage-wise. The Sun was at 24 degrees, approaching 25 degrees Pisces, which was a factor, and the Moon at 12 degrees Scorpio was a sensitive point relating to the upward move. The Sun and Moon were trine, the Sun was conjunct the Moon's North Node and the Moon was trine the North Node. The low on July 21 saw the market drop 7.55 points (7.8 percent). The Sun at 28 degrees Cancer was in a critical zone, and the Moon at 17 degrees Cancer was not a major factor.

In 1934, on January 15, the Dow-Jones dropped 4.53 points (4.6 percent). The Sun was at 24 degrees Capricorn. The Moon at 26 degrees Capricorn was the sensitive point, triggering this advance on the New Moon. The low on July 26 brought the market down 6.6 points (6.6 percent). The Sun was at 2 degrees Leo, a sensitive point, and the Moon was at 5 degrees Aquarius, in opposition, causing the downtrend. Also, the Moon was conjunct Saturn, also in Aquarius; Saturn was also affecting the North Node in Aquarius.

In 1935, the high was on December 3, with the market rising 2.86 points (2 percent). The Sun was at 10 degrees Sagittarius, which was not a prominent influence, but the Moon was at 15 degrees Pisces, which was the major factor of this upward movement. The low on October 2 dropped the market 3.45 points (2.6 percent). The Sun at 8 degrees Libra was not a factor; nor was the Moon at 7 degrees Sagittarius. But the Moon was square Saturn, which caused the minor decline on that day.

In 1936, the high occurred November 4, with the market rising 3.99 points (2.3 percent). The Sun was at 11 degrees of Scorpio, a sensitive point for movement, as was the Moon at 25 degrees Cancer. Jupiter was conjunct the North Node in Sagittarius. All these factors were positive, and the Moon was also trine the Sun. On April 27, the market dropped 4.88 points (3.2 percent). The Sun was approaching 7 degrees Taurus, leaving the 6 degree critical zone; and the Moon was at 28 degrees Cancer, also representing a very negative factor.

In 1937, the high on October 20 resulted in a 7.71 point gain (6.1 percent). The Sun was at 26 degrees Libra, which is not a factor in the movement, and the Moon was at 7 degrees Taurus, which also did not represent a factor. This was another unusual uptrend period that was not stable as far as effects of this upward movement. The low, two days earlier on October 18, dropped the market 10.57 points (7.8 percent). The Sun was at 24 degrees Libra, again not a factor, but the Moon was at 9 degrees Aries which caused the drop. The Moon also was square Jupiter in Capricorn.

In 1938, the high occurred April 9, with the market rising 5.75 points (5.2 percent). The Sun was at 18 degrees Aries, which is not a factor here, but the Moon was at 15 degrees Leo, which represented an uptrend. The Moon was also trine Saturn and the Sun, and this is more or less what caused the rise in this direction. At the low on March 25, when the market dropped 6.07 points (5.3 percent), there was a combination of the Sun at 4 degrees Aries (not a factor) and the Moon at 25 degrees Capricorn square Saturn and Mercury which did relate to the downfall. The Moon was also square the Sun, and 25 degrees is a sensitive point that brought the drop.

1939 brought a high on September 5, with the market rising 10.03 (7.3 percent). The Sun was at 12 degrees Virgo, which was a sensitive point for a rise, and the Moon was at 27 degrees Taurus, another point of advancement. These two planets were in trine aspect. At the low, on January 23, the market lost 5.44 points (3.7 percent). The Sun was at 2 degrees Aquarius, which was not a sensitive factor, but the Moon was at 9 degrees Pisces, which did represent a drop.

The 1940 high, on November 7, saw the market rise 5.77 points (4.4 percent). The Sun was at 14 degrees Scorpio, and the Moon was 24 degrees Aquarius, which was the activating factor of this upward trend. The Moon was also trine the North Node. At the low, which occurred May 14, the market fell 9.36 points (6.8 percent). The Sun was at 23 degrees Taurus and the Moon at 22 degrees Leo, which was the downfall factor. The Moon was also square the Sun, Saturn and Mercury.

In 1941, the high occurred December 30, with a rise of 3.76 points (3.5 percent). The Sun was 8 degrees Capricorn and the Moon at 3 degrees Gemini. Neither one of these degrees represent a major factor for the up movement, but the Moon was conjunct Jupiter in Gemini and Saturn, and the Sun was trine the North Node and Mercury. The low on December 8 resulted in a drop of 4.8 points (3.5 percent). The Sun at 16 degrees Sagittarius was a negative factor for a downfall, and the Moon at 9 degrees Leo also represents a factor for a downfall. The Moon was square Saturn in Taurus.

In 1942, the market rose 2.18 points (2.1 percent) at the high on July 8. The Sun was at 16 degrees Cancer and the Moon at 23 degrees Taurus, both positive zones relating to upswings in the market. The Moon was also trine the North Node. At the low on March 6, the market dropped 2.45 points (2.3 percent). The Sun was at 15 degrees Pisces and the Moon at 4 degrees Scorpio, both negative zones. The Moon was also square Saturn.

In 1943, on March 25, the market rose 2.60 points (2 percent). The Sun at 4 degrees Aries and the Moon at 20 degrees Scorpio were both positive factors for the move up. The low occurred April 9, with the market falling 4.30 points (3.2 percent). The Sun was at 18 degrees Aries, a negative point, and the Moon at 18 degrees of Gemini, also a negative point. The Moon was conjunct Saturn.

In 1944, the market rose 1.76 points (1.26 percent) on December 28. The Sun at 6 degrees Capricorn was a positive factor, as was the Moon at 27 degrees Gemini. The low on September 6 dropped the market 2.14 points (1.5 percent). The Sun was at 13 degrees Virgo, and the Moon was at 5 degrees Taurus, a negative zone causing the drop.

In 1945, the high on August 23 resulted in a rise of 3.1 points (1.9 percent). The Sun was at 29 degrees Leo, which was not a factor. The Moon was at 3 degrees Pisces, also not a factor. It was an unusual pattern becauuse Saturn and the North Node were conjunct. Mercury was retrograde at 24 degrees Leo, affecting the Sun, but there was nothing as far as strong points to bring the uptrend. At the low on July 17, the market dropped 3.39 points (2 percent). The Sun was 24 degrees Cancer, which is not a factor, but the Moon was 29 degrees Libra, a sensitive point bringing the downfall. The Moon was also square Saturn and the North Node.

In 1946, the market rose 6.8 points (3.6 percent) at the high on October 15. The Sun was at 21 degrees Libra, a positive point, and the Moon was at 27 degrees Gemini, another positive point; they were trine and the North Node was conjunct the Moon. The low on September 3 dropped the market 10.51 points (5.6 percent). The Sun was at 10 degrees Virgo, which is a critical point, and the Moon was at 12 degrees Sagittarius, another critical point. The Moon was also opposition the North Node and the Sun was square the North Node in Pisces.

In 1947, the high occurred June 11, with a rise of 3.58 points (2.1 percent). The Sun was at 19 degrees Gemini and the Moon at 15 degrees Pisces, which were positive factors. The North Node was also in Gemini. At the low on April 14, when the market dropped 5.07 points (3 percent), the Sun was at 24 degrees Aries and the Moon at 5 degrees Aquarius, both negative factors. The Moon was also in opposition to Saturn.

In 1948, the high was May 14, when the market rose 3.78 points (2 percent). The Sun was at 23 degrees Taurus, not a factor, but the Moon was at 6 degrees Leo, which was the rising factor. The North Node and Mercury were also in Taurus. At the low on November 3, the Sun was at 10 degrees Scorpio, not a major factor, and the Moon was at 12 degrees Sagittarius, causing the decline. The Sun was also opposition the North Node.

1949 brought a high on January 6, with the market up 3.14 points (1.8 percent). The Sun at 15 degrees Capricorn was not a factor; the Moon at 7 degrees Aries was the rising factor. The low on September 20 brought the market down 3.38 points (1.9 percent). The Sun was at 27 degrees Virgo and the Moon at 2 degrees Libra were not factors. But the Sun and Saturn were conjunct and the Moon was opposition the North Node.

In 1950, the high on December 27 raised the market 4.56 points (2 percent). The Sun was approaching 6 degrees Capricorn, and the Moon was at 15 degrees Leo, both positive aspects. The low on June 26 dropped the market 10.44 points (4.7 percent). The Sun was at 4 degrees Cancer (not a major factor), but the Moon was at 21 degrees Scorpio, causing the downfall.

In 1951, the high on January 2 raised the market 4.51 points (2 percent). The Sun was at 11 degrees Capricorn (a very sensitive point) and the Moon was at 27 degrees Libra. The low on October 22 brought a market drop of 5.13 points (1.9 percent). The Sun was at 28 degrees Libra, a neutral influence, and the Moon was at 28 degrees Cancer, a negative influence. The Moon was also square Saturn.

In 1952, the high occurred March 4 with a rise of 3.87 points (1.5 percent). The Sun was at 13 degrees Pisces, a sensitive factor, and the Moon was at 27 degrees Gemini, another sensitive point. The North Node was in Pisces. The low on February 19, dropped the market 3.98 points (1.50 percent). The Sun was at 29 degrees Aquarius (a critical degree), and the Moon was at 12 degrees Sagittarius, another bad factor. The Moon was also square the North Node.

In 1953, the market rose 3.71 points (1.4 percent) at the high on October 16. The Sun was at 21 degrees Libra, a sensitive point, and the Moon was at 19 degrees Capricorn, another sensitive point. The North Node was conjunct the Moon. The low on April 6 dropped the market 5.93 points (2.1 percent). The Sun was at 16 degrees Aries and the Moon at 8 degrees Capricorn. Neither of these was a major influence to cause the down, but the Moon was square Saturn.

1954 brought a high on November 3, when the market rose 7.54 points (2.1 percent). The Sun was at 11 degrees Scorpio, a sensitive zone, and the Moon was at 9 degrees Aquarius, another sensitive zone. The low on June 8 dropped the market 6.96 points (2.1 percent). The Sun was at 17 degrees Gemini and the Moon at 21 degrees Virgo, both critical points.

In 1955, the high was September 27, raising the market 10.37 points (2.3 percent). The Sun at 3 degrees Libra was not a main factor, nor was the Moon at 10 degrees Aquarius. The Sun and Moon were trine, and Jupiter was trine the North Node. The low on September 26 dropped the market 31.9 points (6.4 points). The Sun was at 2 degrees Libra and the Moon at 5 degrees Aquarius, both critical points.

In 1956, the high occurred May 29, with a rise of 8.87 points (1.9 percent). The Moon was in Aquarius at 6 degrees trine the Sun at 8 degrees Gemini; Jupiter was trine the North Node. The low on April 10 dropped the market 8.48 points (1.6 percent). The Sun at 20 degrees Aries and the Moon at 16 degrees Aries were not factors. Saturn was conjunct the North Node.

In 1957, the high on October 23 raised the market 17.34 (4.1percent). The Sun was at 29 degrees Libra, and the Moon at 12 degrees Scorpio, both positive factors. The Moon was also conjunct the North Node in Scorpio. The low occurred November 26, with a drop of 13.4 points (2.9 percent). The Sun was at 3 degrees Sagittarius, not a major factor. What brought the Dow-Jones down was the Moon at 5 degrees Aquarius, as the aspects were mixed good and bad.

In 1958, the high on November 26 brought the market up 8.63 points (1.6 percent). The Sun was at 3 degrees Sagittarius (a positive factor), and the Moon was at 6 degrees Gemini (not a major factor). The low on November 24 dropped the market 14.68 points (2.6 percent). The Sun was at 1 degree Sagittarius was not a factor, but the Moon at 16 degrees Taurus related to the downfall.

In 1959, the high on December 8 raised the market 9.72 points (1.5 percent). The Sun at 15 degrees Sagittarius was not a factor, but the Moon at 7 degrees Aries was a factor. The low occurred August 10, when the market dropped 14.10 points (2.2 percent). The Sun was at 17 degrees Leo (negative point) and the Moon was at 4 degrees Scorpio, another negative point.

July 28, 1960 brought a high, when the market rose 11.06 points (1.8 percent). The Sun was at 6 degrees Leo and the Moon at 14 degrees Libra, both positive points. The low on March 3 brought the market down 9.33 points (1.5 percent). The Sun at 12 degrees Pisces was not a factor, nor was the Moon at 21 degrees Taurus; but the Sun was in opposition to the North Node.

In 1961, January 4 brought a market high with a rise of 11.24 points (1.8 percent). The Sun was at 13 degrees Capricorn and the Moon at 15 degrees Leo, which was an effective degree causing the uprise. The low on April 24 dropped the market 12.60 points (1.28 percent). The Sun was at 4 degrees Taurus (not a major degree). The Moon was at 22 degrees Leo, which was an effective degree as far as a downfall.

In 1962, the high on May 29 resulted in a market rise of 27.03 points (4.7 percent). The Sun was at 8 degrees Gemini, and the Moon at 16 degrees Aries, both triggers for a strong market. The Moon was trine the North Node. The low, one day before, dropped the market 34.95 points (5.7 percent) on May 28. The Sun was close to 7 degrees Gemini (no factor), and the Moon was just past the critical degree of 29 degrees Pisces; there was a square from Saturn to Mercury.

In 1963, the high point was November 26, when the market rose 32.03 points (4.5 percent). The Sun was at 3 degrees Sagittarius, and the Moon at 7 degrees Aries, both of which were positive factors and the Sun and Moon were trine. The low on November 22 saw the market drop 21.16 points (2.9 percent). The Sun was at 29 degrees Scorpio, approaching the 0 degree mark of Sagittarius. The Moon was at 8 degrees Aquarius; this was not a factor in itself, but it was conjunct Saturn in Aquarius.

In 1964, the high on August 11 brought a rise of 7.6 points (0.9 percent). The Sun was at 18 degrees Leo (a positive zone) and the Moon at 8 degrees Libra was not a factor. When the low occurred on December 1, the market dropped 11.00 points (1.03 percent). The Sun at 9 degrees Sagittarius was not a main factor, but the Moon at 15 degrees Scorpio was the declining factor.

In 1965, the high on June 30 saw the market rise 16.63 points (2.41 percent). The Sun was at 8 degrees Cancer (a positive factor), and the Moon at 0 degrees Leo was no factor at all. The low on June 27 brought the market down 13.77 points (1.6 percent). The Sun was at 6 degrees Cancer (not a factor), but the Moon was at 29 degrees Gemini, which was the declining factor; the Moon was also square Saturn.

In 1966, the high occurred October 12, with a rise of 19.54 points (2.6 percent). The Sun was at 18 degrees Libra (no main factor), but the Moon was at 28 degrees Virgo, which was a positive factor. The Moon was also trine the North Node. The low on July 26 brought the market down 16.32 points (1.9 percent). The Sun at 2 degrees Leo was a major factor, as was the Moon at 15 degrees Scorpio.

In 1967, the market rose 14.95 points (1.8 percent) with the high on June 6. The Sun was at 16 degrees Gemini, and the Moon at 20 degrees Gemini, both positive factors. The low on June 5 dropped the market 15.54 points (1.8 percent). The Sun at 14 degrees Gemini was not really a critical position, but the Moon at 16 degrees Taurus was an effective point of the drop.

In 1968, the high of April 1 raised the market 20.58 points (2.4 percent). The Sun was at 11 degrees Aries, and the Moon was at 23 degrees Taurus, both positive factors. The North Node was also in Taurus. The low on July 22 dropped the market 13.60 points (1.5 percent). The Sun was at 29 degrees Cancer, just one degree past a critical zone, and the Moon was at 29 degrees Gemini, a critical zone.

In 1969, the high was on April 30, and the market rose 16.30 points (1.7 percent). The Sun was at 9 degrees Taurus (not a major factor), and the Moon was at 20 degrees Libra (not a factor). This was just one of those unusual days in the stock market, the most likely influence being Mercury in Taurus. The low on January 6 saw the market drop 15.23 points (1.6 percent). The Sun was at 16 degrees Capricorn, and the Moon was at 9 degrees Leo, both critical points.

In 1970, the market rose 32.04 points (5.1 percent) with the high on May 27. The Sun at 5 degrees Gemini and the Moon were not major factors. But the other planets combined triggered the high, along with the Moon and North Node in Pisces. The low on May 25 dropped the market 20.81 points (3.1 percent). The Sun was at 3 degrees Gemini (no major factor), but the Moon at 5 degrees Aquarius was the factor that caused this drop, along with the Moon square Saturn.

The Moon's position can be found in an astrological calendar or an ephemeris.

Chapter VIII

Year-End Rally

The Sun's position in relation to the stock market can show trends that are more or less active for each year, as the Sun degrees are generally fixed—they fall on about the same date every year. This is why some periods of the year reflect more of a pattern. This means that the Dow-Jones Industrials average will have similar to the same patterns at different sensitive points throughout each year. As an example, let's take the natal chart of the NYSE and the U.S. chart.

In the NYSE chart we find Venus, a prominent planet, along with Jupiter, relating to moves of success. The Sun is trine Venus at 5 degrees Taurus with the Sun at 5 degrees Virgo or 5 degrees Capricorn. This would relate to a sensitive point from the transit of the Sun to the NYSE chart. But in the US chart we have Jupiter at 5 degrees Cancer (the opposition of Cancer is Capricorn) so the transit at 5 degrees Capricorn would affect the market during that orb which would last from 5 degrees through 9 degrees, a 4-degree orb. This orb is in effect around Christmas and has become known as the year-end rally. The percentages are thus strongly in the favor as far as the Dow-Jones coming up on the plus side from Christmas Day to New Year's Day. This trend is more or less dominant year after year.

As an example, if we take the period from 1897 through 2008, there have only been 25 times when the stock market ended on the minus side in this period. But the reason for the minus side during this period can easily be related to sensitive points of the Moon's node. As an example, in 1911, the Dow-Jones ended up on the minus side by .43, when the North Node was in Aries, square Capricorn and also Jupiter in Cancer in the U.S. chart. The North Node was again at that sensitive degree in 1930, a year when the Dow-Jones ended up on the minus side by .62. In 1948, the North Node was leaving Taurus to enter Aries, which resulted in a minus of .12, as the degrees were activated.

The next return aspect of the North Node in Aries was in 1968, and the Dow-Jones ended on the minus side by 8.57. This was the result of the North Node square the Sun in Capricorn and square the Cancer planets in the U.S. chart. Minus points occurred when the North Node was in Cancer in 1925, and the year ended with a minus of .35. Again in 1926, it ended with a minus of 3.26. When in Capricorn in 1953, there was a minus of .02. Overall, the Dow-Jones ends up on the minus side about 14 percent of the time during that period from December 25 to 30.

The greatest point gained during this period was during 2008, when a 307.91 point gain occurred during the year-end rally. The greatest point loss was in 2007, with a 284.51 loss. The years 2007 and 2008 related to the highest and lowest gain for the year-end rally. Out of the 25 times the year-end rally failed, 14 of them were back-to-back under the influence of the cycle they were currently in. If the year-end rally ends on the downside, you might want to use caution the following year, with a stop.

So you can always see this effect in the period from Christmas Eve to New Year's, and it will not be a very hard prediction that the Dow-Jones Industrials will close up that week.

Dow-Jones Industrials

Year	Christmas Eve	New Year's	Gain
1900	70.03	70.71	.68
1901	61.52	64.56	3.04
1902	62.61	64.29	1.68
1903	47.75	49.11	1.36
1904	68.47	69.61	1.14
1905	95.05	96.20	1.15
1906	92.94	94.35	1.41
1907	58.00	58.75	.75
1908	85.68	86.15	.47
1909	98.61	99.05	.44
1910	81.33	$1.36	.03
1911	82.11	81.68	(Loss) -.43
1912	87.36	87.87	.51
1913	78.34	78.78	.44
1914	53.17	54.58	1.41
1915	98.36	99.15	.79
1916	94.60	95.00	.40

Year	Christmas Eve	New Year's	Gain
1917	69.29	74.38	5.09
1918	80.59	82.20	1.64
1919	103.95	107.23	3.28
1920	68.91	71.95	3.04
1921	79.61	81.10	1.49
1922	98.62	98.73	.11
1923	94.42	95.52	1.10
1924	116.74	120.51	3.77
1925	157.01	156.66	(Loss) - .35
1926	160.46	157.20	(Loss) - 3.26
1927	200.30	202.40	2.10
1928	287.89	300.00	12.11
1929	234.07	248.48	14.41
1930	165.20	164.58	(Loss) - .62
1931	75.84	17.90	2.06
1932	57.98	59.93	1.95
1933	98.04	99.90	1.86
1934	100.69	104.04	3.35
1935	141.53	144.13	2.60
1936	178.60	179.90	1.30
1937	127.36	120.85	(Loss) -6.51
1938	151.38	154.76	3.38
1939	149.85	150.24	.39
1940	128.89	131.13	2.24
1941	106.67	110.96	4.29
1942	119.27	119.40	.13
1943	136.24	135.89	(Loss) -.35
1944	150.63	152.32	1.69
1945	190.67	192.91	2.24
1946	176.95	177.20	.25
1947	108.84	180.56	(Loss) -.28
1948	177.42	177.30	(Loss) - .12
1949	198.88	200.13	1.25
1950	231.54	235.41	3.87

Year	Christmas Eve	New Year's	Gain
1951	265.79	269.23	3.44
1952	287.37	291.90	4.53
1953	280.92	280.90	(Loss) - .02
1954	397.15	404.39	7.24
1955	486.59	488.40	1.81
1956	494.38	499.47	5.09
1957	429.11	435.69	6.58
1958	572.73	583.65	10.92
1959	670.69	679.36	8.67
1960	613.23	615.89	2.66
1961	720.87	731.14	10.27
1962	647.71	652.10	4.39
1963	756.86	762.95	6.09
1964	868.16	874.13	5.97
1965	966.36	969.26	2.90
1966	799.10	785.69	(Loss) - 13.41
1967	887.37	905.11	17.74
1968	952.32	943.75	(Loss) - 8.57
1969	794.15	800.36	6.21
1970	828.38	838.92	10.54
1971	881.17	890.20	9.03
1972	1004.21	1020.02	15.81
1973	814.81	850.86	36.05
1974	598.40	616.24	17.84
1975	851.94	852.41	.47
1976	985.62	1004.65	19.03
1977	829.87	831.17	1.30
1978	808.47	805.01	(Loss) -3.46
1979	839.16	838.74	(Loss) - .42
1980	963.05	963.38	.33
1981	873.38	875.00	1.62
1982	1045.06	1046.55	`1.49
1983	1250.52	1258.64	8.12
1984	1210.14	1211.57	1.43

Year	Christmas Eve	New Year's	Gain
1985	1519.15	1546.67	27.52
1986	1926.88	1895.95	(Loss) -30.93
1987	1999.67	1938.83	(Loss) -60.84
1988	2168.93	2168.57	(Loss) -.36
1989	2711.39	2753.20	41.81
1990	2621.29	2633.66	12.37
1991	3050.98	3168.83	117.85
1992	3326.24	3301.11	(Loss) -25.13
1993	3757.72	3754.09	(Loss) -3.63
1994	3833.43	3834.44	1.01
1995	5097.97	5117.12	19.15
1996	6522.85	6448.27	(Loss) -74.58
1997	7660.13	7901.25	248.12
1998	9217.99	9181.43	(Loss) -36.53
1999	11,405.76	11,497.12	91.36
2000	10,635.56	10,786.85	151.29
2001	10,035.34	10,021.50	(Loss) -13.84
2002	8448.11	8341.63	(Loss) -106.48
2003	10,305.19	10,453.92	148.73
2004	10,827.12	10,783.01	(Loss) -44.11
2005	10,883.27	10,717.50	(Loss) -165.77
2006	12,434.22	12,463.15	119.93
2007	13,549.33	13,264.82	(Loss) -284.51
2008	8,468.48	8,776.39	307.91

As you follow each year you will find the same pattern activated. You can see the upward trend because of the trine aspect from Capricorn to the five-degree Venus in the NYSE. Now what about the trine aspect from Virgo? This will work the same way during this period. As an example, if you take the period with the Sun in Virgo from 5 to 10 degrees (you could use a wider orb of nine degrees) what happens during that period will indicate the trend for the rest of the month.

Remember that the Sun is generally at these degrees of Capricorn every year from Christmas to New Year's, only varying a day or so at times, just as the Sun is in 5 degrees Virgo on August 28, with the orb effective through September 3 or 4. Both have the same tendency, the same trend, and what happens in these periods relating to the stock market will indicate what will occur the balance of the month. The reason for this is that we also have a trine from Virgo and Capricorn to Venus in Taurus in the NYSE chart. You can go all the way to the first week of September as an indicator of what will occur the rest of the year because the NYSE chart has Mars at 18 degrees Virgo and the US chart has Neptune at 22 degrees Virgo; transiting planets going through this section will thus activate the market up or down.

To make this easy, watch what happens in the market the first week of September, and then check whether the entire month follows the same trend. If the first week is up, the month is up. If that first week is down, then the month is usually down. And the percentages are way above, close to 80 percent, of this being accurate all the time. The only way it could be inaccurate is if there is a certain affliction at the time, something better left for experts, not novices, because 80 percent is a good average. So use the first week of September as a guide, and do the same from December 25 to New Year's.

Regarding the trend for the year, January can give a good indication because of the later degree sensitive points (Venus in Taurus, and Mars and Neptune in Virgo). This means that January can indicate what the eleven months ahead are going to be, bearish or bullish. Research reveals the success rate to be about 80 percent. This does not work when there are crash periods, certain sensitive zones activated in panics and crashes. This will bring some turmoil, as will Saturn going through Capricorn, which also indicates delays. This is very helpful in determining what an individual stock will do, but there are three factors you need to learn in order to determine which stock to start with for the year. In most cases it's better to buy a stock at the beginning of the year and ride with it because you can get a pretty good indication of the January influence.

Why is the January influence so important? Astrologically speaking, there is the trine aspect related to the year-end rally period. But it's more than that. We have Venus at 5 degrees Taurus, Mercury at 23 degrees Taurus and the Sun at 27 degrees Taurus, and Mars at 18 degrees Virgo. These points are trine Capricorn. So January is important because there is a grand trine, a configuration that occurs when there are three planets, each 120 degrees apart.

As the Sun leaves the 5 degree Capricorn point that relates to the short rally it moves on to a trine to the NYSE Mars at 18 degrees, the NYSE Mercury at 23 degrees and NYSE Sun at 27 degrees. So this is why January is important in anything related to the Dow-Jones averages. The trine also occurs in the U.S. chart with Neptune at 24 degrees Virgo and the Part of Fortune at 25 degrees Taurus. But the opposition to planets in Cancer show a turning point; and Capricorn rules government. These influences can be seen from about January 9 through January 18, as the Sun transits the pertinent degrees. If the market shoots up in January, it will be up in December; if it's low in January, then it's going to be low in December, at year's end.

But it's wise to do your homework before investing in the market. All the facts and figures presented here useful to begin research to find the patterns of individual stocks. You will find, however, that the Dow-Jones is a leader, and just like sheep, everything follows the pattern; whether a movement or a stampede, they all run one way. The Dow-Jones Industrial average thus affects everything on the New York Stock Exchange. When the Dow-Jones drops, everything follows that trend. Not all stocks go down in a down period, but the majority of them do. Gold stocks and some others are exceptions to the rule. But you have to ride with the tide. If the tide is going out, ride with it; don't go against it. If the tide is coming in, ride with it. And these key points of the year alone should help you determine whether to go short or long.

There are three movements in the Dow-Jones Industrial averages. The primary movement, is a broad uptrend or downtrend, known as a bull or a bear market. This can even be as long as several years, especially if there's a strong Saturn movement (a two and a half year uptrend). A secondary movement shows a significant decline in a primary bull market or a primary bear market rally; it generally lasts from three weeks to three months. The three-month point represents a square, or 90 degrees, which is why it does not last for a long duration. The tertiary movement is more or less the daily price fluctuation. This occurs when the Moon-Sun aspect mentioned earlier in the book is active; it relates to up or down trends during the day. So realizing the planetary influence of each trend you are able to stay one step ahead of it. And every time the Dow-Jones broke to a new high, we had the presence of the conjunctions combined with the other planetary influences. Now, recapping the events discussed earlier regarding the Dow-Jones Industrial averages, the breaking point generally comes when there's a cluster or a combination of mutables. This means there are planets either in Sagittarius or Pisces, which are the two strongest mutable points as far as the break of the positive against a negative factor. As an example, on June 12, 1906, the Dow-Jones Industrials hit 100. Saturn was in Pisces, the Moon was in Pisces, the other mutable aspects were Jupiter in Gemini, Mercury in Gemini, Sun in Gemini.

On December 19, 1927 the Dow-Jones Industrials broke 200, with the Sun in Sagittarius, Mercury in Sagittarius, Saturn in Sagittarius, Mars in Sagittarius, Jupiter in Pisces and Uranus in Pisces. On January 2, 1929, the Dow-Jones broke 300, with Saturn in Sagittarius and Mars in Gemini. On December 29, 1959, the Dow-Jones broke 400, with Mars in Pisces. On March 12, 1956, the Dow-Jones broke 500, with the Sun in Pisces, Mercury in Pisces, Moon in Pisces and Saturn in Sagittarius. On February 20, 1959, the Dow-Jones broke 600, with the Sun in Pisces, Venus in Pisces, Mercury in Pisces and Jupiter in Sagittarius. On February 28, 1964, the Dow-Jones broke 800, with the Sun and Mars in Pisces. On January 28, 1965, the Dow-Jones broke 900, with the Moon in Sagittarius and Saturn in Pisces. On January 18, 1966, the Dow-Jones broke 1000, with the Moon in Sagittarius and Saturn in Pisces.

So you will notice that there is always a pattern within the Dow-Jones, and that the mutable aspects are important in relation to changes. By using an ephemeris you will be able to find out when all the planets are in one sign, and this will indicate a turning point. A conjunction of planets in Sagittarius should bring a new high.

CHAPTER IX

Dow-Jones Predictions

In 1979, Jupiter will be in Leo, with gold hitting a new high until October when it enters Virgo. This starts a cluster with Jupiter and Saturn in Virgo, and as we go into November it falls into a pattern with Mars in Virgo. This represents a conjunction, three planets in one sign. It shows the beginning of a new cycle and the energies involved are working together toward a recession aspect relating to a downfall in the stock market.

Early 1979, with Jupiter in Leo trine the Sun in Aries in April will create some high volume and prices, and the Dow-Jones should hit an all-time high during this period with a very heavy month. However, Mercury will be retrograde between March 15 and April 8.

It is after April 8, that we will notice a rise in the market all the way into July 19. Between July 19 and August 9, we will have a sluggish market, and also again when Mercury is retrograde between November 11 and December 2, as it starts to fall into a bearish market. In October the market will be jarred by the general living conditions, inflation, interest rates, unemployment, the working class dissatisfied with conditions, discontent and strikes. This will be a period of panic as October 1979 approaches and we run into the aspects of 1980.

In 1980, Mars will be retrograde between January 16 and April 6. This will be a very bearish trend, and there will be a conjunction between Jupiter and Saturn. The conjunction here is related to this cycle from the cluster point of October-November 1979, with planets in Virgo. The market will be shaky during the entire period of 1980 as many changes are indicated, even indecision in the area of the elections. It shows that the president of the United States prior to this point will either decide not to run or drop out of the race. So 1980, under the influence of Virgo, will not be a very good year because of conditions relating to the changes that will take place.

As we go into 1981, the Jupiter-Saturn conjunction in Libra shows disputes among people in power in connection with finance and trade. This relates to foreign trade conditions concerning the stock exchange that will send the Dow-Jones deeper during this period of scandal. Regarding international affairs, it shows depression in foreign trade and the U.S. dollar in the money market. The influence of 1981 is negative and bearish, and there will be new rules and changes in the stock market itself, especially on margin trades. An upside trend will begin around June 1982.

The period of Mars retrograde, February 21 through May 12, indicates a few changes, a breaking of the trends from the old to the new. Areas that can gain from this are shipping, commercial affairs, anything relating to the Sagittarian type of stocks. Also, Scorpio stocks show restriction when Saturn enters Scorpio. But, 1982 will pave the way for new discoveries that will lead into 1983. This will relate to inventions and scientific discoveries. Many new things will be born that will change the operation of many stocks. Energy could be one related area at this time, and there will be an unusual rate of explosions, accidents. fires on ships, strikes and disputes in shipping areas. But shipping stocks are still prominent during 1982.

In 1983, the market should start on the high side, with Jupiter conjunct Uranus; this is the beginning of a new cycle. It will mean changes of a Uranus nature, and Jupiter will be in Sagittarius that year. The influence is changing and the market will be mixed. The year will begin on the positive but could end on the negative. The first six months of 1983 should show quite a stimulated market due to new enterprises and inventions.

In 1984, the Dow-Jones Industrial average should begin bullish. Mars will be retrograde between April 5 and June 20, which indicates a mixed market and some setbacks. Mercury will be retrograde between April 13 and May 7, which will enhance the retrograde movement of Mars during that period. At the end of 1984, there will again be involvement with debts owned by other countries, the interest rate will be up and there will be a bit of uncertainty because of inflationary aspects. So 1984 will begin bullish, turn bearish, return to and end bearish. In 1985 there are good movements aspected, with the year beginning at a low level and progressing.

Because of the return of Mercury, 1984 will end on the high side. We do have a square aspect between Jupiter and Saturn, which relates to a crisis point, indicating confrontation and obstacles. Obstacles during this period include trying to correct situations in foreign affairs and loans, trying to cut the value of the dollar itself and more or less setting new rules with regard to banking institutions. At this time during 1985 there will be changes within U.S. currency. However, the indications of a good market are prominent during 1985. There will be a rush on stocks related to this Sagittarian influence and the market will have panic-type buying with volume hitting an all-time record during this period.

As we enter 1986, there will be a conjunction between Saturn and Uranus, another new cycle, with the Jupiter-Saturn square still in effect. Mars will be retrograde from June 9 through August 12. Mercury will be retrograde between July 11 and August 4. This is a strong influence connected with this aspect of Mars, and, therefore, the market could begin falling around July. However, the market fall will be temporary, with temporary bullish aspects.

In 1987, Jupiter will be trine Saturn and Uranus, and there is a Saturn-Uranus conjunction. The trine aspect is harmonious, showing growth and expansion. There is no period of retrograde Mars, but Mercury will be retrograde. However, 1987 will be a very good year for the market. The conjunction cycle that was mixed with the bearish and bullish trends will turn 1987 into a bullish market, which will run into 1988, until November, when Saturn enters Capricorn. Mars will be retrograde between June 26 and October. Jupiter will be opposition Saturn, which brings conflicting possibilities related to the stock market. The energies involved are diverse; it's a pullback. During this period there will be a depression, the same as 1929, with the market moving up and then dropping into a crash. This will be a panic.

In 1989, Jupiter will be opposition Saturn, with Saturn conjunct Uranus. In 1990, Jupiter will be opposition Uranus and Saturn, with Saturn conjunct Uranus. These influences are very negative for the market. One of the low periods during this time will be August 28 through October 20, 1988, when Mars will be retrograde. This will be the signal for the depression, and the time to sell short. Everything on the market will drop 75-80 percent. It is a return cycle of what occurred earlier, and when the market goes to the bottom it is time to buy. Sell short, then buy.

In 1992, Jupiter will be trine Uranus, representing corrections and changes related to U.S. financial interests. Employment will be on the rise, and the market will be bullish. This trend will meet with some restrictions from November 30, 1993 to February 16, 1994, when Mars will be retrograde. This will cause some impulsive selling, causing the market to dip, but it should bounce back into the period of 1994. The trine aspect prevails through 1994, and goes into 1995 with a square aspect, when the market will meet a crisis point.

In 1995, between January 4 and March 26, the market will have some disruption. However, it should close the year out with the Mercury influence on the upside. Some of the concerns at that time which will affect the market in general will be a concern with the finances of medical institutions and hospitals. Areas related to public institutions and government spending will bring a depression to the market over a short period. In 1996, the market will be somewhat bearish, especially during the early part of January. Problems related to the market in 1996 will also affect the market in 1997; these problems relate to loss of trade, discontent and a U.S. pull-back in production. In 1997, there will be a conjunction of Jupiter with Uranus, which always starts trends; but during this period it will not be heavy enough because of the lack in the other aspects.

Going into 1998, the market will fall into a bearish trend but pull out in the latter part of 1998 and end on the upside. In 1999, the market will be affected by a square aspect from Saturn to Uranus. This relates to bearish trends which will run to the year 2000. This will affect the financial condition of the country and banks as we know them today will not be operating the same. We will have a complete monetary system change. These changes will emanate from the era of 1988 to 1991 and will even affect the color of money. The 1980 period also relates to disputes—war. Although there are conditions that relate to war, there will be inventions that will benefit the U.S. moving forward into the 21st century.

Looking back over the past 20 years since this book was first published, you've witnessed the power of retrograde Jupiter and Saturn. Jupiter has a 75 percent probability, and Saturn a 70 percent probability, that the Dow-Jones will be higher at the end of the retrograde period—with the exception of the transit of Saturn in Cancer.

As we move forward into the 21st Century, we will go through the process of many changes. Some of the Dow-Jones stocks that are its backbone will no longer be listed. We can expect a foreign country to attack the U.S. in the cycle of 2001-03. This could lead us into a war, like it did in 1942 at Pearl Harbor. The Hetty Green scandal of 1884 will come full circle.

The cycle from 2008 to 2010 will bring unemployment to over 10 percent. This cycle will produce many bank failures, as it did in 1861, when hundreds of banks failed, bringing on a depression. Real estate, publications, and working conditions will crumble under this cycle, leading us to the cycle of 2011-2013, as it played out in the 1880s, with the Federal Cash Surplus of the 1880s as a result of the extravagance of the Harrison administration, and the McKinley Tariff of the 1890s. Expect new rules in the trading of oil and gold, with inflation that could contribute to bankruptcy of states, as well, as the U.S.

After this period, we'll be back in a new bull market as Saturn transits Sagittarius. No matter what trend the stock market is in, you'll always have many cycles that move up and down. When the moon is in a mutable sign, the changes can be extreme. Using the chapter on sensitive degrees of the Moon, the Moon can predetermine the direction of the change.

The dates I've listed under each year (beginning on the next page) are considered air, water, fire, or earth years, according to the sign's element. All three of any of these groups divide the year. The degree of the Moon and sign is given for the opening bell on the New York Stock Exchange. The prediction is that the trend will change on these dates in a new direction for at least 28 days. Looking at the positive and negative degrees of the Moon, you can predetermine the trend, and it's generally in the opposite direction from where it is currently going. Next you'll notice that in some of the years I give a date, followed by SXT (sextile), TRN (trine) or SQ (square). This is the aspect of Mars to a cardinal sign Full Moon. These trends are considered bullish. Over the last 20 years, the trine has been 80 percent accurate; the sextile, 90 percent; and the square, 82 percent.

The end date should be higher than the start date. When it falls into a trend-change date, they will follow up together.

A Jupiter-Saturn sextile or square will aid the trend 16 days before the aspect date (the aspect date will be higher), and also 16 days after, which will be higher than the aspect date. Jupiter and Saturn in trine or opposition aspect is the opposite. At the aspect date, the price will be lower, and the same 16 days after. The predictions listed are through 2050.

2000
February 11; 4 Taurus
June 9; 24 Virgo
November 5; 13 Capricorn

2001
January 31, 0 Taurus
April 8-July 5, SXT
May 29; 3 Virgo
September 24; 3 Capricorn
October 1-December 30, SQ

2002
January 20; 17 Aries
May 18; 11 Leo
September 13; 18 Sagittarius

2003
January 10; 20 Aries
April 16-July 13, SQ
May 9; 19 Leo
July 13-October 10, SXT
September 3; 11 Sagittarius
December 30; 10 Aries

2004
January 7-April 5, SQ
April 5-December 26, TRN
April 26; 23 Cancer
August 22; 17 Scorpio
December 10; 10 Pisces

2005
March 25-July 21, TRN
April 15; 14 Cancer
August 12; 13 Scorpio
December 8; 17 Pisces

2006
January 14-April 13, SXT
April 5; 16 Cancer
July 7; 29 Scorpio
November 28; 10 Pisces

2007
March 26; 14 Cancer
April 2-September 27, TRN
July 20; 14 Scorpio
November 19; 16 Pisces

2008
March 14; 24 Gemini
March 22-July 18, SQ
July 10; 22 Libra
November 5; 19 Aquarius

2009
March 3; 3 Gemini
June 29; 8 Libra
July 7-October 4, TRN
October 4-December 31, SQ
October 26; 9 Aquarius

2010
February 20; 14 Taurus
March 20-June 26, SXT
June 18; 17 Virgo
June 26-September 23, TRN
October 15; 29 Capricorn

2011
February 10; 14 Taurus
June 8; 2 Virgo
October 4; 15 Capricorn

2012
January 9-April 6, SXT
January 29; 22 Aries
May 27; 20 Leo
July 4-September 30, SQ
September 22; 26 Sagittarius

2013
January 18; 14 Aquarius
May 17; 23 Gemini
September 12; 26 Libra

2014
January 8; 22 Aries
January 16-April 16, SQ
May 6; 10 Leo
July 12-October 8, SQ
September 2; 10 Sagittarius

2015
April 24; 18 Cancer
August 21; 14 Scorpio
December 18; 25 Pisces

2016
March 23-October 16, SXT
April 14; 29 Cancer
August 10; 16 Scorpio
December 7; 17 Pisces

2017
January 13-April 11, TRN
April 3; 10 Cancer
July 31; 19 Scorpio
Novemb3er 27; 15 Pisces

2018
January 2-March 31, TRN
March 23; 17 Gemini
March 31-June 28, SQ
July 19; 23 Libra
September 25-December 22, SXT
November 15; 22 Aquarius

2019
March 13; 11 Gemini
July 9; 17 Libra
November 4; 13 Aquarius

2020
March 1; 27 Taurus
April 8-July 5, TRN
June 27; 25 Virgo
July 5-October 1, SQ
October 22; 18 Capricorn

2022
February 8; 20 Taurus
June 6; 4 Virgo
July 13-October 9, TRN
October 2; 4 Capricorn

2024
January 17; 19 Aries
May 5; 26 Leo
June 22-October 17, TRN
September 10; 10 Sagittarius

2026
April 23; 27 Cancer
August 19; 20 Scorpio
December 16; 16 Pisces

2028
April 1; 26 Gemini
July 27; 20 Libra
October 3-December 31, TRN
November 23; 27 Aquarius

2030
March 11; 12 Gemini
July 8; 17 Libra
November 2; 10 Aquarius

2021
February 18; 17 Taurus
March 28-June 25, TRN
June 17; 18 Virgo
October 13; 25 Capricorn

2023
January 27; 24 Aries
April 6-July 3, SQ
May 26; 23 Leo
September 21; 13 Sagittarius

2025
January 6; 9 Aries
April 13-July 10, SQ
May 4; 13 Leo
July 10-October 7, TRN
August 31; 11 Sagittarius
December 26; 15 Aries

2027
March 22-July 18, SXT
April 13; 17 Cancer
July 18-October 15, SQ
August 9; 20 Scorpio
December 6; 18 Pisces

2029
March 22; 25 Leo
June 29-October 21, SQ
July 18; 20 Sagittarius
November 16; 4 Aries

2031
January 8-April 7, SQ
February 28; 3 Gemini
June 27; 1 Libra
July 4-September 30, SXT
September 30-December 28, TRN
October 13; 3 Aquarius

2032
February 17; 22 Taurus
June 15; 19 Virgo
October 11; 10 Capricorn

2033
January 15-April 14, TRN
February 6; 17 Taurus
April 14-July 12, SQ
June 4; 9 Virgo
October 1; 7 Capricorn

2034
January 4-April 3, SXT
January 26; 25 Aries
May 24; 28 Leo
September 20; 25 Sagittarius

2035
January 16; 17 Aries
March 23-July 20, SQ
May 14; 24 Leo
July 20-October 17, SXT
September 9; 16 Sagittarius

2036
January 5; 1 Aries
January 13-April 10, SQ
April 10-July 8, TRN
May 2; 4 Leo
August 28; 5 Sagittarius
December 25; 1 Aries

2037
March 31-June 27, TRN
April 22; 26 Cancer
June 27-September 24, SQ
September 24-December 22, SXT
August 17; 19 Scorpio
December 14; 22 Pisces

2038
April 11; 8 Cancer
April 19-July 16, SQ
August 7; 10 Scorpio
December 3; 11 Pisces

2039
March 31; 26 Gemini
July 6-October 2, TRN
July 27; 18 Libra
October 2-December 30, SQ
November 22; 26 Aquarius

2040
March 20; 28 Gemini
March 28-June 24, SQ
July 16; 14 Libra
November 11; 17 Aquarius

2041
March 9; 26 Cancer
July 5; 27 Scorpio
October 31; 29 Pisces

2042
February 26; 3 Gemini
April 6-July 3, SXT
June 25; 5 Libra
July 3-September 29, TRN
October 22; 5 Aquarius

2043
February 16; 24 Taurus
June 14; 24 Virgo
October 10; 9 Capricorn

2044
January 14-April 12, SXT
February 5; 3 Taurus
June 2; 10 Virgo
July 10-October 7, SQ
September 28; 0 Capricorn

2045
January 26; 11 Taurus
May 23; 3 Virgo
September 18; 2 Capricorn
September 26-December 24, TRN

2046
January 14; 15 Aries
May 12; 10 Leo
July 18-October 14, SXT
September 7; 16 Sagittarius

2047
January 2; 24 Pisces
January 12-April 10, TRN
May 1; 22 Cancer
August 27; 27 Scorpio
December 23; 26 Pisces

2048
January 1-June 26, SXT
April 20; 21 Cancer
August 16; 17 Scorpio
December 12; 23 Pisces

2049
April 9; 12 Cancer
July 15-October 11, SQ
August 6; 10 Scorpio
December 2; 17 Pisces

2050
January 8-April 7, TRN
March 28; 20 Gemini
April 7-July 4, SQ
July 26; 28 Libra
September 30-December 28, SXT
November 21; 26 Aquarius

CHAPTER X

ANALYZING CORPORATE CHARTS

After analyzing the Dow-Jones average as far as its movement up or down, you should incorporate this information into your individual stock choices. If the trend is bearish, knock off 50 percent for the individual stock. If the individual stock is riding at 100 and the prediction is that the market will be bearish, go short and then buy when it is low and ride it to a high. When the market shows an indication of a high, go 50 percent high. Many stocks will rise with the market. Remember to always rate a stock for 25 percent—25 points—upward movement if it is due to the fundamentals of the stock. If a stock shows something good, if it shows it is getting into something, that earnings are up, then rate this 25 percent. Then you can ride it up 25 percent and then sell. If a stock is in a group (oil stock, cardboard container stock, etc.) that is having an up trend, then this is also 25 percent. You can then ride the group up 25 percent on their own worth. If the market shows an upward trend, rate them 100 percent. So if the stock is $50 a share, you would rate it all the way up to 100. This would give you the doubling points. If you have 10 turnovers of a stock and you start with an initial investment of $2000 this would give you more than $1 million after all 10 turnovers are made. But be very careful in rating your stock as far as turnover and going long or selling short. You have to ride with the tide. If the tide is coming in, you ride with it; if the tide is going out, you ride with it. When you go against the tide, you get hurt. So the key factor in speculating on the New York Stock Exchange is riding with the Dow-Jones average. When it starts falling back, everything follows, just like a low or high tide. When you rate a stock on these percentages, you will not get hurt in buying or selling. Also remember that volume of a certain stock will indicate an upward movement due to the type of stock it is or the fundamentals of the stock.

As the cycle of the transiting planets unfolds there will be periods when a stock will appear to be at a standstill. It will maintain its place until the next cycle comes in and causes the motion to change, indicating that the aspects are operating, forcing the stock up or down. When a stock price changes direction, it is indicative that the cycle force has caused the change, and a buyer's emotions are stimulated from this to either to buy or sell, causing a stock to go up or down. Stock prices consists of two parts: the earnings value and the cycle market worth, depending on the high and low cycle prices. As the upward cycle comes in, more stocks go up in price. The urge to buy becomes stronger and people who normally want to buy stock or people who have been watching stock all want to get on the bandwagon and ride with it. And the profits grow because the product is in demand. So the influences of the planets more or less affects the people, causing this reaction in the stock market itself.

As more and more stocks fall in price the urge to sell becomes stronger and the Mars influence becomes more prominent as the would-be seller anticipates losses and decides he has to get out of the market before things get worse. So these are generally the two influences that affect a cycle.

Short cycles in the market reflect the day-to-day balance in buying and selling, and this comes from the Moon-Sun aspect. The longer cycles reflect a longer balance and become in effect a trend which brings on a cycle balance. These longer cycles are due to the transits of Saturn and Jupiter.

You have to remember that a buyer can only buy stock from a pessimistic owner, one who feels the stock is not worth the price and wants to get out—where the person buying the stock feels it is a good price and he is an optimistic buyer. When prices move downward the supply of stock being offered at each down tick increases at the same time as the demand diminishes. Now the would-be sellers can only sell stock to optimistic buyers and as prices decline buyers turn less optimistic and a lot of them withdraw their buy orders and this causes delays and drops in stock.

Each stock has a resistance point, the high part of the cycle and the low point. There are many stocks on the New York Stock Exchange so you can be discriminating as far as your selection. It is always smart to watch for the uptrend as far as the volume and cycle trend of the chart itself, and buy the stock at its low point, not at its high point. The best deals are stocks that don't look too good, stocks that are very weak. As an example, in 1973, I recommended Resorts International, which was $1-3 a share. Many stockbrokers talked people out of it because it was a very, very bad stock at the time. But within a short period Resorts International went to $210 a share. There are many stocks like this on the market. The buyer just has to be aware of them by looking at the cycle influence of the chart, what is moving up with the cycle, whether the product is in demand and the trend of the stock itself. So the early years of a corporation, what the corporation has done in the past, should be of no concern in making a choice of a stock for the future.

A lot of cycles will run ten days, ten weeks, twenty-five weeks, seventy-five weeks and 225 weeks. These are due to certain aspects between the planets and all these cycles correspond with each other. And with these cycles you can dig up the eight and a half year full cycle, the seventeen year, the thirty-four year, all the way down.

Always remember that the key factor in buying stock is volume. As the volume builds, prices rise. When volume declines, prices fall. These two factors are directly involved with each other because they affect both parts of the chart: price and buying. The effect of volume springs from the fundamental side of the market, analysis of the economic outlook. People want to get in on the product. Also, the rise from this type of buying volume comes from the technical side as part of it could be seasonal as there are certain stocks that do better during certain periods of the year.

From New Moon to New Moon, and from aspect to aspect, certain stocks are regulated by certain speeds and changes within these speeds. These are related because there are certain points around its chart which will make a stock go up or down at different intervals and the effect of this movement is from buying and selling.

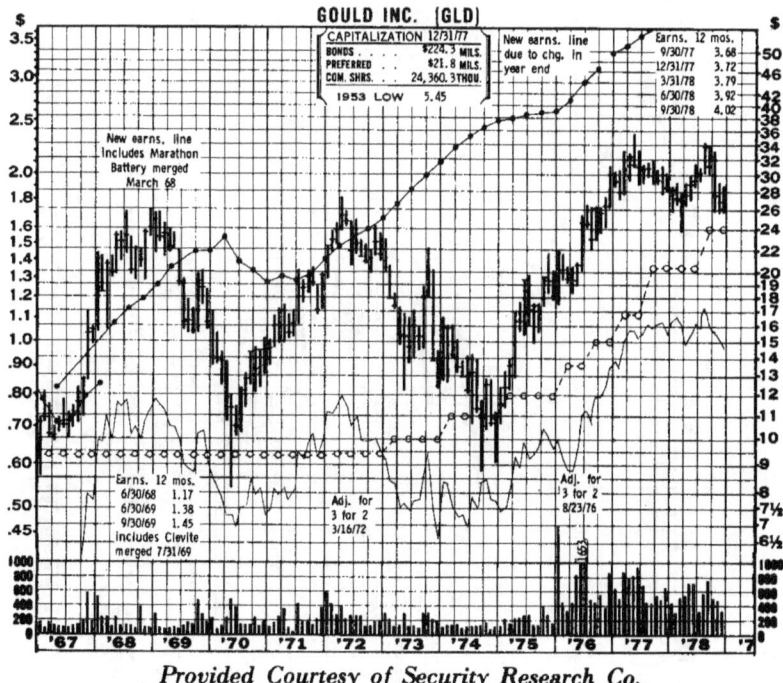

Provided Courtesy of Security Research Co.

Chart courtesy of Security Research Co.

In the one-half speed circumference the stock will have a tendency to shoot up to the first point of the chart, then bound down, then up, then down, as it hits each cusp point of the chart, bringing up and down cycles. This is what is called speed of one-half. A good example of this is Gould, Inc. As you can see in the illustration, the market comes from the low peak, hits a high, drops to the low, and then rises. At its low in 1966, it started its movement upward to a high in 1969, then back down to a low in 1970, back up again to a high in 1972, back down again to a low in 1974 and back up again to a high in 1977. Notice from the price range that this stock would be a good buy at $10, as this seems to be this cycle's breaking point. It is apparent from the high cycle point that a high value of $26 a share is when the stock will meet resistance. Using a 12-year graph like this you would be able to determine the astrological breaking-point and the high point of the cycle as far as the effect of the movement by speed. The low point is generally when the New Moon comes back around.

As an example, we know that in December 1966 and January 1967 the stock ran low to $9 per share. This occurred again in January and February 1970, and its next drop came at the end of the year in December 1974, when it also reached the $9 mark. So you could have picked up this stock at these points and been able to ride it up, using almost the same period each year, either at the very end of December or January-February.

There are actually four major cycles you'll see regarding different stocks. When the stock was at $10 a share there was hardly any volume and no indication regarding what the stock might do. The high volume period came in January 1976, which would have been a signal to buy; but if you bought at that time, you would have had to buy the stock at around $18 a share. So this is the importance of knowing when to pick up on a stock at its low cycle.

Another stock that has this same pattern is PPG Industries, Inc. It had a high point of $30 and dropped down in 1970, where it met a low of $15. It then shot back up, had a high in 1972 of about $33 and then dropped back down to $14. So a price of $14 or $15 a share for this stock would be its purchase price, as it would track back down and could go as low as

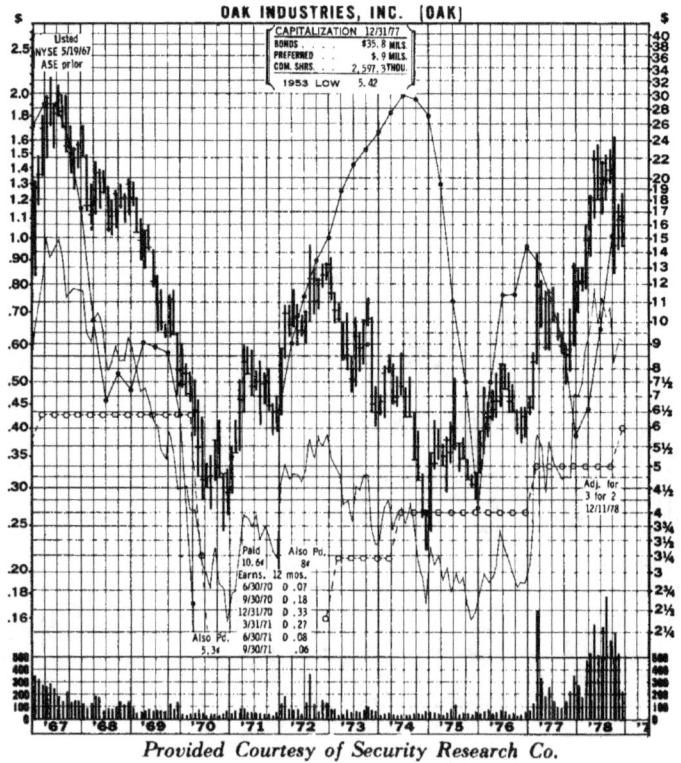

Chart courtesy of Security Research Co.

$14 or $15 in 1979. A stock generally will hit its low point at three different times and will hit its high before it changes its cycle according to other transits related to Uranus. Remember the transit of Jupiter every 12 years. When Jupiter comes back around this could indicate a somewhat different pattern because Uranus stays in one sign for seven years.

Let's look at one other stock with this pattern, Oak Industries. This cycle is a little more erratic, although the pattern is the same one-half speed cycle. Notice that in 1967 it had a high of almost $50, and a low of $5. The stock went back up to $20 a share, back down to $5 and then back up to $36. With this type of stock, a good buying price would be in the area of $6 per share, and the selling price in the area of $20 per share.

Another stock that is a little erratic regarding its high and its low one-half cycle is Super-Scope. This stock has been $7 per share, then shot up top $55, went back to $8.50 per share, back up to $34, back down to $10, back up to $42, back down to $9, back up to $40 and back down to $10 a share. This kind of company will generally maintain the same pattern, so the safe buying price would be $10 per share, which would have occurred five different years within the last 12 years. The selling price would be $40 a share, and there were four years in which you could have sold at that price. This is the pattern of the one-half speed.

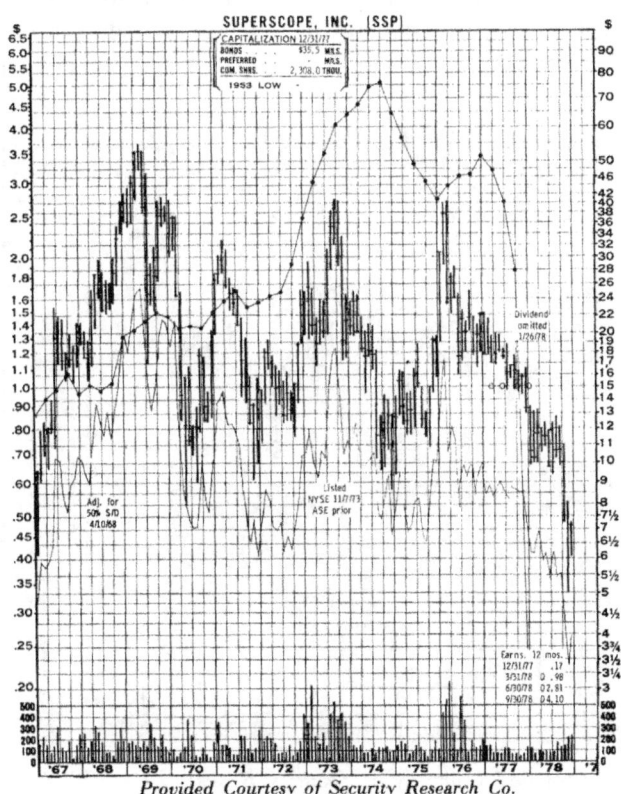

Chart courtesy of Security Research Co.

The next is one-fourth speed, in evidence with a chart where it hits the cusp on a high point on every other house. As an example of the one-half speed, one cusp it hits up, the other one down, the next one up and the next one down. The years in between depend upon the planet that activates it. If Saturn, it's a two and a half year jump; if Jupiter, it's a one-year jump, one year up and one year down. But each cycle can always be determined.

Picture the cusp of each house as the first one going through a stage, passing through one cusp and hitting the top of another one, then starting to go down, passing one and hitting the bottom of the next one; almost every other one is being aspected. So every other house cusp is where this change occurs. Again, this will relate to the buying price as far as the best price to buy. The first company we'll look at with this type of aspect is Kraft, Inc.

The first thing to notice about Kraft is that it has no major move. Generally, a safe buy would be at $32 a share, which would be the low, and the top would be at $46 a share. This is not a stock that would double because it does not have the movement and has been more or less stable. If you look at the chart for the last 12 years you can see a slight uptrend to $69, going slightly downward over a few years and then slightly moving back up, followed by a slight down, etc. This stock is generally good for long-term investment but not a good investment for a fast turnover.

Another company with a one-fourth cycle is Shell Oil. It stayed on an uptrend from 1966 to 1969, and then went down in 1970. A good bottom point for buying is $18 per share, and it has a high level of $34. So it's not a complete 50 percent movement stock, but it is a stock from which money can be made. Notice the cycle moving up slowly, hitting a high of $20, then dropping down, then up slowly again and then starting a downward trend.

Another company that is a good example of this cycle is Tenneco. Notice it moves up and then hits a high of $78, retreats to a low of $70, comes back up slightly all the way through and then hits $77-78. The bottom point of the cycle to buy is $20; the selling point is $30. This is a 50 percent markup.

This kind of stock has a steady trend, and this kind of cycle is usually

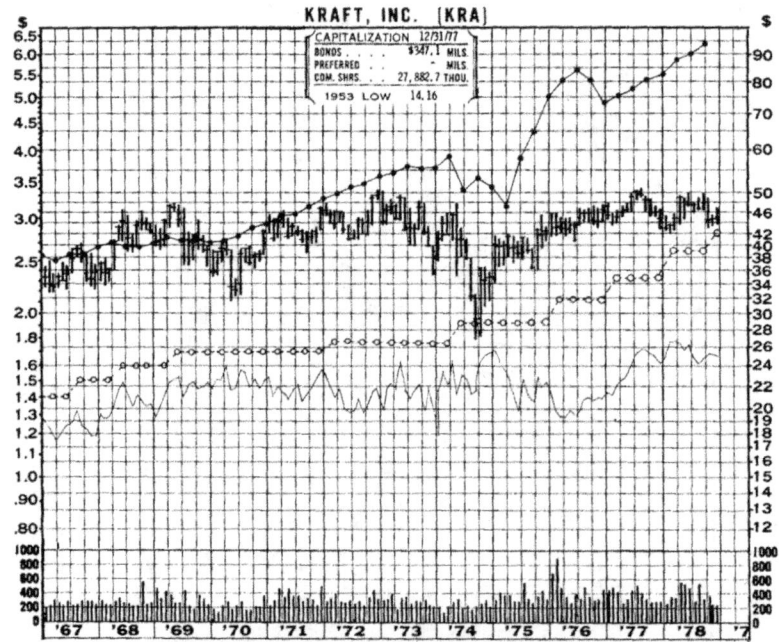

Provided Courtesy of Security Research Co.

Chart courtesy of Security Research Co.

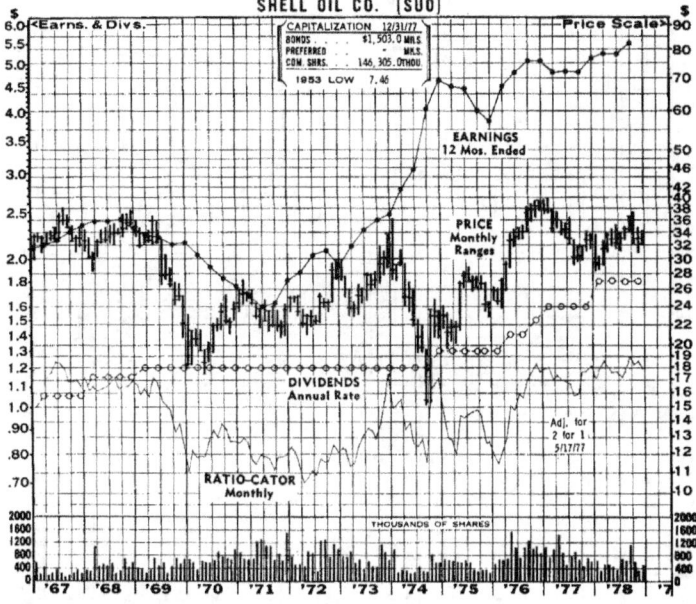

Chart courtesy of Security Research Co.

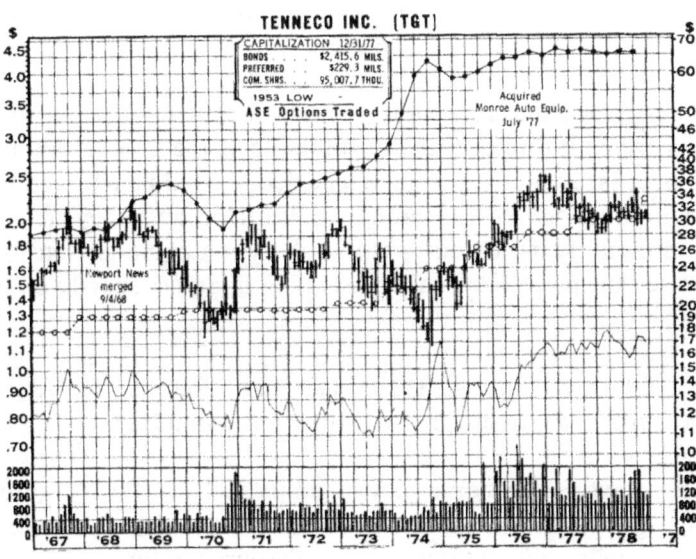

Chart courtesy of Security Research Co.

good for stocks that follow this trend because they don't seem to have potential as far as the possibility of making money by doubling the stock price. But another important factor to watch is earning power. The earning power of Tenneco is all the way up, meaning that when the cycle changes on this stock after the 12-year period, it might take up a different pattern and fluctuate more between the high and low levels.

The next cycle is the three-quarter cycle. It is similar to the one-quarter cycle, but it comes up, misses one house, connects on the next house, starts a down trend passing three houses and then goes back up on the next house cusp.

International Paper Co. is an example of this trend. Its low buying price is $32 per share, and its selling price is $70 per share in the up cycle. Notice that in 1966-1967, there was a gradual gain upwards. Then stock dropped in 1971-1972, but not much. It then kept coming up and passed its next aspect. As soon as it gets to the house cusp that it hits on, it shot up from $32 per share, where it was in December 1974, to a high of almost $80 per share in February 1976. These companies are easy to spot, and can generally be picked up just as they make that final upward move.

Another example is Occidental Petroleum, which also shows when to sell short. In the 1968 period, there is a high of $50 per share. As soon as it passes the high point of that house on that cusp, it has to start going down, moving to a low of $7 per share by 1974. You have to wait for the timing to be right on stocks that have this type of cycle, and there are only certain periods in which they go down.

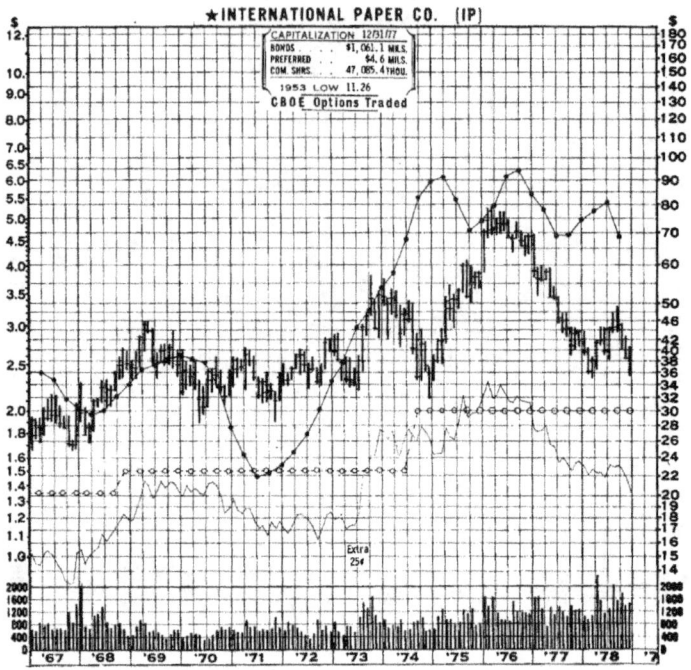

Chart courtesy of Security Research Co.

Don't forget. They're missing three house cusps. This means three different cycles that could be a total of almost six years, especially with the influence of Saturn.

As an example, the change in Occidental became apparent in 1967, 1968, 1969, 1970 and 1972, and then during the period of 1973, when it dropped to $8. But that was the time to buy that stock and then ride back up with it because the selling price of Occidental would have been $28 a share in that area. These stocks will function like this through their life because they are triggered by the different influences in their charts. I won't get into these midpoints or sensitive points because it's easy for you to see the pattern from the past and tell almost exactly on the chart when it's going to break.

The last cycle here is mixed with the three-fourths. It alternates three-fourths, one fourth, one-half cycle, a very erratic cycle or pattern. An example is Minnesota Mining.

Minnesota Mining stays with the basic cycle, then comes down, jumps back up real fast—from $34 to $90 within a couple of years—and then starts its downward motion real fast, then back up, back down and back up. So this company has all three cycles. Missouri Pacific has the same pattern but on a different level. It starts off on the one-half, goes down to a low of $7½, bounces

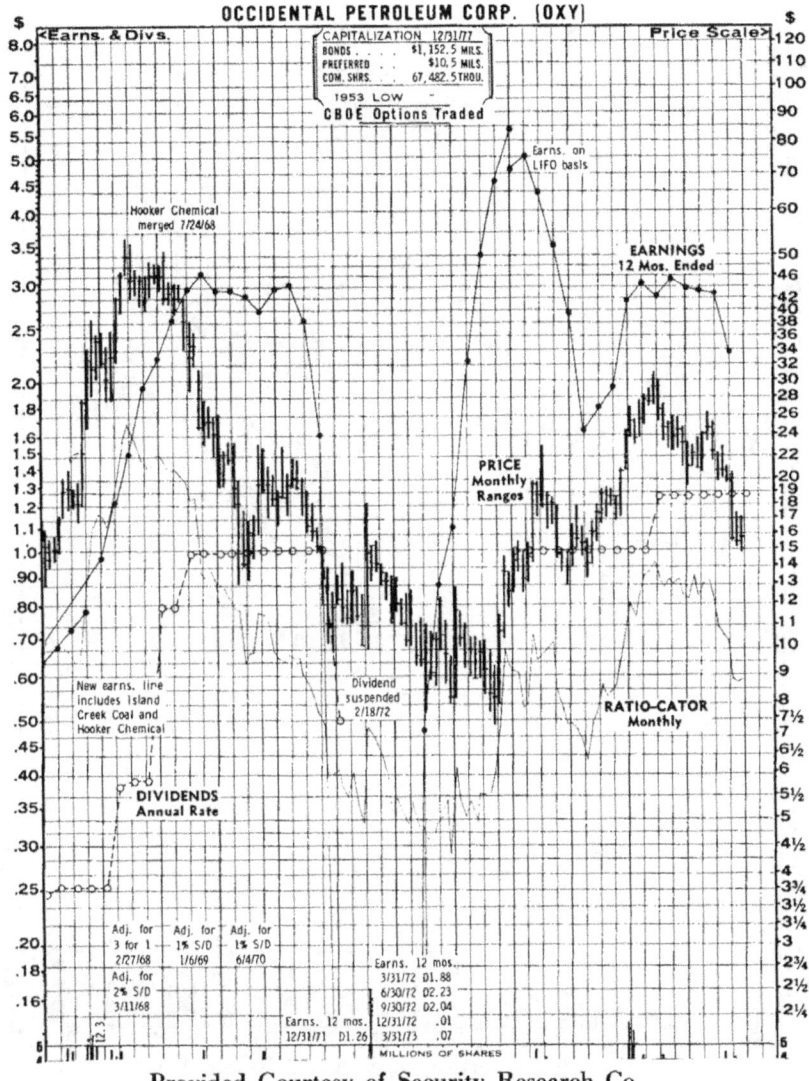

Chart courtesy of Security Research Co.

right back up to $20, down, and then steadily climbs all the way up to $60. These are irregular pattern charts and this is because the midpoints of the cusp areas of the charts are very sensitive to certain triggering events that create more of an erratic movement. Again, these can be spotted by going over the past 12 years of a stock to gain an idea of its cycle movement. The cycle movements are triggered by the 20-day lunar cycle and its effect on the transiting planets, and every 28 days will indicate a notch that will lead the cycle in its direction.

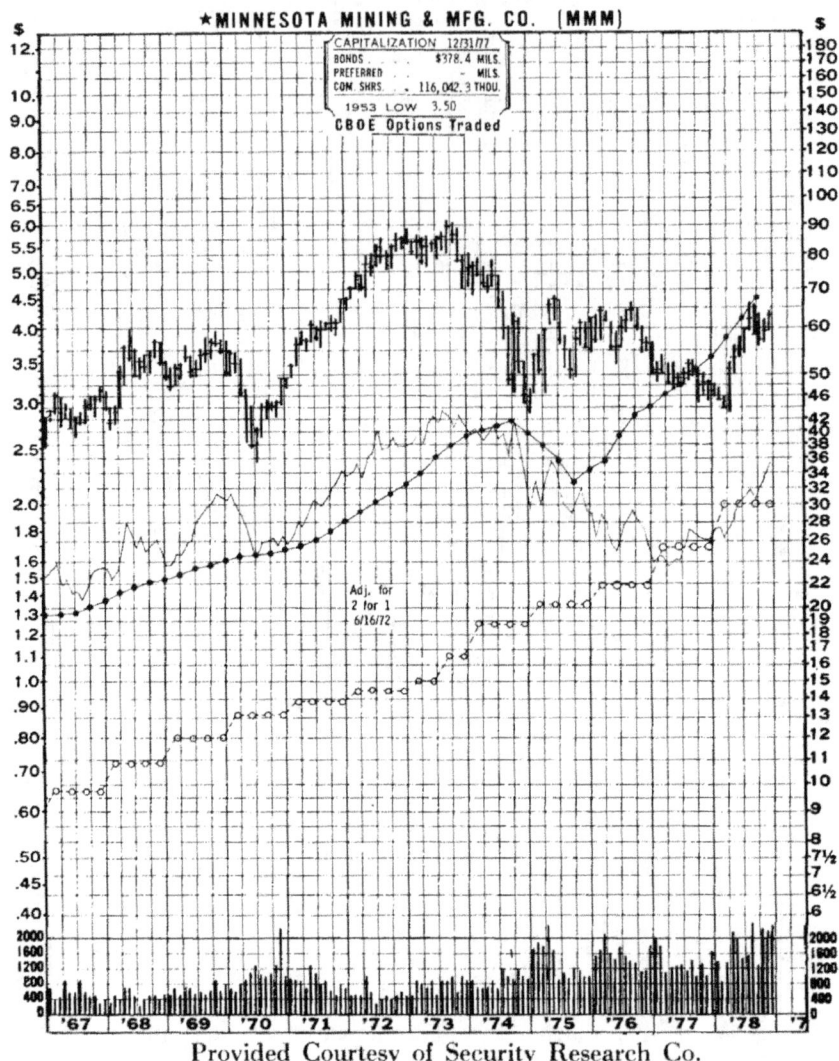

Chart courtesy of Security Research Co.

The zodiac is a 360-degree circle. Early astrologers noticed that when certain planets transit in certain parts of the heavens, different events occurred. This means that the time of birth is the starting place from which the chapters of life begin and proceed. It's just like an individual chart. By age 30, you would first experience the full cycle of Saturn, and at age 31 the cycle would begin again. So things at age 31 would be similar to the first cycle, but affect you as an adult.

A corporation begins a new cycle at age 31. But there are other planetary factors to look at such as the 12-year cycle of Jupiter; this planet returns to the same spot every 12 years. The same events that began when the corporation was born, as far as its expansion, will return when the cycle is repeated. The Saturn cycle generally brings restriction. The Moon returns to its same position at birth every four years. So you'll see these four or four-and-a-half year cycle changes that will affect individual stocks as well as the stock market. The return cycle of Mercury is 10 years. Again, Mercury is the intellectual side of a chart and thus deals with paperwork and contracts. Venus has a return cycle of eight years; it dictates a company's appearance. The Sun has a return cycle of 19 years, which is the corporate structure of the corporation. Mars has a return cycle of 15 years and affects the movement of the corporation.

The most important cycles to look at are the three-year cycles from birth—ages 3, 6, 9, 12, etc. Every three years Saturn will come into a negative position that will cause the corporation to go up or down. Generally the most critical periods are ages 30 and 15, as all the planets seem to meet in these 15-year cycles. Therefore, it's well to check back every 15 years to see the motion.

The zodiac is 360 degrees, which, divided by 12 equals 12 sectors of 30 degrees each, which we know today as the 12 houses. Each house represents the condition, the cycle and a basic part of a corporation.

In looking at many corporations, I find that the aspects for failure and success are always prominent within the chart. This is what led me into the area of studying stock market charts relating to corporations to see if all corporations follow the same pattern. Had the cycle of restrictive Saturn when it was transiting a certain house held the corporation back? Or did Jupiter expand it? As there are many factors in a corporate chart and each one is individual, many corporations will be affected by the trend of the Dow-Jones average, but not all. The type of product involved relates also to a cycle. Is the planet restricting that type of product or is it encouraging expansion? All these things must be taken into consideration when plotting your movements for a stock.

To tell what the stock is going to do and by what percentage, return to the same cycle and take it from the low point that the cycle is moving in, or the specific planetary influence you are working with, and take it to its high point. Break that down by percentage by determining the percentage from the low to the high under that cycle. Update that and do the same thing by adding that percentage onto what you're working with. Say, for example, that in a Jupiter cycle 12 years ago, there was a prominent change in a stock that was $2 per share and went up to $4, or a 100 percent movement. Twelve years later the stock is at $7 per share, so your prediction or projection for the stock would be $14 a share under this new cycle.

Its period of growth and expansion can be determined from its movement, along with the Dow-Jones average, as to how many weeks, months, or years it took for this growth, when the pattern occurred, the time frame when it was it at its fastest growth and during what months.

When you analyze the full chart, it will give you an idea of what the stock is capable of doing, how long you will have to wait in order to make your projected price of the stock, and what to look for as far as negative factors relating to the stock. Is it a time to sell short or buy long?

Each house has a meaning, and the planet going through it indicates changes. For example, Saturn restricts. If the planet is Jupiter, it brings expansion. All stocks on the NYSE are generally born somewhere between 9:00 a.m. and 3:00 p.m, You will be unable to get the exact time for many stocks, but you can rectify a chart very easily by using the table in this section. The ascending sign changes every two hours, so you only have about three possible ascending signs during that period. Take the first one within the first two periods and bring it backwards. Continue doing this until you get the cycle pattern. You can see when certain things were restricted by volume, prices, etc. This will give you a fairly good idea of what a stock's birth time is.

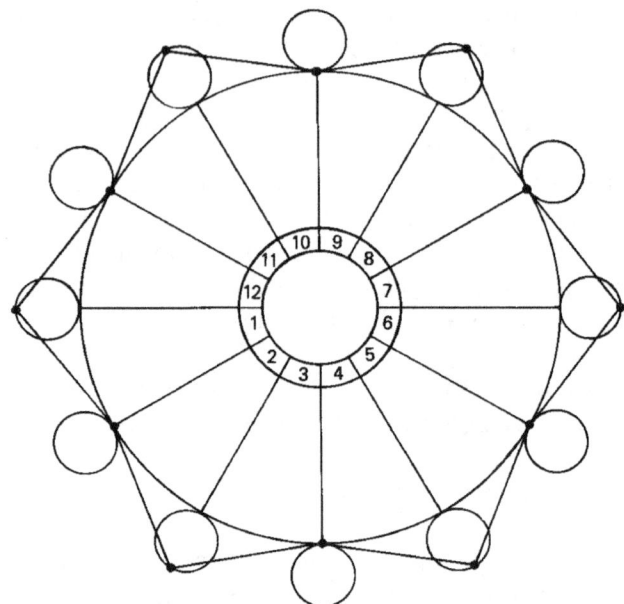

Speed: One-half Circumference

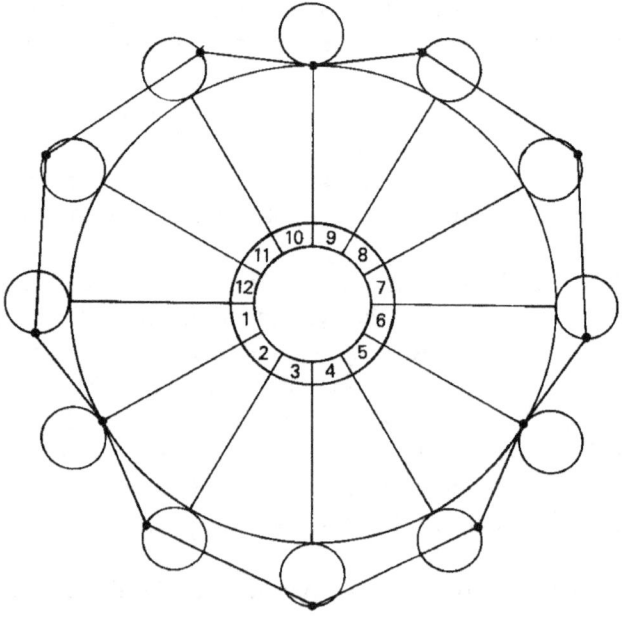

Speed: One-quarter Circumference

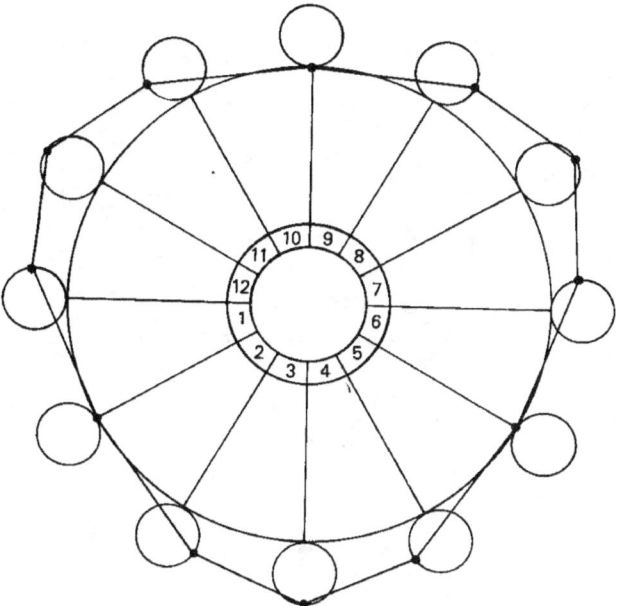

Speed: Three-quarter Circumference

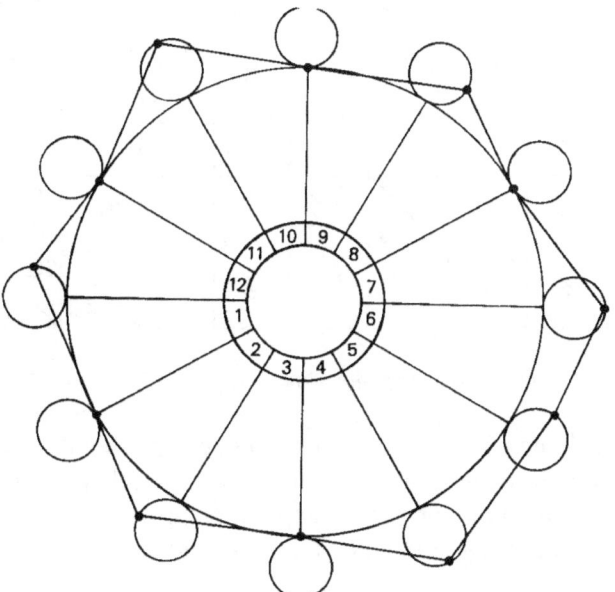

Speed: Alternating Three-quarter, One-quarter, One-half Circumference

As an example, let's take December 28 at 9:00 a.m. If you go to the reference you can see that for December 28 we would have to go to the date that says "12/23 to 1/20." For 9:00 a.m., go to "9:00 a.m. to 10:00 a.m.," where in the box you'll see "No. 11." So if it was from 8:00 a.m. to 9:00 a.m. you would use chart 11. If it was from 9:00 a.m. to 10:00 a.m., you would use chart 12, and so on. (See pages 119-120 for charts 1 through 12.) So these would be the Ascendant points to work with. Then, if Cancer is in the seventh house, for example, you would put the transiting planets in Cancer in the seventh house. One thing to remember, however, is that if a transiting planet can also affect the following house if it's in a late degree.

It is always best to start with noon because most corporations have a birth time between 11:00 a.m. and 1:00 p.m. What you're really looking for is a cycle, the cycle under which that stock is being activated, what's making that stock move, and at what time.

After determining the ascending sign, take that planet and its meaning backwards to see if it applies to the stock. If not, then go to the next ascending sign un-

Birthdate → / Birthtime ↓	3/21 TO 4/20	4/21 TO 5/20	5/21 TO 6/21	6/22 TO 7/23	7/23 TO 8/23	8/24 TO 9/23	9/24 TO 10/23	10/24 TO 11/22	11/23 TO 12/22	12/23 TO 1/20	1/21 TO 2/19	2/19 TO 3/20
6-8 am	1/2	3	4	5	5/6	6/7	7/8	8	9	10	10/11	12
8-10 am	3	4	5	5/6	6/7	7/8	8	9	10	11/12	12/1	1/2
10-12 am	4	5	5/6	6/7	7	8	9	10	11/12	12/1	1/2	3
12-2 pm	5	5/6	6/7	7	8	9	9/10	11	12/1	2/3	3	4
2-4 pm	5/6	6/7	7	8	9	9/10	11	12/1	2/3	3/4	4	5
4-6 pm	6/7	8	8	9	9/10	11	12/1	2/3	3/4	4	5	5/6
6-8 pm	7	8	9	9/10	11	12/1	2	3/4	4	5	5/6	6/7
8-10 pm	8	9	9/10	11	12/1	2	3/4	4	5	6	6/7	7/8
10-12 pm	8/9	9/10	10/11	12/1	2	3/4	4	5	6	6/7	7	8
12-2 am	9/10	10/11	12/1	2	3	4	5	5/6	6/7	7/8	8	9
2-4 am	10/11	12/1	1/2	3	4	5	5/6	6/7	7/8	8	9	9/10
4-6 am	12/1	1/2	3	4	5	5/6	6/7	7/8	8	9	9/10	10/11

Chart courtesy of Astrology Researcher

til you reach the one that has the pattern. Once you have the pattern, you can predict the growth of the corporation, what it will do and how it relates to the New York Stock Exchange. If it reverses on a negative trend, and goes up, then you know how to apply it on upward trends, what type of product is involved and then the long-range projections in those signs.

Let's go into the meaning of each house, what it represents and what it means as far as a corporation is concerned. For example, if Saturn is transiting the first house, you know the earnings will

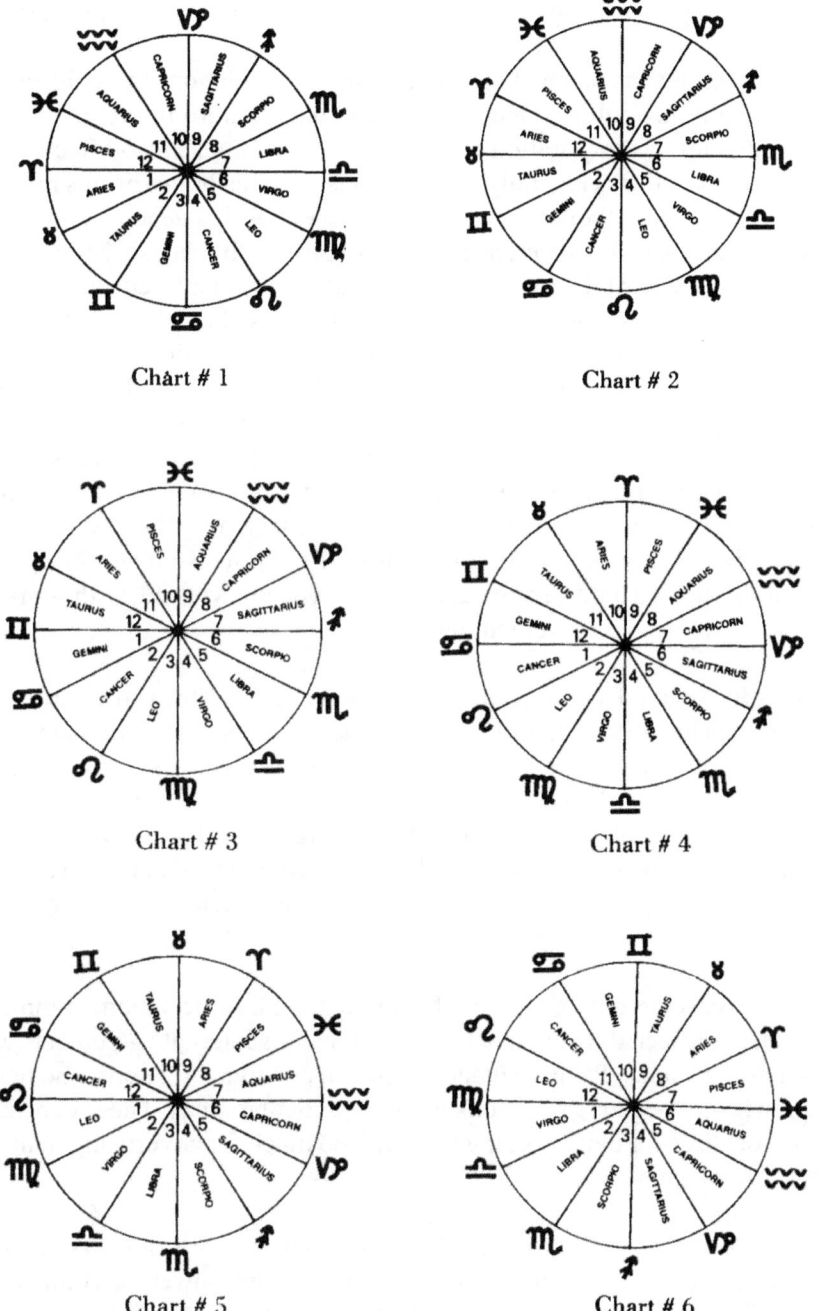

Chart # 1

Chart # 2

Chart # 3

Chart # 4

Chart # 5

Chart # 6

be restricted; if Jupiter is in the first house, earnings will be good. Also remember that when Mercury is retrograde, companies having this aspect are more affected than companies that do not.

The first house represents the place of incorporation and its relationship to the public. The location is the area usually favorable or incompatible. Usually Saturn in the first house shows that the location can hinder the corporation's success. The first house also affects how the. stockholders view the corporation. Generally, Jupiter transiting this house brings more stockholders and they are more optimistic about the company. With Venus, it's generally a young crowd. The Moon brings changes, much turnover, as it goes through the first house. Mercury, if retrograde, affects the public's opinion of the stock. So the stockholders are influenced by the transits in the first house, which also affects the price of the stock. The stockholders' buying and selling has a direct relationship to moving the stock up or down. It also affects the company's earnings, what it is capable of earning. Usually, with Jupiter, it expands, things go well; but with Saturn they're usually restricted. You must remember in using the transits with relation to these companies to use Saturn as the hour hand and Jupiter as the minute hand. Uranus in this case would represent the alarm hand, the explosive factor. If Jupiter hits Uranus, the explosion is usually positive; if Saturn hits Uranus, it is generally negative. Prices are affected by the first house, so watch the influence of a planet as it goes into the first house. If the price starts to drop the first day the planet enters this house, it would be advisable to sell if you are working with short-term gains on the stock, or buy if it shows a movement upwards.

Earnings and profit potential are affected by the second house. This shows the company's ability to earn and brings in the aspects influencing money matters. It is also important to check the company's quarterly earnings. If a negative planet transits this house and the earnings start to drop, it is best to sell short, or if you have the stock at that time, it is best to sell it. In most graphs this will show the earnings of a corporation. The earnings should be above the price of the individual stock, indicating higher potential for the price of the stock. Quarterly earnings also relate to the effect of the Sun, Moon, or other planets that are affected in the second house of the corporation.

The third house affects the relationship with competitors, transportation, communication, and advertising. It also is affected from the ratio-cator. It covers internal agreements within the corporation as to new decisions. Positive planets bring on positive directions, and negative planets bring on impulsive and negative decisions in these particular areas. These decisions can hurt a corporation. If you discover they're going to spend too much for advertising in the wrong areas, then it is a time to sell short.

The fourth house rules the tangible assets of the corporation and its direct competition, how far ahead of its competitors the corporation is in research and what power the competitors have over the corporation. With negative planets, competitors would be ahead of the corporation, but with positive planets the bind would be broken. It also causes hazards involving property. This could be due to bad weather, storms, fire, anything that could damage the property or affect business.

The fifth house rules subsidiaries, branches and franchises, the corporation's advertising success or failure and income from invested capital. It also deals with earnings, prices and the motivation of the corporation itself. It is more of a speculative position in which the company spends its money, either for other stocks or for expansion.

The sixth house affects the employees as to strikes, etc. This house represents the characteristics and health of the employees who work for the corporation, as well as work and equipment, how far advanced the corporation is with its fixtures, equipment or things the corporation needs to expand its profits. It relates to health plans or insurance the corporation would buy to protect itself.

The seventh house affects the trading volume, how much stock is being purchased. The stock market in general will affect the corporation at the time of a transit going through the third house. When a stock jumps in volume in trading it is generally the seventh house being affected. If it is buying volume, this is the signal to buy the stock; if it is selling volume, then this is the time to sell. This house covers sales appeal, putting across the product, and adjustments. Whether the adjustments will be positive or negative can be determined by the transiting planets.

The eighth house deals with the corporation's credit, how much money it owes. It affects dividends, whether they will be paid and in what amount. If dividends are omitted, this is a signal to sell. Upon news of this, look for negative influences and negative planets related to the eighth house. Usually Jupiter transiting through this house will bring healthy dividends; with Saturn transiting the dividends are delayed, denied or cancelled. This is also the house of trade secrets. It deals with the board of directors, the net earnings of the corporation and information that is kept from the. public. A lot of times under certain aspects with Mercury, secret information will leak and this affects the volume and sales of the corporation.

The ninth house deals with contracts with other corporations, mergers, litigation, audits, its correspondence, its dealings with people and other corporations at a distance. Many companies generally merge under this influence, ss you will see from some examples given in the following pages.

The tenth house rules the corporate head, the administrative department, the corporation's relationship with the government and higher heads of other corporations, and the corporations general business conditions as far as its public image.

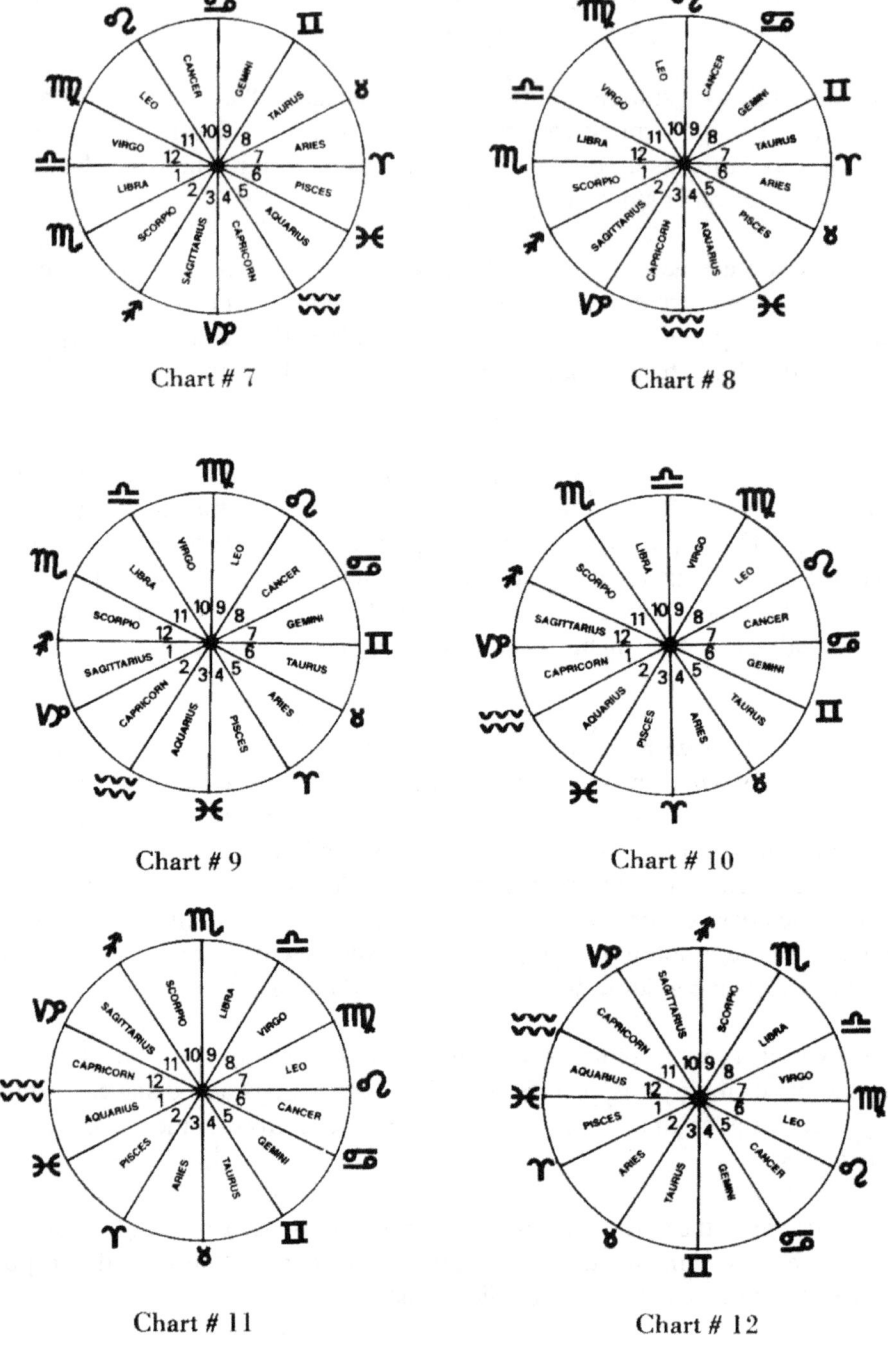

Chart # 7

Chart # 8

Chart # 9

Chart # 10

Chart # 11

Chart # 12

The eleventh house is the house of the corporation's public relations, its resources related to the head of the corporation, its political connections, its intangible assets, its indebtedness and mortgages and other money that is owed.

The twelfth house deals with experimentation, research and trade secrets. This can also affect litigation, things that are hidden from the public and the corporation's actions relating to these things.

Bear in mind that before you even look at the transits, it is good to look at the corporation from the point of its related birthday to determine the condition of the corporation and whether it will make it as a corporation. This is more important in over-the-counter stocks. Almost all stocks on the New York Stock Exchange have proved themselves as to their assets, their potential, and their growth possibilities. So on the New York Stock Exchange we are mainly concerned with the transits of the planets in relation to the corporation's progress.

To better understand this, let's take the chart of the New York Stock Exchange, born May 17, 1792, 8:52 a.m. (shown on the next page). The NYSE has Cancer on the Ascendant (first house). This is the starting point for this chart and the first house would be between Cancer and Leo.

First, we know that when Saturn is in Capricorn we always have a bad market; this is the sign of depression. Let's take a look at Saturn's position relative to the earlier discussion about panics and crashes, and different combinations.

The seventh house rules the volume of sales, the trade and volume on the market. What happened during the depression? The volume dropped. Let's return to times when Saturn was in Capricorn. In 1873, Saturn was transiting the seventh house and the stock market dropped in volume. Remember that the seventh house is also the house of adjustments, sales appeal, and it wasn't very good. In 1901, it again related to the same thing—volume. In 1929, it was again the volume. Volume again pretty well fit into the period of 1960, when the stock market was again affected regarding volume. So volume—volume buying and the shares traded—were the big issues related to all these cycles because of the seventh house. Saturn through the seventh house has never been good for the stock market. It has always caused it to drop.

But Jupiter is a planet of expansion. In 1972, Jupiter was in Capricorn and volume shot to new highs; it all happened during 1971-72 when Jupiter occupied Capricorn. Therefore, Jupiter affected the market during most of 1972, causing a rise due to the volume of sales. In 1960, Jupiter was cancelled out because Saturn was also in Capricorn, causing the volume to be somewhat steady but the market to be affected by the overall negativity of this aspect. So there was a loss of Jupiter's power under this transit because of Saturn also moving into the seventh house.

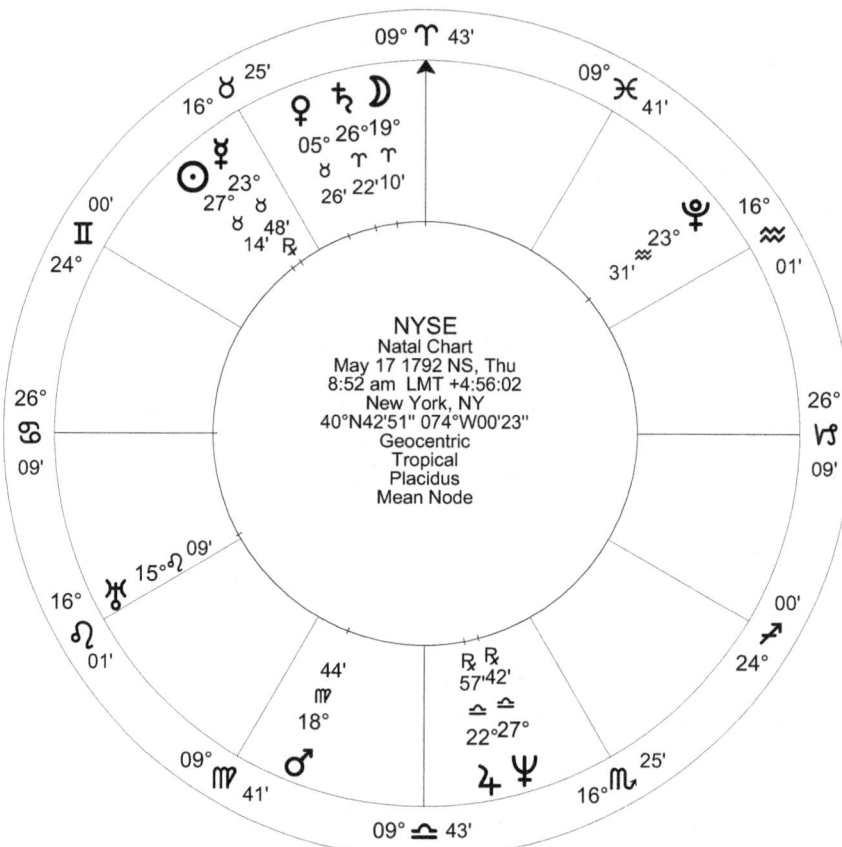

In 1949, Jupiter was retrograde but went direct on September 20, which caused an upswing in volume and a rise in the market. The 12-year cycles of Jupiter have always been prominent through the seventh house. From 1936 through most of 1937, Jupiter was in Capricorn. Again, volume increased and sales went up. As Jupiter left Capricorn at the end of 1937, the market was affected by Jupiter's retrograde motion, and then its direct motion into Aquarius caused a downswing in the market. During the period of 1925, again Jupiter in Capricorn, again growth in volume and the market went to the top.

You can go back to these two houses using just these two planets to see these patterns, not only with individual stocks but the entire New York Stock Exchange. Each aspect and each planet is affected by its growth, volume, sales and prices.

In the chapter on panics and crashes, notice that there are problems when Saturn is in Libra, the fourth house of the New York Stock Exchange. This affected control, tangible assets, competition and, more or less, government control. As you go through these things, you will learn more about the transits, and then can apply Mercury, Mars, Venus as triggers of a short duration. In the balance of this chapter I will take a few corporations and show the transits and how they relate to changes.

In selecting a stock you should look at the stock market as the ocean. This means that you should ride with the tide and go out with the tide. If the tide is coming in, you fish with those fish that are coming in with the tide. When the tide is going out, you fish for the fish that are going out with the tide. Never go against the tide because you'll generally end up being hurt.

Always buy a stock at its lowest possible point. This is the importance of knowing a cycle because in fishing for a stock you have to go through many to find the right one, the one that is going to be big enough for you. What you look for in a stock is generally a stock that will double within a year, and every year on the NYSE there are always those stocks that will double. Why doesn't anybody pick them? Why can't the stockbrokers see them? Why can't other people in the financial world spot these? Because they come up overnight, they come up by some event that happens, a need for a certain product gained from unforeseen areas. This is why by going back in the chart to certain points, certain cycles, you can spot them. As I mentioned earlier, the 12-year cycle of Jupiter is very important. The 2½-year cycle of Saturn in each sign, the 30-year cycle of Saturn through the zodiac, the 3½-year cycle related to Jupiter and Uranus—there are so many factors involved and there are so many different types of cycles.

So in determining a stock for the present year try at first to select those stocks under the sign currently occupied by Jupiter. As an example, in 1978, Jupiter was in Leo, so you would want stocks to be in Leo or one of the other two fire signs, Aries and Sagittarius. The reason for this is that Jupiter was trine the natal Sun of these corporations and as long as you don't have any afflictions in the natal chart from these transiting planets, they will expand. You can even make money on a lot of stocks being influenced by Saturn. Saturn will send some stocks to the bottom, while with other stocks you'll find restrictions and shortages that can cause prices to rise. So these are the main factors that you want to look for: find out why, how and when. In 1974, we sent a mailing to 100 people to find out how many would go all the way on speculating on the stock market regarding a doubling factor, suggesting that they take $2,000 and buy each stock at the price that we gave them. As soon as that stock doubled, it was recommended they sell it and buy another one. At that time we were looking in terms of 10 years, a double a year, because from this doubling factor, after 10 turnovers you would make more than $1 million.

Our first stock recommended for January 1975 was British Petroleum at 4½, because this was the bottom point. In February 1975, it went up to $9. Our next stock was American Bakeries. In March 1975 it was $3¼, and by June 1975 it had gone up to $8; it more than doubled. Our next selection was Anthony Industries. It took a while for this stock to drop to $3¼, but it did in September 1975. After that it jumped up to $8 in January 1976. Our next selection was Singer, at $9, in January 1976; it jumped in February 1976 to 20. Our next selection was AVCO. In March 1976, it was $4; in April it jumped to $8½.

We had other stocks during this period, one of which was ChrisCraft, which was $4 and jumped to around $10 in November 1977. We had Resorts International, a stock that we gave many people, not only on this mailing list but thousands of others. Not everybody took advantage of it, but we gave that at $2½, and in 1978 it jumped to $210. By cycle we were also able to call the split and its downfall as far as dropping back. We also had Ramada Inn; in March 1978 it was $4½, and in June 1978 it rose to $10. Todd Shipyards, in June 1978, was at $16, and doubled to $32 in July 1978. Allied Artists, one of the last on the list, and one we recommended at $2, jumped to $8 overnight. On this special list no one went all the way. A lot of them doubled and doubled, but then they panicked when they began getting into too much money. And this is what happens in the market itself. People get scared. The market is always there, it's always playable and we always recommend that if a stock starts to drop, don't panic and sell and take a loss but buy more at the bottom because the cycle will return to the top. And usually when people run scared, this is the element of loss. If you make a bad decision, then it may take three or four years to recoup, but it's still better than losing.

It is not wise to speculate in the stock market with "scared" money. It is best to put it into savings, retirement or, if you're playing for fast return, play for a 25 percent or 50 percent markup and buy and sell real fast. There are many ways to play the market. One is a speculative venture where you buy and sell each month, one on a long term where you double and use the doubling system. This is where the element of astrology is very important and where it becomes more of a game because you are making decisions. When I gave many people advice about Resorts International, they were talked out of it by their brokers; but there are a lot of people who became wealthy by it. A lot of times you'll make mistakes, but you will learn from these mistakes.

Now, as the first example, let's take Walker-Gooderham and Worts Ltd. As we look at the low points of the chart, we can figure that a safe bet would be $24 per share at its low period. We know the stock has a potential of $32 per share, and it's been as high as almost $60. Now let's look at the 12-year cycle of Jupiter and pretend that we are looking at this in 1966, the low point that we would as yet be unaware of. So we know that in December 1966 the stock hit a low of $24 a share. The company was born December 31, 1926, around 1:38 p.m, and by rectifying the chart from the tables we can see that the Ascendant sign is Taurus.

The second house, which rules the price of the stock and earnings, is in Cancer. We know that Mars is an aggravating planet, that it triggers things, but that it's not a long-term influence. So we know we're not going to have this price long, that the pattern is going to move up. Don't forget it takes almost 12 years for Jupiter to return with Mars. In that period again Mars moves into Cancer with Jupiter, and around the same month at the same time, it goes just below $24 a share.

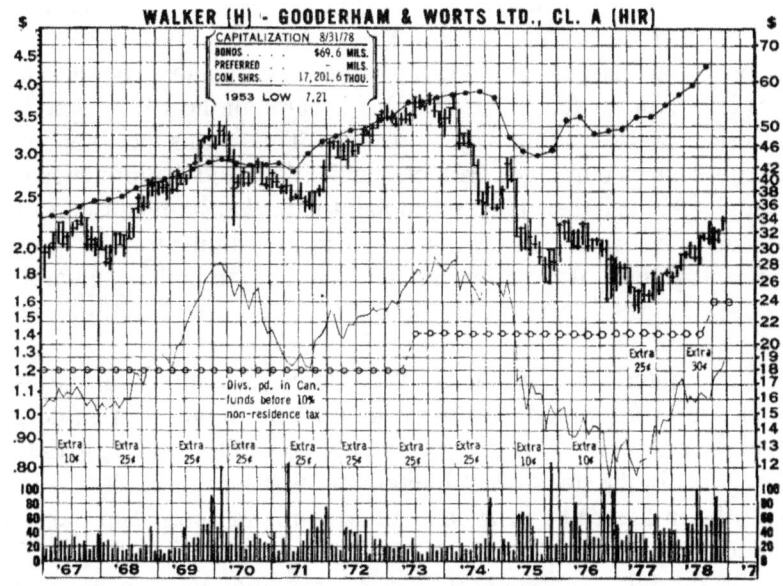

Chart courtesy of Security Research Co.

But now I want you to look backward to September 1966 to see the pattern of this company. What did it do after it hit $24? It started moving upward. Now look at the pattern in September 1977. It is almost a carbon copy of what happened when the same two planets were there before. Conjunctions represent a new start, a change, and with this conjunction in the second house, it concerns price and finances and shows there is a change. So in 1966 you know it would be wise to go short just prior to September 1977, and go short all the way down to $24 per share, from almost $60 per share, which would have been 2½ years.

Also, if you notice that with the recession of 1974, when the general market was very depressed, this stock was not affected as it only dropped about 28 percent. This means the same effect will happen in another bad cycle under the same influence.

You have to relate what the market is doing to the individual stock. If you notice the earnings ability of the stock is still moving upward to the upper black line, the stock should follow the same trend. These are easy points to pick out.

You also can go into the chart on each high point. As an example, let's look at 1973, when it was at its highest level in the 1974 period. We know that Jupiter was in Aquarius and this was affecting the ninth and tenth houses. You can see that the public image of the stock was at an all-time high, and when Aquarius was trine the Libra factor going into the months of October and November when the Sun was in Scorpio in the seventh house, that was the highest volume peak of the year. This stock's volume has always been good near the end of the year, and only in the years under afflictions to the seventh house was the volume not that active.

Saturn is the planet of restriction in everything, and it was in the first house but also trine Jupiter in Aquarius. All the combinations there were positive. Mars was in Aquarius, and Uranus was in Libra. So the slow-transiting planets in harmony would send this corporation to its point of new highs. Now as Uranus moves into Scorpio and Saturn into Virgo through the 1978-79 period, this will affect the company's sixth house dealing with employees. This means the company is susceptible to unexpected events such as employee problems and strikes and the influence will be prominent all the way through 1979 and then again when Saturn hits that sixth house in 1983 and 1984. So looking at the map of a corporation the main concern is with the transits of each planet. When we look at the natal planets of the corporation it will help to understand certain events.

Why was the stock so good when Jupiter was in Aquarius? Well, Jupiter was also in Aquarius at the time of birth. Any time you see a corporation's birthday, look where Jupiter is in the corporate chart and then check the placement of transiting Jupiter. If Jupiter is well-aspected in the natal chart, then this will be very good for the stock when Jupiter returns to that point. Why is it effective with employees under the influence of Scorpio? The Moon is in Scorpio in the sixth house dealing with its employees, and it has the Sun and Venus in Capricorn. This is why Jupiter and Mars in Cancer were so bad for this corporation; they were opposition the Sun and Venus and transiting from the second house in opposition to the eighth. Mercury and Saturn are in Sagittarius, which is the seventh house. Uranus is in Pisces in the eleventh house. And Neptune in Leo is in the third house. But Neptune deals with alcoholic beverages and the placement of the third house is very good for this corporation. So, analyzing the chart, look at the natal aspects as well as the transiting planets.

The next company is Standard Brands, Inc. This is a major company dealing with packaging of consumer food and food-related products. It's a natural company for it because Virgo, which rules food products, is on the Ascendant. With Virgo on the Ascendant any combination or cluster of four planets aggravating the Ascendant, the second house or the eighth house (because the eighth house is in opposition to the second) will drive this stock down very fast and will cause it to be erratic even though the aspects in this corporation are very steady. This corporation has the Sun in Cancer, Venus in Taurus, Mercury and Jupiter in Gemini, the Moon in Pisces, Saturn in Sagittarius, Mars in Leo, Uranus in Aries and Neptune in Leo. The North Node is in Taurus. So any time you have an aggravation from Taurus, Virgo on the Ascendant, or Scorpio in the second house, this triggers the stock. In the past 12 years there were six chances to buy this stock at a low of $20 a share, and fifteen chances to sell it at $28 a share, or a 40percent profit. This is a speculative stock, something that's fast-moving, and you can buy it and expect to sell a few months later at $28. Let's go back and look at the influence. We'll only take it from 1968, even though it was earlier under the same influence. So actually in the last 10 years there were six chances to buy it at $20 and 15 chances to sell it at $28. In the period of May 1968 the Sun, Venus Mercury and Mars were in Taurus, which triggered the stock drop to $20. In August 1969,

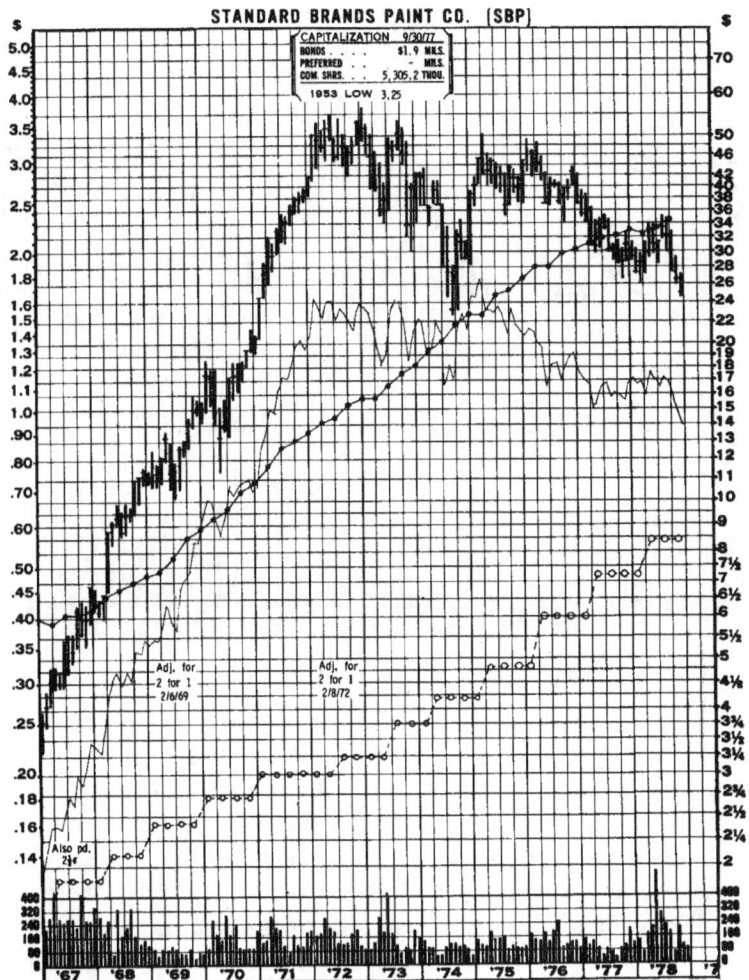

Chart courtesy of Security Research Co.

there was a cluster in Virgo: Sun, Mercury, Venus and Jupiter. Again the stock dropped to $20. In September 1970, the same effect occurred with the cluster in Virgo: Sun, Mercury, Mars and the Moon. In November 1971, it again this was affected by the second house with a Scorpio cluster: Sun, Mercury, Venus and the Moon. And then again in 1974, the Sun, Mercury, Venus and Mars were in Scorpio, and the stock returned to $20 per share. Now every time it hit this low point, being that these were fast-moving planets, it did not stay there; it shot right back up. Its highest level was in January 1976, when Jupiter was in Aries conjunction its natal Uranus. On October 14, 1975, with Jupiter in Aries trine Saturn in Leo and Jupiter in Aries in the eighth house (the house of dividends), it was no surprise that the company announced a stock split of 2 for 1. This Jupiter transit affected it and took it all the way up.

Now the reason that Jupiter in Gemini cannot be a strong factor in this chart is because at birth Jupiter in Sagittarius was under heavy affliction. Jupiter in Sagittarius is in bad aspect with Jupiter in Gemini, but Uranus in Aries was the main factor as it was trine Saturn in Sagittarius, with the fire element being prominent for this corporation. The 12-year cycle will not be as prominent as the three-year cycle because it is aspected every three years because of the Jupiter turning point. As an example, look at 1966 through 1968, then 1969 through 1971 (slight drop), then 1972 through 1974 (drop), and then 1975 through 1977 (drop). So this has a three-year pattern which has been affected by the three-year movement of Jupiter. Any time Jupiter becomes an affliction, the stock drops somewhat. But the main thing with this stock is knowing the bottom point and watching for the clusters, the conjunctions in Taurus, Virgo and Scorpio, which would be the signal to buy.

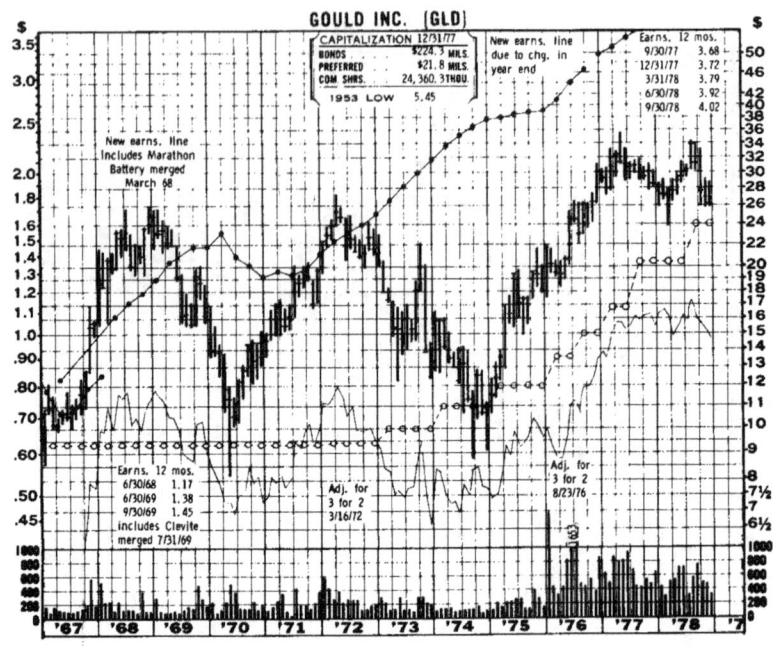

Chart courtesy of Security Research Co.

Our next company is Gould, Inc. (see graph), born October 15, 1928, in Delaware, with Capricorn rising. The cardinal signs of the zodiac are Aries, Capricorn, Libra and Cancer, so the Capricorn effect hits the Ascendant, Nadir, Descendant and Midheaven. These are all sensitive points. The Sun is in bad aspect to the Ascendant, so every time Jupiter goes into Aries, Cancer, Libra or Capricorn, its effect would be for the stock to go down. In the last 12 years, there were four in which you could have picked up Gould, Inc. at $10 or under per share and sold it almost overnight for $20 even though the stock has hit a high of almost $30 per share. In 1967, Jupiter was in Cancer and all year the stock was somewhat repressed and stayed around the $10 mark. In 1970, Jupiter went into Libra and Gould dropped to its low of $10 per share but went right back up again. In 1974, Jupiter went into Aries, and again it dropped back down but moved back up.

The only one it seemed to bypass at times was Capricorn, but in the early part of that transit it did drop to almost $13 per share. In 1973, when Saturn moved into Cancer, also a cardinal sign, the lowest point of the cycle affected Gould and Great American Investors. They both started their downward trend. So Saturn in the cardinal signs seems to have an effect on Jupiter. Jupiter was more prominent with Gould, Inc. as far as its fast moves up and down, but the Saturn aspect, also in a cardinal sign, proved to be devastating to both these companies. Both are just a little bit apart as far as relating to time and both of them have a natural trend as far as following each other price-wise.

Another factor in determining the influence of where problems might relate to a stock's volume or prices is the aspect relating to the negative planet itself. For example, if Saturn were transiting the first house and were in opposition to Mars in the seventh house, the opposition would be 180 degrees away or in the opposite sign. This would mean that the earnings would go down or be affected because of volume. The signs that are in opposition are Aries and Libra. For example, if you have Saturn in Aries and Mars in Libra, this combination is an opposition. Therefore, any planets in Aries or Libra are in opposition to each other. Taurus and Scorpio are oppositions, Gemini and Sagittarius are opposition, Cancer and Capricorn are opposition, Leo and Aquarius are opposition and Virgo and Pisces are opposition. Oppositions are considered negative aspects.

Appendix I

New York Stock Exchange Stock Birthdates

Aquarius Stocks (January 20 - February 18)

Company	Date of Birth	Place of Birth
Alberto Culver	January 30, 1961	Delaware
Allegheny Corp.	January 26, 1929	Maryland
Allied Supermarkets, Inc.	January 26, 1926	Delaware
Amerada Hess Corp.	February 7, 1920	Delaware
American Home Products Corp.	February 4, 1926	Delaware
AMIC, Inc.	January 22, 1970	North Carolina
(Acquired American Mortgage Insurance Co.)		
Amstar Corp.	February 7, 1966	Delaware
ARA Services, Inc.	February 17, 1959	Delaware
Arizona Public Service Co.	February 16, 1920	Arizona
Armada Corp.	February 5, 1926	Michigan
ARO Corp.	January 23, 1930	Ohio
(Merged parent s/s November 30, 1965, Delaware)		
Applied Digital Data, Inc.	January 22, 1969	Delaware
Avon Products, Inc.	January 27, 1916	New York
Barnes Group, Inc.	January 30, 1925	Delaware
Bay Colony Property Co. Dec of Trust	January 21, 1971	Massachusetts
Bundy Corp.	January 30, 1929	Michigan
Burlington Industries	February 15, 1937	Delaware
Canadian Pacific Railway Co.	February 16, 1881	Canada

Company	Date of Birth	Place of Birth
Carolina Clinchfield & Ohio Ry.	January 26, 1905	Virginia
Certain-Teed Products Corp.	January 30, 1917	Maryland
Chase Manhattan Corp.	January 22, 1969	Delaware
Chelsea Industries, Inc.	February 18, 1964	Delaware
(Merged parent s/s January 6, 1976)		
Chris-Craft Industries, Inc.	January 23, 1928	Delaware
C.I.T. Financial Corp.	January 28, 1924	Delaware
C.L.C. of America, Inc.	January 25, 1962	Delaware
Cluett Peabody & Co., Inc.	February 4, 1913	New York
Coca Cola Bottling Co. consolidated	January 27, 1969	North Carolina
Colonial Stores, Inc.	January 24, 1901	Virginia
Columbia Broadcasting System, Inc.	January 27, 1927	New York
Communications Satellite Corp.	February 1, 1963	Washington DC
Connecticut General Mortgage & Realty Investments Trust	February 18, 1970	Massachusetts
Continental Illinois Realty	February 7, 1969	California
Cox Broadcasting Corp.	February 6, 1964	Georgia
Crane Co.	February 15, 1865	Illinois
CTS Corp.	February 8, 1929	Indiana
Cummins Engine Co., Inc.	February 3, 1919	Indiana
Dart Industries, Inc.	Fbruary 11, 1928	Delaware
Dentsply, Intl.	February 15, 1983	Delaware
Dial Finance Co.	January 30, 1924	Iowa
(Merged parent s/s June 10, 1977, Iowa)		
Dictaphone Corp.	January 20, 1923	New York
Elgin National Industries, Inc.	February 15, 1865	Illinois
(Elgin National of Delaware wholly owned subsidiary March 22, 1962, Delaware; merged August 30, 1968, Delaware)		
Enviro Tech. Corp.	February 6, 1969	Delaware
Ethyl Corp.	February 15, 1887	Virginia
Facet Enterprises, Inc.	January 29, 1962	Delaware
First Chicago Corp.	January 23, 1969	Delaware
Flexi-Van Corp.	February 16, 1955	New York

Company	Date of Birth	Place of Birth
Fluor	January 23, 1978	Delaware
Foster Wheeler Corp.	February 6, 1900	New York
Gateway Ind. Inc.	February 5, 1951	Illinois
(Merged parent s/s March 20, 1970, Delaware)		
Gearheart-Owens Industries, Inc.	January 25, 1955	Texas
General Foods Corp.	February 11, 1922	Delaware
G.F. Business Equipment, Inc.	January 28, 1902	Ohio
Gino's, Inc.	February 15, 1960	Maryland
Harris Bankcorp.	February 2, 1907	Illinois
Hatteras Income Securities, Inc.	February 2, 1973	North Carolina
Hazeltine Corp.	February 1, 1924	Delaware
Heller (Walter E.) Int'l Corp.	February 3, 1969	Delaware
Helmerich & Payne, Inc.	February 3, 1940	Delaware
Houdaille Industries, Inc.	January 30, 1929	Michigan
(Merged parent s/s April 1, 1968, Delaware)		
Intuit, Inc.	Fewbruary 1, 1993	Delaware
Iowa-Illinois Gas & Electric Co.	February 13, 1940	Illinois
IPCO Hospital Supply Co.	January 20, 1950	New York
(Merged parent s/s July 1, 1951, Delaware)		
Jantzen, Inc.	January 20, 1947	Nevada
Joy Manufacturing Co.	February 7, 1939	Pennsylvania
Kaiser Cement & Gypsum Corp.	February 10, 1939	California
Kaneb Services	January 23, 1953	Delaware
Kane-Miller	January 26, 1920	New York
(Merged parent s/s ASeptember 25, 1964, Delaware)		
Kansas City Southern Industries, Inc.	January 29, 1962	Delaware
Levitz Furniture Corp.	February 1, 1965	Pennsylvania
Mead Corp.	February 17, 1930	Ohio
Memorex Corp.	February 9, 1961	California
Merck, Inc.	January 31, 1991	Delaware
Microchip Tech.	February 14, 1989	Delaware
Milton Bradley Co.	January 21, 1884	Massachusetts
Minnesota Power & Light Co.	January 29, 1906	Minnesota

Company	Date of Birth	Place of Birth
Nabisco	February 3, 1898	New Jersey
National City Lines, Inc.	February 5, 1936	Delaware
National Tea Co.	February 6, 1902	Illinois
Nevada Power	February 9, 1929	Nevada
North American Coal Corp.	February 18, 1913	Ohio
Northwest Bancorp.	January 24, 1929	Delaware
N.W. Mutual Life Mtge. & Realty	February 18, 1971	Massachusetts
Opelika Mfg. Corp.	January 24, 1946	Illinois
Pacific Petroleum, Ltd.	January 21, 1939	British Columbia
(Reincorporated June 2, 1977, Canada, affiliate of Canada of Phillips Petroleum Co.)		
Peoples Gas Co.	February 12, 1855	Illinois
(Merged parent s/s August 3, 1967, Illinois)		
Petrolane Corp.	February 10, 1930	California
Pier I Imports	February 10, 1969	Delaware
Planning Research Corp.	February 9, 1954	California
(Merged parent s/s September 4, 1973, Delaware)		
Plessey Co. Ltd.	February 14, 1925	England
Raymond International, Inc.	January 20, 1897	Nebraska
(Reincorporated August 18, 1902, New Jersey)		
Reliance Electric & Eng. Co.	January 28, 1907	Ohio
(Merged parent *sis* January 15, 1969, Delaware)		
Republic of Texas Corp.	February 7, 1974	Delaware
Revco D.S. Inc.	February 8, 1956	Michigan
St. Regis Paper Co.	February 4, 1899	New York
Sav-A-Stop, Inc.	February 4, 1953	Florida
Sav-On Drugs, Inc.	February 1, 1946	California
SCOA Industries, Inc.	January 31, 1920	Ohio
(Merged parent s/s January 25, 1969, Delaware)		
Scot-Lad Foods, Inc.	January 25, 1961	Delaware
Scott Forgsman & Co.	February 13, 1896	Florida
(Merged parent s/s June 30, 1969, Delaware)		
Seagrave Corp.	January 26, 1925	Michigan
(Merged parent s/s April 12, 1965, Delaware)		

Company	Date of Birth	Place of Birth
Sealed Power Corp.	February 9, 1968	Delaware
Seligman & Latz, Inc.	January 20, 1953	Delaware
Shell Oil Co.	February 8-22	Delaware
Standard Oil of California	January 27, 1926	Delaware
Staples, Inc.	January 23, 1986	Delaware
Supermarkets General Corp.	February 2, 1966	Delaware
Talley Industries, Inc.	February 3, 1960	Delaware
Tellabs, Inc.	February 10, 1992	Delaware
Texas Eastern Corp.	January 30, 1947	Delaware
(Merged parent Tex Eastern Transmission February 2, January 26, 1976, Delaware)		
Texas Pacific Land Trust	February 1, 1888	Texas
Tidewater, Inc.	February 7, 1956	Delaware
Trans America Income Shares Inc.	February 14, 1972	Delaware
Tucson Gas & Electric	January 25, 1902	Colorado
Twentieth Century Fox Film Corp.	February 1, 1915	New York
(Reorganized & reincorporated April 22, 1952, Delaware)		
Tyler Corp.	January 28, 1966	Delaware
Union Pacific Corp.	February 3, 1969	Utah
(Formed to take over Union Pacific RR Inc., July 1, 1897, Utah)		
Unitrode Corp.	February 11, 1960	Maryland
Universal Leaf Tobacco Co. Inc.	January 25, 1918	Virginia
Vendo Co.	January 26, 1937	Missouri
Wallgreen Co.	February 15, 1909	Illinois
Williams, Cos.	February 13, 1949	Nevada

Pisces Stocks (February 19 - March 20)

Company	Date of Birth	Place of Birth
Abbot Laboratories, Inc.	March 6, 1900	Illinois
ACF Industries, Inc.	February 20, 1899	New Jersey
Albany International Corp.	March 11, 1895	New York
Allegheny Airlines, Inc.	March 5, 1937	Delaware
Allis-Chalmers Mfg. Co.	March 15, 1913	Delaware
Altera, Corp.	March 1, 1985	Virginia

Company	Date of Birth	Place of Birth
American Can Co.	March 19, 1901	New Jersey
American Power Conversion Corp.	March 11, 1981	Massachusetts
American Ship Building Co.	March 16, 1899	New Jersey
Amgen Convertible Securities Inc.	March 20, 1972	Maryland
AMPCO-Pittsburg Corp.	March 19, 1929	Pennsylvania
Arkansas-Louisiana Gas Co.	March 9, 1928	Delaware
A.T.&T.Co.	March 3, 1885	New York
Automatic Industries, Inc.	March 4, 1955	California
AVCO Corp.	March 1, 1929	Delaware
Avery International Corp.	February 22, 1977	Delaware
Baldwin (D.H.) Co.	February 19, 1898	Ohio
Bausch & Lomb Inc.	March 20, 1908	New York
Beatrice Foods Co.	March 1, 1905	Iowa
(Merged parent s/s November 20, 1924, Delaware)		
Bell & Howell Co.	February 20, 1907	Illinois
(Merged parent s/s April 14, 1977, Delaware)		
Blair (John) & Co.	March 6, 1935	Delaware
Braun (C.F.) & Co.	February 28, 1975	Delaware
Canal Randolph Corp.	March 2, 1955	Delaware
Carolina Freight & Carriers Corp.	February 25, 1937	North Carolina
Charter N.Y. Corp.	March 12, 1965	New York
Chessie System Inc.	February 26, 1973	Virginia
(Merger Chesapeake & Ohio RR)		
Citigroup	March 3, 1988	Delaware
Coca Cola Bottling Co. of NY	March 18, 1920	Delaware
Combined Communications Corp.	February 26, 1968	Arizona
Comcast Corp.	March 5, 1969	Pennsylvania
Conwood Corp.	March 12, 1900	New Jersey
(Merged parent American Snuff s/s October 19, 1966, Delaware)		
Crompton Knowles Corp.	March 3, 1900	Massachusetts
Cyprus Mines Corp.	March 10, 1916	New York
Dayco Corp.	February 28, 1966	Delaware
Ebay, Inc.	March 13, 1998	Delaware

Company	Date of Birth	Place of Birth
Edison Brothers Stores, Inc.	March 13, 1929	Delaware
Emhart Corp.	March 19, 1902	Connecticut
(Merged parent s/s February 25, 1976, Virginia)		
Empire Gas Corp.	March 4, 1963	Missouri
Engelhard Minerals & Chemicals Corp.	March 14, 1960	Delaware
Essex Chemical Corp.	March 16, 1955	New Jersey
Excelsior Income Shares, Inc.	March 16, 1973	New York
Express Scripts	March 20, 1992	Delaware
Fabri-Centers of America	February 28, 1951	Ohio
Fairmont Foods Co.	March 5, 1929	Delaware
Federal Paper Board Co.	March 3, 1916	New York
Fidelity Union Bancorporation	March 3, 1970	New Jersey
Financial Federation Inc.	March 11, 1959	Delaware
Firestone Tire & Rubber Co.	March 4, 1910	Ohio
First Charter Financial Corp.	March 18, 1955	California
First City Bancorporation of Texas, Inc.	March 20, 1950	Texas
First Mississippi Corp.	March 19, 1957	Mississippi
First Pennsylvania Banking & Trust	March 1, 1812	Pennsylvania
(Incorporated October 24, 1968, Pennsylvania)		
Florida Gas Co.	March 19, 1957	Florida
FLServ Inc.	February 19, 1992	Delaware
Fruehauf Corp.	February 27, 1918	Michigan
Gelco	March 1, 1956	Minnesota
General Dynamics Corp.	February 21, 1952	Delaware
General Instruments Corp.	February 24, 1937	New Jersey
(Merged parent s/s June 12, 1967, Delaware)		
General Portland Cement Co.	February 19, 1947	Delaware
General Public Utilities Corp.	March 19, 1906	New York
(Merged parent s/s April 2, 1969, Pennsylvania)		
General Telephone & Electronics Corp.	February 25, 1935	New York
Gerber Products Co.	March 27, 1901	Michigan
Giant Port/Masonry Cement	March 4, 1913	Delaware
GMR Properties SBI Dec of Trust	March 20, 1970	Massachusetts

Company	Date of Birth	Place of Birth
Hackensack Water Co.	March 12, 1869	New Jersey
Harsco Corp.	February 28, 1946	Delaware
Hobart Mfg. Co.	March 15, 1913	Ohio
Hoover Universal	March 12, 1913	Michigan
(Merged parent Hoover Ball Bearing s/s September 23, 1975, Michigan)		
Howard Johnson Co.	March 10, 1961	Maryland
Hutton (E.F.) Group, Inc.	February 23, 1973	Delaware
Indiana & Michigan Electric Co.	February 2, 21 1925	Indiana
Intel	March 1, 1989	Delaware
Interco, Inc.	March 16, 1921	Delaware
Iowa Beef Processors, Inc.	March 17, 1960	Iowa
Kansas Power & Light Co.	March 6, 1924	Kansas
Kidde (Walter) & Co. Inc.	March 15, 1968	Delaware
Koehring Co.	March 5, 1907	Wisconsin
Koracorp Industries	February 27, 1970	Delaware
LaClede Gas Co.	March 2, 1857	Missouri
Liberty Media	March 16, 2004	Delaware
Lomas & Nettleton Financial Corp.	March 7, 1960	Delaware
Loral Corp.	February 24, 1948	New York
Marshall Field & Co.	March 7, 1901	Delaware
McIntyre Mines Ltd.	March 16, 1911	Ontario, Canada
Mckee Corporation	February 24, 1920	Delaware
(Merged parent s/s January 24, 1977, Delaware)		
Medusa Corp.	March 4, 1910	Ohio
Mesa Petroleum Co.	February 21, 1964	Delaware
Mirro Aluminum Co.	March 2, 1909	New Jersey
Montana Dakota Utilities Co.	March 14, 1924	Delaware
MONY Mtge Investors SBI Dec	February 25, 1970	Massachusetts
National Can Corp.	March 16, 1937	Delaware
National Standard	February 26, 1926	Michigan
(Merged parent s/s September 30, 1955, Delaware)		
Newxtel Communications	February 22, 1994	Delaware
Northrop Corp.	March 7, 1939	California

Company	Date of Birth	Place of Birth
Northwest Industries, Inc.	March 17, 1947	Delaware
(Became holding company of Chicago & Northwestern RR August 3, 1967, Delaware)		
Northwestern Steel & Wire Co.	February 28, 1879	Illinois
OKC Corp.	March 12, 1959	Delaware
Oklahoma Gas & Electric Co.	Febraury 27, 1902	Oklahoma
Pacific Tin Consolidated Corp.	Febraury 28, 1907	Maine
Pan American World Airways, Inc.	March 14, 1927	New York
Parker Pen Co.	February 23, 1892	Wisconsin
(Merged parent s/s April 12, 1971, Delaware)		
Patrick Petroleum Co.	February 24, 1970	Delaware
Phillip Morris, Inc.	February 21, 1919	Virginia
Puerto Rico Cement Co., Inc.	February 21, 1938	Puerto Rico
Research In Motion	March 7, 1984	Canada
Reserve Oil & Gas Co.	March 16, 1932	California
Rexnord, Inc.	February 23, 1892	Wisconsin
Richardson Co.	March 1, 1898	Ohio
Rochester Telephone Corp.	Febraury 25, 1920	New York
Rollins, Inc.	February 21, 1948	Delaware
Sabine Corp.	February 24, 1933	Texas
(Merged parent s/s November 1, 1976, Louisiana)		
Scovill Mfg. Co.	March 8, 1880	Connecticut
Shapell Industries, Inc.	March 17, 1969	Delaware
Singer Co.	February 20, 1873	New Jersey
Southern Pacific Co.	March 17, 1884	Kentucky
(Merged parent March 21, 1947, Delaware; merged and reorganized, February 20, 1969, Delaware)		
Southern Railway Co.	February 20, 1894	Virginia
Southwest Airlines	March 9, 1967	Texas
Standard Pacific Corp.	March 9, 1961	California
Superscope, Inc.	March 3, 1954	California
Transcon Lines	March 14, 1946	California
Tyco Laboratories	March 1, 1952	Massachusetts

Company	Date of Birth	Place of Birth
Unarco Industries. Inc.	March 19, 1918	Illinois
(Merged parent s/s May 27, 1970, Delaware)		
Union Commerce Corp.	February 21, 1938	Ohio
(Merged parent Union Commerce Bank February 2 January 17, 1970, Delaware)		
U.S. Fidelity & Guaranty Co.	March 19, 1896	Maryland
U.S. Industries, Inc.	March 5, 1951	Delaware
U.S. Realty Investments SBI Dec. of Trust	March 20, 1961	Ohio
U.S. Steel Corp.	February 25, 1901	NewJersey
(Merged parent s/s September 13, 1965, Delaware)		
Washington National Corp.	February 26, 1968	Delaware
Washington Water Power Co.	March 15, 1889	Washington
Webb (Del E.) Corp.	March 16, 1946	Arizona
Wells Fargo & Co.	March 18, 1852	California
(Merged W.F. National Bank & parent November 15, 1968, California)		
West Penn Power Co.	March 1, 1916	Pennsylvania
Wisconsin Power & Light	February 21, 1917	Wisconsin
Yates Industries, Inc.	March 18, 1955	New Jersey

Aries Stocks (March 21-April 19)

Company	Date of Birth	Place of Birth
Addressograph-Multigraph Corp	April 7, 1924	Delaware
Alabama Gas Corp.	March 21, 1919	Alabama
Allergan Pharmaceuticals	February 26, 1948	California
(Merged parent s/s April 14, 1977, Delaware)		
Alpha Portland Industries, Inc.	April 9, 1895	New Jersey
American Airlines Inc.	April 11, 1934	Delaware
American Building Maint. Industries	April 1, 1955	California
American General Conv. Securitirs Inv.	March 20, 1972	Maryland
American Standard	March 26, 1929	Delaware
American Stores	March 29, 1917	Delaware
Ames Department Stores	March 30, 1962	Delaware
Ametek, Inc.	March 27, 1930	Delaware
Amtel Company	April 15, 1964	Rhode Island

Company	Date of Birth	Place of Birth
Ansul Company Inc.	April 19, 1915	Wisconsin
Arctic Enterprises, Inc.	April 19, 1962	Minnesota
Armour & Company	April 7, 1900	Illinois
(Reincorporated with parent Decenber 23, 1947, Delaware)		
Asarco	March 26, 1929	Delaware
Babcox & Wilcox Company	April 1, 1881	New Jersey
Baker International Corporation	March 26, 1913	California
Bendix Corporation	April 13, 1929	Delaware
Blue Bell, Inc.	April 2, 1962	Delaware
Bobbie Brooks Inc.	April 13, 1946	Ohio
British Petroleum Co. Ltd.	April 14, 1909	UK
Brown Company	March 29, 1888	Maine
(Merged parent sls February 15, 1965, Delaware)		
Brown & Sharpe Mnf	March 26, 1969	Delaware
Buttes Gas & Oil	April 16, 1954	California
Capital Cities Communication Corp.	April 5, 1946	New York
Capital Holding Corporation	March 26, 1969	Delaware
Carolina Power & Light Company	April 6, 1926	North Carolina

Company	Date of Birth	Place of Birth
Caterpillar Tractor Company	April 15, 1925	California
Central Illinois Light Company	April 11, 1913	Illinois
Charter Company	April 1, 1959	Florida
Chase Manhattan Mortgage & Realty Trust, Dec of Trust	April 16, 1970	Massachusetts
Church's Fried Chicken	April 2, 1965	Texas
Cincinnati Gas & Electric Company	April 3, 1837	Ohio
Citrix Systems	April 17, 1989	Delaware
Cognizant Technology	April 6, 1988	Delaware
Combustion Equipment Associates, Inc.	March 31, 1959	New York
Computer Sciences Corporation	April 16, 1959	Nevada
Consumers Company	April 14, 1910	Maine
(Parent Consumers Power Company s/s January 22, 1968, Michigan)		

Company	Date of Birth	Place of Birth
Continental Copper & Steel Industries	April 19, 1944	Delaware
Cooper Tire & Rubber Company	March 26, 1930	Delaware
Crump and Foster	March 29, 1907	New York
Data General Corporation	April 15, 1968	Delaware
Dayton Power & Light Company	March 23, 1911	Ohio
Dennison Manufacturing Company	April 12, 1962	Nevada
Dorsey Corporation	April 7, 1927	Delaware
Dynamics Corporation of America	March 21, 1924	New York
Eastern Air Lines, Inc.	March 29, 1938	Delaware
Eastern Utilities Associates	April 2, 1928	Massachusetts
El Paso Corp.	April 17, 1998	Delaware
Emery Air Freight Corporation	April, 18, 1946	Delaware
Equitable Gas Company	March 31, 1926	Pennsylvania
Esquire Inc.	March 31, 1937	Delaware
Fidelity Financial Corporation	April 1, 1969	California
Financial Corporation of America	April 5, 1968	Delaware
First Pennsylvania Mortgage Trust SBI Dec of Trust	March 31, 1970	Massachusetts
Fotomat Corporation	April 15, 1971	Delaware
General Cable Corporation	April 15, 1902	New Jersey
General Electric Company	April 15, 1892	New York
General Public Utilities Corporatio	April 2, 1969	Pennsylvania
Gerber Products Company	March 27, 1901	Michigan
Globe-Union	April 2, 1928	Delaware
Guardian Industries Corporation	April 10, 1968	Delaware
Gulton Industries Inc. (Merged s/s parent May 10, 1968, Delaware)	March 25, 1942	New Jersey
Hall (W.F.) Printing Company	April 14, 1971	Delaware
Hanna Mining Company	March 27, 1927	Delaware
Hayes Albien Corporation (Merged s/s with parent November 21, 1968, Delaware)	April 4, 1935	Michigan
Heileman (G) Brewing Company, Inc.	April 2, 1918	Wisconsin
Holly Sugar Corporation	April 4, 1916	New York

Company	Date of Birth	Place of Birth
Hospital Corporation of America	April 25, 1960	New York
Hospital Corporation of America	April 25, 1960	Tennessee
Houdaille Industries, Inc.	April 1, 1968	Delaware
House of Fabrics	April 12, 1946	California
Ideal Basic Industries, Inc.	April 10, 1908	Colorado
(Parent Cement Securities s/s January 8, 1924, Colorado)		
Ideal Toy Corporation April 10, 1972	Delaware	
Industrial National Corporation	March 16, 1970	Rhode Island
Inexco Oil Company	April 1, 1968	Delaware
Integon Corporation	March 28, 1968	North Carolina
Interstate Power Company	April 18, 1925	Delaware
Jamesway	March 22, 1966	New York
Jersey Central Power & Light Company	March 27, 1925	New Jersey
Keene Corporation	April 8, 1967	Delaware
Kollmorgen	March 22, 1916	New York
Kroehler Manufacturing Company	April 13, 1915	Illinois
(Merged s/s SN February 24, 1969, Delaware)		
Kroger Company	April 3, 1902	Ohio
M/A Com Inc.	March 7, 1950	Massachusetts
Massachusetts Mutual Corporate Investors, Inc.	April 12, 1971	Delaware
Maremont Corporation	April 10, 1933	Illinois
McDermott (J. Ray) & Company, Inc.	April 15, 1946	Delaware
Michigan Gas Utilities Company	March 28, 1928	Michigan
Midland Ross Corporation	March 21, 1923	Ohio
Milton Roy Company	March 25, 1946	Pennsylvania
Missouri Pacific Corporation	February 8, 1928	Delaware
(Incorporated as Mississippi River Fuel Corp., now owns Missouri Pacific RR as of December 31, 1977		
Monsanto Company	April 19, 1933	Delaware
Morton-Norwich Products, Inc.	March 31, 1890	New York
Myers (L.E.) Company	April 18, 1914	Delaware
National Distillers & Chemical Corp.	April 18, 1924	Virginia
Norris Industries	March 26, 1940	California

Company	Date of Birth	Place of Birth
Novell US Systems	April 11, 1984	California
Pacific Northwest Bell Telephone Co.	March 27, 1961	Washington
Payless Drug Stores Northwest, Inc.	April 13, 1967	Maryland
Penn Central Company	April 13, 1846	Pennsylvania
Pennzoil	April 1, 1968	Delaware
Peoples Drug Stores, Inc.	April 2, 1928	Maryland
Pet, Inc.	March 21, 1925	Delaware
Pioneer Corporation (Pioneer Natural Gas)	April 16, 1906	Texas
Portee, Inc.	April 4, 1928	Delaware
Pueblo International	March 25, 1955	Puerto Rico
Reliance Insurance Company	March 27, 1820	Pennsylvania
Reynolds (R.J.) Industries, Inc. (Reincorporated March 4, 1970, Delaware)	April 4, 1899	New Jersey
Rite Aid Company	April 15, 1968	Delaware
Ross Stores	March 29, 1989	Delaware
Ryder System, Inc.	March 22, 1955	Florida
Safeway Stores, Inc.	March 24, 1926	Maryland
Sargent-Welch Scientific Company	March 26, 1906	Illinois
St. Joe Minerals Corporation	March 25, 1864	New York
St. Paul Securities, Inc.	March 27, 1972	Minnesota
San Diego Gas & Electric Co.	April 6, 1905	California
Schlitz (J.) Brewing	April 16, 1920	Wisconsin
Seaboard Coast Line Railroad (Reincorporated parent Seaboard Airline Ry January 26, 1944, Virginia; merged parent s/s August 1, 1968, Virginia; merged parent s/s May 9, 1969, Delaware)	April 10, 1900	Virginia
Sealed Power Corporation	April 16, 1968	Delaware
Searle (G.D.) & Company (Reincorporated November 2, 1955, Delaware)	April 10, 1908	Illinois
Simmonds Precision Products, Inc.	April 13, 1936	New York
Southdown, Inc.	April 4, 1930	Louisiana
Southern New England Telephone Co.	April 19, 1982	Connecticut
Snap On Tools Corporation	April 7, 1930	Delaware
Standard Brands Paint Co.	March 30, 1961	Maryland

Company	Date of Birth	Place of Birth
Sterchi Bros. Stores, Inc.	March 22, 1929	Delaware
Sterling Drug, Inc.	April 9, 1932	Delaware
Sunbeam Corporation	April 1, 1897	Illinois
(Merged parent 3 for 2 split April 1, 1969; March 17,1897 (Moody), Delaware)		
Sun Chemical Corporation	March 28, 1929	Delaware
Swank, Inc.	April 17, 1936	Delaware
Symantec Corp.	April 19, 1988	Delaware
Textron, Inc.	April 16, 1928	Rhode Island
(Merged s/s parent July 31, 1967, Delaware)		
Tenneco, Ind.	April 1, 1940	Tennessee
(Consolidated parent Ten Gastraws Co. June 9, 1947, Delaware)		
Trane Company	April 2, 1913	Wisconsin
Tropicana Products, Inc.	March 30, 1949	Florida
UMC Industries, Inc.	March 31, 1937	Delaware
Uniroyal, Inc.	March 30, 1892	New Jersey
United Brands Company	March 30, 1899	New Jersey
Union Bancorp, Inc.	April 3, 1973	Delaware
United Guaranty Corporation	April 5, 1963	North Carolina
(Merged s/s parent 1st Mortgage Insurance Company)		
Varo, Inc.	April 4, 1946	Texas
Verisign, Inc.	April 12, 1995	Delaware
Warnaco (reincorporated)	March 28, 1961	Connecticut
Washington Steel Corporation	April 16, 1945	Pennsylvania
Wayne-Gossard Corporation	April 18, 1891	Indiana
Wells Fargo Mortgage Investors Dec of Trust	April 2, 1970	Massachusetts
Western Union Corporation	April 8, 1851	New York
(Merged s/s parent December 25, 1969, Delaware)		
Wisconsin Gas Company	March 27, 1852	Wisconsin
World Airways, Inc.	March 29, 1948	Delaware
Wurlitzer Company	March 28, 1890	Ohio
(Merged s/s parent February 13, 1968 Delaware)		
Xerox Corporation	April 18, 1906	New York
Yahoo	March 24, 1999	Delaware

Company	Date of Birth	Place of Birth
Zale Corporation	April 19, 1924	Texas
Zayre Corporation	April 18, 1962	Delaware

Taurus Stocks (April 20-May 20)

Company	Date of Birth	Place of Birth
Adams Express Company	May 3, 1968	New York
(Merged parent s/s February 10, 1976, Maryland)		
Adams Millis Corporation	May 3, 1928	North Carolina
Adobe Systems	May 9, 1997	Delaware
Advanced Micro	May 1, 1969	Delaware
Airborne Freight Corp., Inc.	May 10, 1969	Delaware
Akzona, Inc.	May 1, 1928	Delaware
Alcon Laboratories	May 16, 1947	Texas
Alexanders, Inc.	May 2, 1955	Delaware
Allegheny Ludlum Steel Corpor tion	May 11, 1905	Pennsylvania
(Parent Allegheny Steel & Iron; reincorporated and merged with Penn Steel Company May 6, 1929, Pennsylvania; merged Ludlum Steel Company August 16, 1938, Pennsylvania)		
Allied Stores Corporation	May 10, 1928	Delaware
Allright Auto Parks, Inc.	May 7, 1962	Delaware
Amerace	May 9, 1957	Delaware
American Century Mortgage SBI Dec of Trust	May 14, 1969	Florida
American General Insurance Company	May 8, 1926	Texas
American Hoist & Derrick Company	April 21, 1928	Delaware
American Seating	April 23, 1906	New Jersey
(Merged parent s/s June 21, 1926, New Jersey; merged parent s/s March 14, 1966, Delaware)		
Amoco Pipeline Company	April 25, 1916	Maine
Ampex Corporation	May 2, 1946	California
Angelica Corporation	April 28, 1904	Missouri
(Merged parent sls March 11, 1968, Missouri)		
Archer-Daniels-Midland Company	May 2, 1923	Delaware
Aristar, Inc.	May 2, 1927	Delaware
(Controlled by Gamble Skogmo, Inc.)		
Arkansas Best Corporation	May 11, 1966	Delaware

Company	Date	State/Country
Atlantic Richfield Company	April 29, 1870	Pennsylvania
AutoDesk	April 26, 1982	Delaware
Bally Manufacturing Company	May 15, 1968	Delaware
Bankers Trust N.Y. Corp., Inc.	May 12, 1965	New York
Barber Oil Corporation	April 30, 1947	Delaware
Bates Mgf. Co., Inc.	May 2, 1938	Delaware
Beech Creek R.R. Co., Ltd.	May 11, 1898	Pennsylvania
Bell Industries, Inc.	May 7, 1959	California
Bell Telephone of Canada	April 29, 1880	Canada
Bemis Company, Inc.	May 18, 1885	Missouri
Beneficial Corporation	May 9, 1929	Delaware
Benguet Consolidated (Reincorporated June 18, 1956, Pillippines)	May 19, 1903	Phillippines
Boise Cascade Corporation	April 23, 1934	Delaware
Borden, Inc. April 24, 1899 (Merged parent s/s April 17, 1966, Delaware)		New Jersey
Borg Warner Corporation (Reincorporated same name September 20, 1967, Delaware)	May 9, 1928	Illinois
Burlington Northern	May 14, 1981	Delaware
California Pacific Utilities Company	May 7, 1928	California
Champion International Corporation	April 28, 1937	New York
Chesebrough-Ponds, Inc.	May 11, 1880	New York
Chromallow American Corporation (Reincorporated August 26, 1968, Delaware)	May 3, 1951	New York
Clark Equipment Credit Corporation	May 17, 1954	Michigan
CMI Corporation	April 21, 1970	Ohio
Colonel Penn Group	April 25, 1963	Delaware
Cousins Mtge & Equity Dec of Trust	May 18, 1970	Georgia
Connecticut Natural Gas Corporation	May 3, 1948	Connecticut
Costco Co.	May 12, 1987	California
C P National Corporation	May 7, 1928	California
Culbro Corporation (General Cigar)	April 28, 1906	New York
Culligan, Inc.	May 1, 1945	Delaware
Dayton Hudson Corporation	May 4, 1902	Minnesota

Company	Date of Birth	Place of Birth
Deere & Company	April 25, 1958	Delaware
Delmarve Power & Light Company	April 22, 1909	Delaware
Denny's, Inc.	May 11, 1959	California
Dillon Companies, Inc.	May 13, 1921	Kansas
Dorr-Oliver	May 13, 1931	Delaware
Dover Corporation	April 21, 1947	Delaware
Dresser Industries, Inc.	April 23, 1956	Delaware
Duke Power Company	May 1, 1917	New Jersey
Echostar Communications	April 26, 1995	Nevada
Edwards, M.G. & Sons, Inc.	May 11, 1967	Delaware
Electronic Arts	May 8, 1991	Delaware
G.M.I., Ltd.	April 20, 1931	England
Fedders	April 21, 1913	New York
Federal Mogul Corporation	May 1, 1924	Michigan
First International Bankshares, Inc.	May 3, 1972	Delaware
Fluor Corporation	April 28, 1924	California
G.A.F. Corporation	April 26, 1929	Delaware
General Growth Properties SB Dec of Trust	May 19, 1970	Massachusetts
Genstar, Ltd.	May 9, 1951	Canada
Genuine Parts Company	May 7, 1928	Georgia
Gibraltar Financial Corp of California	May 18, 1959	Delaware
Goodrich Company	May 2, 1912	New York
Great Lakes Dredge & Dock Company	May 2, 1905	New Jersey
Gulf United Corporation	May 7, 1968	Florida
Handleman Company (Reincorporated July 11, 1969, Delaware)	May 13, 1946	Michigan
Handy & Harman	April 29, 1905	New York
Heath Teena	April 25, 1958	Washington
Hecks, Inc.	May 18, 1959	West Virginia
Hemisphere Fund, Inc.	April 20, 1967	Delaware
Hewlett-Packard	May 20, 1998	Delaware
Honeywell, Intl.	May 13, 1985	Delaware
Horizon Corporation	May 11, 1959	Delaware

Company	Date of Birth	Place of Birth
Holiday Inns, Inc.	April 30, 1954	Tennessee
Houghton Mifflin Company	May 18, 1908	Massachusetts
Idaho Power Company	May 6, 1915	Maine
Illinois Tool Works, Inc.	May 23, 1915	Illinois
Insilco Corporation	April 30, 1946	Connecticut
Invitro Corp.	May 21, 1997	Delaware
Kansas Nebraska Natural Gas Co.	May 18, 1927	Kansas
Kennecott Copper Corporation	April 29, 1915	New York
Keystone Consolidated Industries	May 18, 1955	Delaware
Kings Department Stores	April 21, 1961	Delaware
K-Mart Corporation	April 30, 1912	Delaware
(Reincorporated March 9, 1916, Michigan; former Kresge's, Inc.)		
Lenox, Inc.	May 16, 1889	New Jersey
Libbey-Owens-Ford	May 18, 1916	Ohio
LFE Corporation	May 15, 1946	Delaware
MacAndrews & Forbes Company	May 8, 1902	New Jersey
MacMillan, Inc.	May 6, 1920	Delaware
Madison Fund, Inc.	April 24, 1925	Delaware
Mark Controls Corporation	April 29, 1931	Delaware
MBPXL Corporation	April 24, 1974	Delaware
(Merged MEP, Inc. November 19, 1964, Missouri and KBI, Inc. July 13, 1969, Delaware)		
McDonald's Corporation	April 27, 1956	Illinois
(Reincorporated March 1, 1965, Delaware)		
McLouth Steel Corporation	April 27, 1934	Michigan
Medtronic Inc.	May 1, 1957	Minnesota
Melville Corporation	May 1, 1914	New York
Merrill Lynch, Inc.	May 16, 1973	Delaware
MGIC Investment Corporation	May 6, 1968	Delaware
(Merged s/s parent Mortgage Guaranty Ins. Co. March 26, 1976, Wisconsin)		
Midland Mortgage Investors Trust	May 5, 1969	Oklahoma
Minnesota Gas Company	May 3, 1928	Delaware
Mountain Fuel Supply Company	May 7, 1935	Utah

Company	Date of Birth	Place of Birth
Munsingwear	May 8, 1923	Delaware
Nalco Chemical Company	April 21, 1928	Delaware
Nashua Corporation	April 29, 1904	Massachusetts
(Merged parent s/s November 15, 1957, Delaware)		
New England Power Company	April 27, 1916	Massachusetts
Newmont Mining Corporation	May 2, 1921	Delaware
New Park Resources, Inc.	May 4, 1932	West Virginia
North Central Airlines, Inc.	May 15, 1944	Wisconsin
Northern Natural Gas Company	April 25, 1930	Delaware
Northwest Airlines, Inc.	April 24, 1934	Minnesota
Ohio Power Company	May 8, 1907	Ohio
Oxford Industries, Inc.	April 27, 1960	Georgia
PayChex, Inc.	April 26, 1979	Delaware
Peabody International	May 10, 1946	Delaware
Pfizer, Inc.	April 21, 1900	New Jersey
Pioneer Electronic Corporation	May 8, 1947	Japan
Pitney-Bowes, Inc.	April 23, 1920	Delaware
Plantronics	May 8, 1961	California
Potomac Electric Power Company	April 28, 1896	Delaware
Proctor & Gamble Company	May 5, 1905	Ohio
Products Research & Chemical Corp.	May 17, 1945	California
Proler International Corporation	April 22, 1966	Delaware
Public Service Company of New Mexico	May 9, 1917	New Mexico
Purolator, Inc.	May 2, 1923	Delaware
Quanex Corporation	April 25, 1927	Michigan
(Parent Michigan Seamless Tube s/s June 3, 1968, Delaware)		
Ranco, Inc.	May 15, 1913	Ohio
Rapid American	April 21, 1920	Pennsylvania
(Merged Glen Alden Company s/s September 29, 1966, Delaware)		
Realty Refund Trust SBI Dec of Trust	April 28, 1971	Ohio
Republic Corporation	May 15, 1927	New York
Republic Steel Corporation	May 3, 1899	New Jersey
Riegel Textile Corporation	May 20, 1946	Delaware

Company	Date of Birth	Place of Birth
RLC Corporation	April 27, 1954	Delaware
Rohm & Hass Company	April 23, 1917	Delaware
Ronson Corporation	May 10, 1928	New Jersey
Rubbermaid, Inc.	April 30, 1920	Ohio
Sambo's Restaurants, Inc.	May 9, 1961	California
San Juan Racing Association, Inc.	April 20, 1954	Puerto Rico
Sannmina-Sci, Corp.	May 9, 1989	Delaware
Savin Business Machines Corporation	April 28, 1959	New York
Saxon Industries	May 5, 1924	New York
(Merged s/s with parent August 28, 1975, Delaware)		
Scotty's, Inc.	May 6, 1925	Florida
Siebel Systems	May 9, 1996	Delaware
Sigma-Aldrich	May 12, 1975	Delaware
Sony	May 7, 1946	Japan
Sparton Corporation	May 1, 1916	Ohio
(Reorganized December 29, 1919, Ohio)		
Standard Prudential Corporation	May 6, 1966	New York
Sun Company, Inc.	May 2, 1901	New Jersey
(Merged parent Sun Oil Company August 4, 1971, Pennsylvania)		
Synopsys	May 7, 1987	Delaware
Tandy Corporation	May 3, 1899	New Jersey
(Merged parent s/s December 19, 1967, Delaware)		
Telex Corporation	May 2, 1940	Minnesota
(Merged parent s/s February 13, 1963, Delaware)		
Texas International	May 19, 1930	Delaware
Transwav International Corporation	May 15, 1925	Delaware
United Financial Corporation of Cal	May 8, 1959	Delaware
United Inns, Inc.	May 10, 1956	Tennessee
United Park City Mines Company	May 8, 1953	Delaware
Varian Associates	Apil 20, 1948	California
(Merged parent s/s February 1, 1976, Delaware)		
Westcoast Transmission Company, Ltd.	April 30, 1949	Canada
Western Company of North America	April 28, 1950	Delaware

Company	Date of Birth	Place of Birth
XM Satellite Radio	May 16, 1997	Delaware
YUM, Inc.	May 16, 2002	North Carolina

Gemini Stocks (May 21- June 20)

Company	Date of Birth	Place of Birth
Abbott Laboratories	June 6, 1900	New York
Affiliate Computer	June 8, 1988	Delaware
Alcan Aluminum, Ltd.	May 31, 1928	Canada
Alter Corp.	June 19, 1997	Delaware
Amax, Inc.	June 17, 1887	New York
Amazon, Inc.	May 28, 1996	Delaware
American Express	June 10, 1965	New York
Anheuser-Busch, Inc.	June 20, 1925	Missouri
ASA, Ltd.	June 12, 1958	South Africa
Associated Dry Goods, Corporation	May 24, 1916	Virginia
Automatic Data Processing, Inc.	June 12, 1961	Delaware
Baltimore Gas & Electric	June 20, 1906	Maryland
Basic, Inc.	May 29, 1931	Ohio
Bayuk Cigars, Inc.	May 21, 1920	Maryland
Benguet Consolidated, Inc.	June 18, 1956	Phillipines
Borman's, Inc.	June 6, 1950	Michigan
(Merged parent s/s March 28, 1969, Delaware)		
Bristol-Myers, Inc.	June 9, 1900	New York
(Reincorporated s/s with parent September 11, 1933, Delaware)		
Brockway Glass Co., Inc.	June 20, 1907	New York
Bulova Watch Co., Inc.	June 7, 1911	New York
Bunker Hill Income Securities, Inc.	June 21, 1973	Maryland
Caesars World, Inc.	June 4, 1958	Florida
Callahan Mining Corporation	June 12, 1912	Arizona
Capital Mortgage Investment SBI Dec of Trust	May 28, 1969	Maryland
Central Illinois Public Service Co.	May 26, 1902	Illinois
Chicago & Western Indiana RR, Inc.	June 5, 1879	Illinois
Chrysler Corporation	June 6, 1928	Delaware

Company	Date of Birth	Place of Birth
Control Data Corporation (Parent Commercial Credit)	May 31, 1912	Delaware
DeSoto, Inc.	June 10, 1927	Delaware
Donnelley (R.R.) & Sons Company	June 1, 1956	Delaware
Dow Chemical Company	June 11, 1947	Delaware
DPF, Inc.	June 14, 1961	Delaware
Drexel Bond Debenture Trading Fund	June 7, 1971	Delaware
Elixir Industries	June 12, 1953	California
Expeditors, Intl.	May 29,1 979	Washington
Fisher Foods, Inc.	June 17, 1908	Ohio
Flextronics	May 31, 1990	Singapore
Florida East Coast Railroad Company	May 28, 1892	Florida
Gamble-Skogmo, Inc.	May 28, 1928	Delaware
General Host Corporation	June 6, 1911	New York
General Mills, Inc.	June 20, 1928	Delaware
General Signal Corporation	June 13, 1904	New York
General Telephone Co. of Florida	June 20, 1901	Florida
Golden West Financial	May 29, 1959	Delaware
Grace (W.R.) & Company	June 20, 1899	Connecticut
Great Atlantic & Pacific Tea Co., Inc.	May 29, 1925	Maryland
Grow Chemical Corporation	June 20, 1950	New York
Harrah's	June 7, 1971	Nevada
Hilton Hotels Corporation	May 29, 1946	Delaware
Houston Natural Gas Corporation	May 29, 1930	Texas
Illinois Power Company	May 25, 1923	Illinois
Ingersoll-Rand Company	June 1, 1905	New Jersey
Institutional Investors Trust SBI Dec of Trust	May 22, 1970	Massachusetts
International Business Machine Corp.	June 15, 1911	New York
International Tel & Tel Corporation (Merged parent sls January 26, 1968, Delaware)	June 10, 1928	Maryland
Intersil Corp.	June 2, 1999	Delaware
Iowa Electric Light & Power Co.	May 25, 1925	Iowa
Jewelcor, Inc.	June 15, 1960	Pennsylvania

Company	Date of Birth	Place of Birth
Kuhlman	June 1, 1915	Michigan
Lane Bryant	May 28, 1920	Delaware
Leeds & Northrop Company Leesona Corp.	June 1, 1903	Pennsylvania
Lincoln National Corporation	June 12, 1905	Indiana
(merged s/s January 5, 1968, Indiana)		
Litco	June 16, 1972	New York
Lowenstein (M.) & Sons, Inc.	June 1, 1948	New York
LSI Corp.	June 11, 1987	California
Luckey Stores, Inc.	May 23, 1931	California
MacDonald (E.F.) Company	May 31, 1961	Delaware
Macy (R.H.) & Company	May 28, 1919	New York
Manhattan Ind., Inc.	June 15, 1912	New York
Marion Laboratories, Inc.	June 17, 1952	Missouri
(Merged parent s/s July 9, 1964, Delaware)		
Massachusetts Mutual Mortgage	June 15, 1970	Massachusetts
May Department Stores Co.	June 4, 1910	New York
Mayer (Oscar) & Company, Inc.	May 26, 1911	Illinois
(Merged s/s parent January 2, 1970, Delaware)		
Mid-Continent Telephone Corporation	June 6, 1960	Ohio
Middle South Utilities, Inc.	May 27, 1949	Florida
Mobile Home Industries, Inc.	May 24, 1968	Florida
Monogram Industries, Inc.	May 26, 1947	California
Mortgage Trust of America SBI Dec of Trust	May 23, 1969	California
Murphy Oil Corporation	May 24, 1950	Louisiana
(Merged parent s/s May 20, 1963, Delaware)		
National Chemsearch Corporation	May 21, 1965	Delaware
(Now NCH Corporation; Moody says May 2, 1965)		
National Medical Enterprises, Inc.	June 11, 1968	California
(Merged parent s/s November 7, 1975, Nevada)		
National Semi Conductor	May 27, 1959	Delaware
New Hall Land & Farming Company	June 1, 1883	California
(Merged parent s/s April 20, 1976, Delaware)		
Niagra Share Corporation	June 18, 1929	Maryland

Company	Date of Birth	Place of Birth
Northern States Power Company	June 16, 1909	Minnesota
Northwest Energy Company	June 10, 1965	Delaware
(Merged parent Northwest, Pipeline s/s February 7, 1974, Delaware)		
Norton Company	June 20, 1885	Massachusetts
Oak Industries, Inc.	June 3, 1932	Illinois
(Merged parent s/s February 4, 1960, Delaware)		
Occidental Petroleum Corporation	May 21, 1920	California
Orange Co. Inc.	June 17, 1968	Ohio
(Merged parent s/s August 14, 1969, Delaware)		
Orange & Rockland Utilities, Inc.	May 21, 1926	New York
Overhead Door Corporation	June 15, 1923	Indiana
Pacific Lighting Corporation	April 21, 1907	California
Pacific Power & Light Company	June 16, 1910	Maine
Patterson Cos., Inc.	June 15, 1992	Minnesota
Pennsylvania Power & Light	June 4, 1920	Pennsylvania
(Consolidated merger of companies May 31, 1930, Pennsylvania)		
Phillips Petroleum Company	June 13, 1917	Delaware
Piedmont Natural Gas Company, Inc.	May 22, 1950	New York
Premier Industrial Corporation	June 1, 1946	Ohio
Puritan Fashions Corporation	June 10, 1958	New York
Raytheon Company	May 22, 1928	Delaware
Rochester Gas & Electric Corporation	June 11, 1904	New York
Royal Dutch Petroleum	May 28, 1890	Netherlands
Saga Corporation	June 17, 1957	New York
Sandisk Corp.	June 1, 1988	Delaware
Schaefer (F.M.) Corporation	June 10, 1968	New York
Sears Roebuck & Company	June 16, 1906	New York
Seatrain Lines, Inc.	June 13, 1931	Delaware
Skyline Corporation	May 29, 1959	Indiana
South Atlantic Trust Dec of Trust	May 29, 1969	Massachusetts
Southeastern Public Service Company	May 26, 1947	Delaware
Southern Indiana Gas & Electric Co.	June 10, 1912	Indiana
Standard Oil Company (Indiana)	June 18, 1889	Indiana

Company	Date of Birth	Place of Birth
Sunshine Mining Company	May 28, 1918	Washington
Taft Broadcasting Company	June 3, 1959	Delaware
Talcott National Corporation	May 24, 1968	New York
Tandy Crafts, Inc.	June 10, 1975	Delaware
Texas Industries, Inc.	June 7, 1946	Texas
(Reorganized parent TLA Company April 19, 1951, Delaware)		
Thompson, J. Walter	June 13, 1907	New York
Todd Shipyards, Corporation	June 14, 1916	New York
Transco Companies, Inc.	June 18, 1973	Delaware
Travelers Corporation (The)	June 17, 1863	Connecticut
(Merged parent Travelers Insurance Company, Inc. July 26, 1965, Connecticut)		
T.R.E. Corporation	June 10, 1959	Delaware
T.R.W., Inc.	June 17, 1916	Ohio
UARCO, Inc.	June 5, 1894	Illinois
(Merged parent UARCO s/s September 11, 1969, Delaware)		
UGI Corporation	June 1, 1882	Pennsylvania
U.S. Leasing International, Inc.	May 29, 1952	California
Western Pacific Industries	June 6, 1916	California
(Formed to take over Western Pacific Railroad December 21, 1970, Delaware)		
Weyenberg Shoe Manufacturing Co.	June 1, 1906	Wisconsin
Winter (Jack), Inc.	June 9, 1936	Wisconsin
(Merged parent s/s October 14, 1975, Delaware)		
Witco Chemical Corporation	June 12, 1956	Delaware
Wynn Resorts, Ltd.	June 3, 2002	Nevada

Cancer Stocks (June 21-July 22)

Company	Date of Birth	Place of Birth
Adams Express	July 1, 1854	New York
American Credit Corporation	June 24, 1946	North Carolina
American Cyanamid Company	July 22, 1907	Maine
American General Bond Fund, Inc.	June 30, 1977	Texas
Amfac, Inc.	July 20, 1918	Hawaii
Amsted	June 28, 1902	New Jersey
(Merged parent American Steel Foundry s/s January 31, 1968, Delaware)		

Company	Date of Birth	Place of Birth
Apollo Group	June 30, 1981	Arizona
Armco Steel Corporation	June 29, 1917	Ohio
Avnet, Inc.	July 22, 1955	New York
Bank of New York Co., Inc.	July 9, 1968	New York
Bethlehem Steel Corporation	July 1, 1919	Delaware
Boeing Company	July 19, 1934	Delaware
Briggs & Stratton Corporation	June 30, 1924	Delaware
Burndy Corporation	July 1, 1924	New York
Cadence Industries Corporation	July 13, 1937	Delaware
Campbell Red Lake Mines, Ltd.	July 18, 1944	Ontario
Campbell Taggart, Inc.	July 14, 1927	Delaware
Carter-Hawley Hale Stores, Inc.	July 8, 1897	California
CCI Corporation	July 13, 1959	Delaware
Central Maine Power Company	July 20, 1905	Maine
Centronics Data Computer Corp.	July 3, 1968	Delaware
Checkpoint Software	July 5, 1993	Israel
Chesapeake & Ohio RR Company Virginia	July 1, 1878	Virginia, West
Chicago Milwaukee Corporation	June 24, 1971	Delaware
Chubb Corp.	June 27, 1967	Delaware
Cincinnati Bell, Inc.	July 5, 1873	Ohio
Clark Oil & Refineries Corporation	July 12, 1934	Wisconsin
Cleveland Cliffs Iron Company	July 9, 1947	Ohio
Coldwell-Banker & Company	July 1, 1961	California
Coleco Industries	June 30, 1961	Connecticut
Collins & Aikman Corporation	July 8, 1927	Delaware
Cone-Mills Corporation	July 20, 1895	North Carolina
Consolidated Natural Gas Company	July 21, 1942	Delaware
Cooper Laboratories, Inc.	July 18, 1961	Delaware
Craig Corporation	July 11, 1960	Delaware
Cyclops Corporation	June 22, 1908	Pennsylvania

(Merged parent Universal Steel s/s September 30, 1936, Pennsylvania)

Company	Date of Birth	Place of Birth
Dentsphy Intl., Inc.	June 23, 1899	New York
(Merged parent Dentists Supply Company s/s March 13, 1969, Delaware)		
Diversified Mtg.Investors SBI Dec of Trust	July 14, 1969	Massachusetts
Dome Mines, Ltd.	July 7, 1923	Canada
EASCO	June 26, 1919	Maryland
Eastern Gas & Fuel Associates	July 18, 1929	Massachusetts
Eckerd Jack Corporation	June 23, 1961	Florida
Electronic Data Systems Corporation	June 27, 1962	Texas
Electronic Memories & Magneti Corp.	July 11, 1969	Delaware
Emery Industries, Inc.	June 29, 1935	Ohio
Ex-Cell-O Corporation	July 10, 1919	Michigan
Faberge, Inc.	July 1, 1939	Minnesota
First National Boston Corporation	July 1, 1970	Massachusetts
Fleetwood Enterprises, Inc.	July 12, 1957	California
(Merged parent s/s July 1, 1977, Delaware)		
Flinkote Company	July 12, 1917	Massachusetts
Florida Power Corporation	July 18, 1899	Florida
Ford Motor Company	July 9, 1919	Delaware
Franklin Mint Corporation	July 22, 1964	Pennsylvania
GAP Stores, Inc. (The)	July 3, 1969	California
Garfinkle, Brooks Bros., Miller & Rhodes, Inc.	June 30, 1939	Virginia
GATX Corporation	July 5, 1976	New York
General American Oil Co. of Texas	July 1, 1936	Delaware
General Bancshares Corporation	June 29, 1946	Missouri
Genesco, Inc.	July 7, 1925	Tennessee
Gilead Sciences	June 22, 1987	Delaware
Great Western Financial Corporation	June 22, 1955	Delaware
Halliburton Company	July 1, 1924	Delaware
Home Depot	June 29, 1978	Delaware
Necla Mining Company	July 12, 1898	Delaware
Hecla Mining Company	July 12, 1898	Idaho
Host International, Inc.	June 23, 1914	Delaware
Household Finance Corporation	July 21, 1925	Delaware

Company	Date of Birth	Place of Birth
Hubbard Real Estate Investment	July 7, 1969	Massachusetts
INA Investment Securities, Inc.	June 28, 1972	Delaware
Indiana Gas Company	July 16, 1945	Indiana
Interlake, Inc.	June 23, 1905	New York
(Merged parent Interlake Iron s/s December 18, 1969, Delaware)		
International Paper Company	June 23, 1941	New York
Iowa Public Service Company	July 2, 1901	Iowa
JDS Uniphase	June 23, 1993	Delaware
Jostens, Inc.	June 25, 1943	Minnesota
Kennometal, Inc.	June 25, 1943	Pennsylvania
Kimberly Clark Corporation	June 30, 1928	Delaware
KLA-Tencor Corp.	July 9, 1975	Delaware
Kysor Industrial Corporation	July 1, 1925	Michigan
(Merged parent s/s August 15, 1969, Delaware)		
Lamar Advertising Co.	July 16, 1999	Delaware
LeHigh Valley Industries, Inc.	June 29, 1928	Delaware
Leslie Fay, Inc.	June 29, 1959	New York
Liberty Acquisition	June 27, 2007	Delaware
Lionel Corporation	July 22, 1918	New York
Lockheed Aircraft Corporation	June 21, 1932	California
Lomas & Nettleton Mtg. SBI Dec of Trust	June 26, 1969	Massachusetts
Louisiana-Pacific Corporation	July 20, 1972	Louisiana
Louisville Gas & Electric Company	July 2, 1913	Kentucky
Lynch Communications Systems, Inc.	July 1, 1950	California
(Merged parent s/s April 15, 1954, Delaware)		
Mallory (P.R.) & Co., Inc.	July 1, 1935	Delaware
Malone & Hyde	July 13, 1911	Tennessee
Marriott Corporation	July 10, 1929	Delaware
Massey-Ferguson, Ltd.	July 22, 1891	Canada
Mays (J.W.), Inc.	July 6, 1927	New York
McDonnell-Douglas Corporation	July 6, 1939	Maryland
McDonough Company	July 15, 1931	Delaware

Company	Date of Birth	Place of Birth
MEI Corporation	June 21, 1939	Minnesota
(Merged parent s/s March 21, 1969, Delaware)		
Merck & Company	June 27, 1927	New Jersey
Mesabi Trust SBI	July 18, 1961	Minnesota
Minnesota Mining & Mfg. Co.	June 25, 1929	Delaware
Mission Insurance Group	July 19, 1960	California
Molecula Vaccines, Inc.	June 29, 1987	Delaware
Monarch Machine Tool Company	June 24, 1909	Ohio
Morrison-Knudsen Co., Inc.	July 19, 1932	Delaware
Mountain States Tel & Tel	July 17, 1911	Colorado
(Controlled by AT&T)		
Nabisco Brands	July 6, 1981	Delaware
National Air Lines, Inc.	July 8, 1937	Florida
National Aviation & Tech.	June 28, 1928	New York
National Detroit Corporation	July 14, 1972	Delaware
National Homes Corporation	June 25, 1940	Indiana
National Medical Care, Inc.	June 25, 1968	Massachusetts
(Merged parent s/s July 28, 1969, Delaware)		
National Starch & Chemical Corp.	July 5, 1928	Delaware
Neptune International Corporation	June 25, 1892	New Jersey
Northern California Savings & Loan	July 1, 1969	California
Norton Simon, Inc.	July 17, 1968	Delaware
(Merged Canada Dry-Hunt Foods-McCall Corp.)		
Ohio Edison Company	July 5, 1930	Ohio
Overseas Shipholding Group	July 22, 1969	Delaware
Pope & Talbot, Inc.	June 29, 1940	California
Puget Sound Power & Light	August 8, 1912	Massachusetts
(Reincorporated November 6, 1960, Wshington)		
Pullman, Inc.	June 21, 1927	Delaware
Quaker State Oil Refining Corporation	June 23, 1931	Delaware
Raybestos Manhattan, Inc.	July 5, 1929	New Jersey
(Merged parent s/s February 24, 1976, Connecticut)		
Reece Corporation	June 28, 1948	Massachusetts

Company	Date of Birth	Place of Birth
Reliance Group, Inc.	June 24, 1965	Delaware
Reynolds Metal Company	July 18, 1928	Delaware
DEDCO, Inc.	July 21, 1950	Texas
Service Corporation International	July 5, 1962	Texas
Sherwin Williams Company	July 18, 1884	Ohio
Signal Co., Inc.	June 25, 1928	Delaware
Smith Kline Corporation	July 1, 1967	Florida
South Carolina Electric & Gas	July 19, 1924	South Carolina
Southeast Banking Corporation	July 1, 1967	Florida
Southern California Edison	July 6, 1909	California
Southland Royalty Company	June 26, 1924	Delaware
Sperry Rand Corporation	June 30, 1955	Delaware
Springs Mills, Inc.	July 2, 1966	Delaware
Stanley Works	July 1, 1852	Connecticut
Stone & Webster, Inc.	June 25, 1929	Delaware
Storer Broadcasting Company	July 11, 1927	Ohio
Sutro Mortgage Investment Trust Dec of Trust	June 26, 1962	California
Thomas & Betts Corporation	June 22, 1917	New Jersey
Tiger International	June 25, 1945	Delaware
(Merged parent Flying Tiger s/s July 28, 1969, Delaware)		
Toledo Edison Company	July 1, 1901	Ohio
Tootsie Roll Industries, Inc.	June 28, 1919	Virginia
Twentieth Century Fox Film Corp.	July 22, 1952	Delaware
Unilever, Ltd.	June 21, 1894	UK
Union Camp Corporation	July 12, 1956	Virginia
UAL Inc.	July 20, 1934	Delaware
(Merged parent United Airlines s/s December 30, 1968, Delaware)		
United Nuclear Corporation	July 16, 1954	Delaware
United Refining Company	June 23, 1902	Pennsylvania
United Technologies Corporation	July 21, 1934	Delaware
U.V. Industries, Inc.	July 15, 1965	Maine
Valley Industries	July 16, 1961	New Jersey
Venice Industries, Inc.	July 15, 1968	Delaware

Company	Date of Birth	Place of Birth
Verizon Communications	June 30, 2000	Delaware
Virginia Electric & Power Co.	June 29, 1909	Virginia
Ward Foods, Inc.	June 21, 1912	New York
Washington Gas & Light Company	July 8, 1848	Washington DC
Wean United, Inc.	June 28, 1929	Ohio
West Virginia Company Corporation	July 10, 1899	Delaware
Wheeling Pittsburgh Steel Corp.	June 21, 1920	Delaware
Wieboldt Stores, Inc.	June 26, 1907	Illinois
Wisconsin Public Service Corpor tion	July 17, 1883	Wisconsin
Wometco Enterprises, Inc.	July 14, 1925	Florida
Woods Corporation	July 13, 1959	Delaware
(Merged parent Woods Industries s/s June 16, 1966, Delaware)		
Zenith Radio Corporation	July 5, 1923	Illinois
(Merged parent s/s March 31, 1958, Delaware)		

Leo Stocks (July 23-August 22)

Company	Date of Birth	Place of Birth
Alaska Interstate Company	August 11, 1966	Alaska
American Distilling Company	July 29, 1933	Maryland
American Investment Company	August 1, 1925	Delaware
American Motors Corporation	July 29, 1916	Maryland
Amicor, Inc.	August 21, 1958	Florida
(Merged parent s/s May 20, 1974, Delaware)		
Arcata National Corporation	August 2, 1939	California
ATI Technologies	August 20, 1985	Ontario, Canada
Bank of America	July 31, 1998	Delaware
Belco Petroleum Corporation	July 28, 1959	Delaware
Block (H&R), Inc.	July 27, 1955	Missouri
Broadcom Corp.	August 16, 1991	California
B. T. Mortgage Investors Dec of Trust	August 5, 1970	Massachusetts
Carriers & General Corporation	August 6, 1929	Maryland
Central & Southwest Corporation	July 31, 1925	Delaware
Chicago Bridge & Iron Company	August 8, 1889	Illinois

Company	Date of Birth	Place of Birth
C.H. Robinson Worldwide	August 11, 1997	Delaware
Colgate-Palmolive Company	July 25, 1923	Delaware
Collins Foods International, Inc.	August 13, 1968	California
Copperweld Corporation	August 16, 1915	Pennsylvania
Curtiss-Wright Corporation	August 9, 1929	Delaware
Dan River Mills, Inc.	August 20, 1909	Virginia
Data Point Corporation	July 26, 1968	Texas
(Merged parent s/s September 20, 1976, Delaware)		
Diversified Industries, Inc.	August 9, 1967	Delaware
Entex, Inc.	July 29, 1966	Texas
Esterline Corporation	August 22, 1967	Delaware
Exxon	August 5, 1882	New Jersey
Farah Mfg. Co., Inc.	July 31, 1947	Texas
First Union Real Estate Equity & Mortgage Investments SBI Dec of Trust	August 1, 1961	Ohio
FMC Corporation	August 10, 1928	Delaware
Foremost McKesson, Inc.	August 4, 1928	Maryland
Gardner Denver Company	August 17, 1927	Delaware
Garmin, Ltd.	July 24, 2000	Cayman Islands
Gas Service Company	August 22, 1925	Delaware
Gulf Oil Corporation	August 9, 1922	Pennsylvania
Gulf Resources & Chemical Corp	August 1, 1951	Delaware
(Merged parent s/s April 24, 1956, Delaware)		
Harcourt-Brace/Jovanovich	July 29, 1919	New York
Heinz (H.J.) Co.	July 27, 1900	Pennsylvania
Hewlett Packard Co.	August 18, 1947	California
Hillenbrand Industries, Inc.	August 7, 1969	Indiana
Humana, Inc.	July 28, 1964	Delaware
Huyck Corp.	August 8, 1907	New York
IAC/Interactive	July 28, 1986	Delaware
Inco, Ltd.	July 25, 1916	Canada
(Reorganized December 31, 1928, New Jersey)		

Company	Date of Birth	Place of Birth
Ingredient Technology	August 18, 1905	New York
(Merged parent s/s April 18, 1978, Delaware)		
Japan Fund, Inc.	August 10, 1961	Maryland
Jim Walter Corporation	August 22, 1955	Florida
Kansas City Power & Light Company	July 29, 1922	Missouri
Kaufman & Broad, Inc.	July 26, 1961	Maryland
Keller Industries, Inc.	August 1, 1951	Florida
Kentucky Utilities Company	August 17, 1912	Kentucky
Knight Ridder News, Inc.	August 6, 1941	Ohio
Lubrizol Corporation	July 3, 1928	Ohio
Marathon Oil Company	August 1, 1887	Ohio
Marley Company	August 15, 1952	Delaware
Martha Stewart	July 26, 1999	Delaware
Maxim Integrated Products	August 19, 1987	Delaware
Maytag Company	August 15, 1925	Delaware
Mercury Interactive Corp.	July 26, 1989	Delaware
Meredith Corporation	August 9, 1905	Iowa
Metropolitan Edison Company	July 24, 1922	Pennsylvania
Mobil Oil Corporation	August 10, 1882	New York
(Merged parent s/s March 3, 1976, Delaware)		
Mohawk Data Sciences	August 16, 1964	New York
National Service Industries, Inc	August 20, 1928	Delaware
Niagara Mohawk Power Corporation	July 31, 1937	New York
North Indiana Public Service Company	August 2, 1912	Indiana
Oakite Products, Inc.	August 14, 1926	New York
Ogden Corporation	August 4, 1939	Delaware
Olin Corporation	August 13, 1892	Virginia
Outlet Company	July 30, 1925	Rhode Island
Pacific Lumber Company	August 11, 1905	Maine
PetSmart	August 11, 1986	Delaware
Phelps Dodge Corporation	August 10, 1885	New York
Phillips Van Huesen Corp.	August 14, 1919	New York
(Merged parent s/s April 2, 1976, Delaware)		

Company	Date of Birth	Place of Birth
Ponderosa System, Inc.	August 12, 1968	Delaware
Portland General Electric	July 25, 1930	Oregon
Potlatch Corporation	August 10, 1955	Delaware
Public Service Electric & Gas Co.	July 25, 1924	New Jersey
Public Service Co. of New Hampshire	August 16, 1926	New Hampshire
Richardson-Merrell, Inc.	August 12, 1933	Delaware
Sanders Associates, Inc.	July 24, 1951	Massachusetts
Saul (BF) Real Estate Investment Trust	July 31, 1962	Washington DC
Savannah Electric & Power Co.	August 5, 1921	Georgia
Schering-Plough Corp.	July 28, 1970	New Jersey
Seaboard Coastline Indust. Inc.	August 1, 1968	Virginia
(Merged parent s/s May 9, 1969, Delaware)		
Smurfit-Stone Container Co.	August 4, 1989	Delaware
Southwestern Public Service Co.	August 17, 1921	N.Mex.
Starret (L.S.) Co.	July 29, 192?	Massachusetts
Stauffer Chemical Co.	July 24, 1953	Delaware
Sterndent Corp.	July 26, 1965	New York
Stokely-Van Camp, Inc.	August 13, 1936	Indiana
Stop & Shop Companies	August 15, 1925	Massachusetts
Storage Technology Corp.	August 11, 1969	Delaware
Technicare Corp.	July 26, 1960	Massachusetts
(Merged parent BCC Industries s/s December 5, 1972, Delaware)		
Tobin Packing Co., Inc.	July 30, 1942	Delaware
Triangle Pacific Corp.	August 18, 1943	New York
Viacom International, Inc.	August 20, 1970	Delaware
(Merged parent s/s March 11, 1975, Ohio)		
Whirlpool Corp.	August 10, 1955	Delaware
Whittaker Corp.	July 31, 1947	California
Whole Foods Market	August 15, 1978	Texas
Whyly Corp.	July 23, 1963	Texas
(Merged parent University Computer s/s April 3, 1972, Delaware)		

Company	Date of Birth	Place of Birth

Virgo Stocks (August 23-September 22)

Company	Date of Birth	Place of Birth
Aetna Life & Casualty Co.	August 25, 1967	Connecticut
Aluminum Co. of America	September 18, 1888	Pennsylvania
American Heritage Life Ins. Corp. Inc.	September 11, 1956	Florida
(Acquired parent American Heritage Life Ins. November 30, 1968, Florida)		
American Water Works Co., Inc.	August 28, 1936	Delaware
Ameriprise Finance, Inc.	September 15, 1941	Delaware
Ameron, Inc.	September 13, 1961	California
AMF, Inc.	September 15, 1941	New Jersey
Anchor Hocking Corporation	September 13, 1928	Delaware
Bache Group, Inc.	September-17-74 Delaware	
Bluebird, Inc.	September 9, 1929	New York
(Merged parent s/s May 4, 1970, Pennsylvania)		
Brooklyn Union Gas	September 9, 1895	New York
Buffalo Forge Co.	September 5, 1901	New York
Cameron-Brown Investment Corp.	September 4, 1969	Massachusetts
Carlisle Corp.	September 12, 1917	Delaware
Genco Instruments	September 2, 1948	Delaware
Central Illinois Public Service	September 1, 1923	Illinois
Central Telephone & Utilities Corp.	September 22, 1909	Kansas
Cessna Aircraft Co.	September 7, 1927	Kansas
Chase Convertible Fund of Boston	September 9, 1971	Massachusetts
Cities Service Co.	September 2, 1910	Delaware
Clevepak Corp.	September 6, 1962	Delaware
Central States Gas Corp.	September 7, 1972	Delaware
CNA	September 8, 1967	Delaware
Coca Cola Company (The)	September 5, 1919	Delaware
Community Psychiatric Center	September 4, 1962	California
(Merged parent s/s April 11, 1972, Nevada)		
Compugraphic Corp.	September 14, 1960	Massachusetts
Consolidated Foods Corp.	September 4, 1941	Maryland

Company	Date of Birth	Place of Birth
Consolidated Freightways, Inc.	August 28, 1929	Washington
(Merged parent s/s August 13, 1958, Delaware)		
Copeland Corporation	September 14, 1933	Michigan
(Merged parent s/s July 26, 1971, Delaware)		
Crown Zellerbach Corp.	August 28, 1924	Nevada
Cunningham Drug Stores, Inc.	September 1, 1931	Michigan
Curtis Noll Corp.	September 9, 1934	Ohio
Damon Corp.	September 1, 1961	Delaware
Dick (A.B.) Co.	September 14, 1971	Delaware
Digital Equipment Corporation	August 23, 1957	Massachusetts
DuPont de Nemours & Co.	September 4, 1915	Delaware
Eaton Corp., Inc.	August 28, 1916	Ohio
Equitable Life Mortgage Dec of Trust	September 15, 1970	Massachusetts
Federal Company	September 5, 1925	Delaware
Florida Steel Corp.	August 24, 1956	Florida
Fort Dearborn Income Securi ies, Inc.	September 20, 1972	Delaware
Georgia Pacific Corp.	September 22, 1927	Georgia
Geosource, Inc.	September 8, 1972	Delaware
Gillette Co.	September 10, 1917	Delaware
Goodyear Tire & Rubber Co.	August 29, 1898	Ohio
Google, Inc.	September 4, 1998	California
Greyhound Corporation	September 20, 1926	Delaware
(Merged parent s/s October 27, 1977, Ar izona)		
Gulf States Utilities Co.	August 25, 1925	Texas
Honda Motor Co., Ltd.	September 24, 1948	Japan
Hunt International Resources	August 26, 1885	Colorado
(Parent Colo. Milling & Elevator s/s Great West United April 4, 1967, Delaware; Great West United s/s Hunt Intl. Resources February 2, 1977, Delaware)		
I.C. Industries	August 31, 1962	Delaware
International Aluminum	September 19, 1963	California
Interpublic Group Companies	September 18, 1930	Delaware
(Parent McKann-Erickson)		
Juniper Networks	September 10, 1997	Delaware

Company	Date of Birth	Place of Birth
Katy Industries, Inc.	August 24, 1967	Delaware
Kellwood Company	August 28, 1961	Delaware
LAM Research	September 8, 1989	Delaware
Lanier Business Products	September 1, 1959	Georgia
Lee Enterprises	September 22, 1950	Delaware
Lehman Corp.	September 11, 1929	Delaware
Loew's Corporation	August 26, 1954	New York
(Reincorporated parent Loew's Theatres, Inc.	November 12, 1969, Delaware)	
Ludlow Corp.	August 25, 1928	Massachusetts
Manufacturers-Hanover Corp.	September 18, 1905	New York
(Merged partner s/s December 5, 1968, Delaware)		
Mary Kay Cosmetics	August 28, 1963	Texas
Masonite Corp.	September 1, 1925	Delaware
McNeil Corp.	September 8, 1932	Ohio
Metromedia, Inc.	August 23, 1955	Delaware
Microsoft Corp.	September 22, 1993	Delaware
Miller-Wohl, Inc.	September 16, 1932	Delaware
Molex, Inc.	September 8, 1972	Delaware
Moore & McCormack Res. Inc.	September 12, 1927	Delaware
National Gypsum Co.	August 29, 1925	Delaware
Owens-Illinois, Inc.	September 3, 1903	New Jersey
(Merged parent s/s December 16, 1907, New Jersey)		
Penn-Dixi Industries, Inc.	September 16, 1926	Delaware
Penwalt Corp.	September 12, 1950	Pennsylvania
Pepsi Co., Inc.	September 18, 1919	Delaware
Pertee Computer Corp.	September 11, 1967	California
(Merged parent s/s July 1, 1976, Delaware)		
Philips Industries, Inc.	August 29, 1912	Ohio
(Reincorporated September 12, 1957, Ohio)		
Playboy Enterprises, Inc.	August 31, 1964	Delaware
Pneumo Corp.	August 27, 1959	Delaware
Polaroid Corp.	September 13, 1937	Delaware
PPG Industries, Inc.	August 24, 1883	Pennsylvania

Company	Date of Birth	Place of Birth
Prime Computer, Inc.	September 16, 1971	Massachusetts
(Merged parent ICS, Inc. s/s June 9, 1972, Delaware)		
Public Service Co. of Colorado	August 25, 1969	Colorado
Public Service Co. of Indiana	September 6, 1941	Indiana
Quaker Oats Co.	September 21, 1901	New Jersey
Qualcomm, Inc.	September 11, 1991	Delaware
Rexham Corp.	September 16, 1971	Delaware
Royal Crown Cola Co.	September 8, 1928	Delaware
R.T.E. Corp.	September 16, 1955	Wisconsin
Safeguard Industries, Inc.	September 11, 1953	Pennsylvania
St. Louis-San Francisco Ry. Co.	August 24, 1916	Missouri
SCA Services. Inc.	August 25, 1969	Delaware
Seaboard World Airlines. Inc.	September 12, 1946	Delaware
Skil Corporation	August 26, 1937	Delaware
Spartan Food Systems, Inc.	September 6, 1961	South Carolina
Squibb Corporation	August 24, 1967	Delaware
Studebaker-Worthington. Inc.	September 1, 1909	Michigan
Sun Microsystems	September 17, 1986	Delaware
Tappan Co.	September 13, 1918	Ohio
Technicolor. Inc.	September 12, 1922	Delaware
Texaco, Inc.	August 26, 1926	Delaware
Texas Oil & Gas Corporation	September 19, 1955	Delaware
Texas Utilities Co.	September 4, 1945	Texas
Tonka Corp.	September 18, 1946	Minnesota
Triangle Industries, Inc.	August 30, 1939	Delaware
Twin Disc	September 12, 1918	Wisconsin
Union Corporation (The)	August 23, 1938	New Jersey
United Energy Resources, Inc.	September 3, 1937	Delaware
(Merged parent s/s United Gas Pipeline June 10, 1976, Delaware)		
Univer Corp. (Formerly V.W.R. Unite)	September 16, 1966	Delaware
U.S. Home Corp.	August 26, 1959	Delaware
U.S. Steel	September 10, 1965	Delaware

Company	Date of Birth	Place of Birth
Utah Power & Light	September 6, 1912	Maine
(Merged parent s/s May 5, 1976, Utah)		
Wachovia Corp., Inc.	September 19, 1968	North Carolina
(Bank chartered June 16, 1879)		
West Point Pepperell, Inc.	August 29, 1955	Georgia

Libra Stocks (September 23–October 22)

Company	Date of Birth	Place of Birth
Abercrombie & Fitch	September 26, 1996	New York
Air Products & Chemicals, Inc.	October 1, 1940	Michigan
Allied Products Corp.	October 6, 1937	Michigan
(Merged parent s/s November 21, 1967, Michigan)		
Allied Maintenance Corp.	October 13, 1944	New York
American Brands, Inc.	October 19, 1904	New Jersey
American Medical Inn, Inc.	October 19, 1956	California
(Merged parent Medical Labs Inc., s/s June 25, 1976, Delaware)		
Apple	October 15, 2004	Delaware
Armstrong Rubber Co.	September 24, 1940	Connecticut
Ashland Oil, Inc.	October 22, 1936	Kentucky
Atlantic City Electric Co.	October 4, 1907	New Jersey
Baxter Travenol Labs	October 19, 1931	Delaware
Bed Bath & Beyond	October 5, 1971	New York
Belden Corporation	September 25, 1902	Idaho
(Merged parent s/s March 11, 1975, Delaware)		
Belding-Heminway	October 1, 1947	Delaware
Black & Decker Mfg. Co.	September 27, 1910	Missouri
Carborundum Co.	September 28, 1891	Pennsylvania
(Merged parent s/s October 22, 1936, Delaware)		
Carson, Pirie Scott & Co.	October 9, 1969	Delaware
Carter Wallace, Inc.	September 23, 1937	Missouri
(Merged parent s/s June 25, 1968, Delaware)		
Citizens & Southern Corp.	October 2, 1968	Delaware
Cleveland Electric Illuminating	September 29, 1892	Ohio

Company	Date of Birth	Place of Birth
Columbia Gas System, Inc.	September 30, 1926	Delaware
Commonwealth Edison Co.	October 17, 1913	Illinois
Comverse Technology, Inc.	October 4,1 984	New York
ConAgra	September 29, 1919	Nebraska
(Merged parent s/s December 5, 1975, Delaware)		
Congoleum	October 21, 1927	Maine
(Merged parent Bath Iron Works May 11, 1967, Delaware)		
Conrac Corporation	October 7, 1935	New York
Continental Illinois Properties Dec of Trust	September 23, 1971	California
Continental Oil Co.	October 8, 1920	Delaware
Cowles Communication, Inc.	October 2, 1919	Iowa
(Merged parent s/s October 14, 1936, Iowa)		
Crocker National Corp.	October 7, 1968	Delaware
CPC International, Inc.	September 30, 1958	New Jersey
(Merged parent s/s May 11, 1959, Delaware)		
Dana Corp.	October 12, 1916	Virginia
Dell, Inc.	October 22, 1987	Delaware
Del Monte Corp.	October 19, 1916	New York
Deltona	September 24, 1962	Delaware
Disney (Walt) Productions	September 29, 1938	California
Donaldson Lufkin & Jenrette, Inc.	October 20, 1959	Delaware
Emerson Electric Co.	September 24, 1890	Missouri
Empire District Electric Co.	October, 16 1909	Kansas
Equimark Corp.	October 3, 1968	Pennsylvania
FedEx Corp.	October 2, 1997	Delaware
Ferro Corporation	October 13, 1919	Ohio
Fieldcrest Mills, Inc.	September 25, 1953	Delaware
First Virginia Bankshares Corp.	October 21, 1949	Virginia
Freeport Minerals	September 30, 1913	Delaware
GCA	October 15, 1958	Massachusetts
(Merged parent s/s July 20, 1960, Delaware)		
General American Investors Co. Inc.	October 15, 1928	Delaware
General Motors Corp.	October 13, 1916	Delaware

Company	Date of Birth	Place of Birth
General Tire & Rubber Co.	September 29, 1915	Ohio
Global Marine Inc.	October 7, 1964	Delaware
Gould National Batteries, Inc.	October 15, 1928	Delaware
Great Northern Wekoosa	October 17, 1898	Maine
Hammermill Paper Co.	October 18, 1916	Pennsylvania
Hancock (John) Income Securities Corp.	October 20, 1972	Maryland
Harte Hanks	October 1, 1970	Delaware
Hawaiian Electric Co., Inc.	October 13, 1891	Hawaii
Hercules, Inc.	October 18, 1912	Delaware
Houston Industries	October 5, 1976	Texas
Iowa Power & Light Co.	October 22, 1924	Iowa
Itek Corp.	September 26, 1957	Massachusetts
(Merged parent s/s February 10, 1960, Delaware)		
I.U. International	October 8, 1924	Maryland
KLM Royal Dutch Airlines	October 7, 1919	Netherlands
Koppers Co., Inc.	September 30, 1944	Delaware
Linear Technology Corp.	October 20, 2000	Delaware
Longs Drug Stores	October 4, 1946	California
Macke Co.	October 15, 1935	Delaware
Mapco, Inc.	October 3, 1958	Delaware
Marathon Mfg. Co.	September 24, 1959	Maryland
(Merged parent s/s February 6, 1969, Delaware)		
Marine Midland Banks Inc.	September 23, 1929	Delaware
Martin-Marietta Corp.	October 10, 1961	Maryland
Maryland Cup Corp	October 1, 1926	Maryland
Metro-Goldwyn-Mayer, Inc.	October 18, 1919	Delaware
Motorola, Inc.	September 25, 1928	Illinois
National Mine Service Co.	September 23, 1919	West Virginia
New England Tel & Tel Co.	October 19, 1883	New York
NLT	September 30, 1968	Tennessee
Norlin Corp.	October 6, 1937	Bahamas
(Reincorporated June 2, 1969, Panama)		
North American Philips Corp.	October 16, 1959	Delaware

Company	Date of Birth	Place of Birth
Outboard Marine Corp.	September 30, 1936	Delaware
Overnite Transportation Co.	October 9, 1947	Virginia
Pacific Gas & Electric Co.	October 10, 1905	California
Parker Drilling Co.	September 23, 1954	Oklahoma
(Merged parent s/s August 4, 1970, Delaware)		
Pillsbury Co.	September 25, 1935	Delaware
PNB Mtg. & Realty Investors SBI Dec of Trust	October 8, 1970	Maryland
R.C.A. Corporation	October 17, 1919	Delaware
Reading & Bates Offshore Drilling Co.	October 19, 1955	Delaware
Republic Mortgage Investors Dec of Trust	October 3, 1968	Massachusetts
Rio Grande Industries, Inc.	October 1, 1968	Delaware
Robins (A.H.) Co., Inc.	September 24, 1948	Virginia
Rohr Industries, Inc.	October 18, 1949	California
(Merged parent s/s August 8, 1969, Delaware)		
Roper Corp.	October 14, 1963	Delaware
Sea Containers, Inc.	October 16, 1965	New York
Servomation Corp.	October 18, 1960	Delaware
Shell Transport & Trading Co., Ltd.	October 18, 1887	UK
Skaggs Companies, Inc.	October 6, 1965	Delaware
Smuckers (J.M.) Co.	September 26, 1921	Ohio
Soo Line Railroad Co.	October 19, 1949	Minnesota
Southwest Forest Industries, Inc.	October 1, 1935	Nevada
Suave Shoe Corp.	September 28, 1960	Florida
Sunstrand Corp.	October 19, 1910	Illinois
(Merged parent s/s December 15, 1966, Delaware)		
Technicon Corp.	October 9, 1969	Delaware
Telecor, Inc.	September 29, 1969	Delaware
Texfi Industries, Inc.	October-16-63	Delaware
Times-Mirror	October 6, 1884	California
Trans America Corp.	October 11, 1928	Delaware
TransContinental Gas Pipeline Corp.	October 5, 1948	Delaware
Trinity Industries, Inc.	October 17, 1933	Texas
Tri-South Mortgage Investors SBI Dec of Trust	September 30, 1970	Massachusetts

Company	Date of Birth	Place of Birth
Union Oil of California	October 17, 1890	California
United Industrial Corp.	October 22, 1951	California

(Merged parent s/s September 14, 1959, Delaware)

U.S. & Foreign Securities Corp.	October 9, 1924	Maryland
Vestaur Securities, Inc.	October 10, 1972	Delaware
Waste Management, Inc.	September 23, 1968	Delaware
Western Airlines	October 1, 1928	Delaware
Western Bancorp	September 27, 1957	Delaware
Wickes Corp.	October 3, 1947	Michigan

(Merged parent s/s March 17, 1971, Delaware)

Wrigley Company	October 19, 1927	Delaware

Scorpio Stocks (October 23–November 21)

Acme Cleveland Corp.	November 17, 1916	Ohio
Air Products & Chemicals	November 13, 1961	Pennsylvania
Alabama Power Company	November 10, 1927	Alabama
Allstate	November 5, 1992	Delaware
Amerace Corp.	October 25, 1946	Delaware
American Air Filter Co., Inc.	October 26, 1925	Delaware
American Broadcasting Co.	November 15, 1949	New York
American District Telegraph Co.	November 1, 1901	New Jersey
American Family Corp.	November 17, 1955	Georgia

(Acquired all stock of American Family Life Assurance Co. April 27, 1973, Georgia)

American Sterilizer Co.	October 28, 1902	Pennsylvania
AMGEN	October 31, 1986	Delaware
Anixter Bros. Inc.	October 25, 1967	Delaware
Applied Magnetics Corp.	October 28, 1957	California
Applied Materials	November 10, 1917	California
Atlas Corp.	October 31, 1936	Delaware
Baker Hughes	November 3, 1986	Delaware
Bank of America Corporation	November 1, 1930	California

(Merged parent s/s October 7, 1968, Delaware; also see Leo stocks)

Company	Date of Birth	Place of Birth
Banner Industries, Inc. November 19, 1928	Delaware	
Bearings, Inc.	November 19, 1928	Delaware
Belton-Dickinson & Co.	November 13, 1906	New Jersey
Best Products Co., Inc.	October 29, 1969	Virginia
BIOGEN IDEC, Inc.	November 12, 2003	Delaware
Braniff International	November 3, 1930	Oklahoma
(Merged parent s/s August 31, 1966, Nevada; merged parent s/s November 1, 1971, Nevada)		
B.F.I.; Inc.	October 1, 1949	Texas
(Merged Browning-Ferris Industries October 26, 1970, Delaware)		
Bucyrus-Erie Company	November 3, 1927	Delaware
Burns (R.L.) Corp.	November 17, 1969	New York
Carpenter Technology Corp.	November 1, 1904	New Jersey
Carrier Corp.	October 31, 1930	Delaware
Central Soya Co.	November 2, 1934	Indiana
Chemical New York Corp.	October 28, 1968	Delaware
Chesapeake Corp. of Virginia	October 25, 1918	Virginia
Chock Full O'Nuts	November 7, 1932	New York
Cigna Corp.	November 3, 1981	Delaware
Cincinnati Milacron, Inc.	November 21, 1922	Ohio
Cintas Corp.	November 13, 1986	Washington
CI Realty Investments SBI Dec of Trust	November 10, 1971	Massachusetts
City Investing Company	December 2, 1904	New York
(Merged parent s/s February 7, 1968, Delaware)		
Colt Industries, Inc.	November 11, 1911	Pennsylvania
(Merged parent s/s October 17, 1968, Delaware; merged parent s/s May 6, 1976, Pennsylvania)		
Combustion Engineering, Inc.	October 25, 1912	Delaware
Consolidated Edison Co. of New York	November 10, 1884	New York
Continental Illinois Corp.	November 14, 1968	Delaware
Core Industries, Inc.	November 16, 1964	Nevada
CSX	November 1, 1980	Virginia
Current Income Shares	November 15, 1972	Delaware

Company	Date of Birth	Place of Birth
Dean Witter Reynolds Organization	November 9, 1973	Delaware
Denver & Rio Grande Western R.R.	November 15, 1920	Delaware
Diamond M Company	November 10, 1958	Texas
(Merged parent s/s April 17, 1972, Delaware)		
Dutch Boy, Inc.	November 3, 1933	Pennsylvania
Eastman Kodak Co.	October 25, 1901	New Jersey
Electronics Associates	October 31, 1945	New Jersey
Fairchild Industries	November 4, 1936	Missouri
Far West Financial, Inc.	November 13, 1959	Delaware
Filmways	November 21, 1968	Delaware
Frigitronics, Inc.	October 30, 1967	Delaware
General Cinema Corp.	November 1, 1950	Delaware
General Refractories Co.	October 24, 1922	Pennsylvania
GENZYME Corp.	November 21, 1991	Massachusetts
Getty Oil Co.	November 10, 1928	Delaware
Gordon Jewelry Corp.	November 8, 1957	Delaware
Gray Drug Stores, Inc.	November 1, 1928	Ohio
Gulf & Western Industries	November 8, 1934	Michigan
Hancock (John) Investors, Inc.	October 26, 1970	Delaware
Heller (Walter E.) Intl.	November 20, 1919	Delaware
Merged parent s/s February 3, 1969, Delaware)		
Hershey Foods Corp.	October 24, 1927	Delaware
Homestake Mining Co.	November 5, 1877	California
Honeywell, Inc.	October 27, 1927	Delaware
Hudson Pulp & Paper Corp.	November 6, 1937	Maine
Imperial Corp. of America	November 9, 1956	California
Indianapolis Power & Light Co.	October 27, 1926	Indiana
Inland Steel	October 30, 1893	Illinois
(Reincorporated February 16, 1917, Delaware)		
Kerr McGee Corp.	November 9, 1932	Delaware
Lamson & Sessions Co.	November 5, 1883	Ohio
Leaseway Transportation Corp.	November 9, 1960	Delaware
Lexmark Intl., Inc.	November 15, 1985	Delaware

Company	Date of Birth	Place of Birth
Lincar Holdings, Inc.	November 2, 1990	Delaware
Lincoln Natl Direct Placement Fund	October 28, 1970	Delaware
Litton Industries, Inc.	November 2, 1953	Delaware
Lone Star Industries	November 12, 1919	Maine
(Merged parent s/s October 10, 1968, Delaware)		
L.T.V. Corp.	November 4, 1953	California
M.C.A., Inc.	November 10, 1958	Delaware
McGraw-Edison Co.	November 17, 1926	Delaware
Merrill Lynch	November 15, 1958	Delaware
(Merged parent sls March 27, 1973, Delaware)		
Mesta Machine Co.	November 21, 1898	Pennsylvania
Missouri Public Service Co.	November 20, 1936	Delaware
(Merged parent s/s May 31, 1950, Missouri)		
Modern Merchandising	October 23, 1968	Minnesota
Mutual of Omaha Interest Shares, Inc.	November 3, 1971	Nebraska
National Can Corp.	November 20, 1929	Delaware
(Reincorporated March 16, 1937, Delaware, on merger of McKeesport Tin Plate Corp., the parent company; name changed back to National Can Corp.)		
National Presto Industries	November 10, 1905	Wisconsin
National Steel Corp.	November 7, 1929	Delaware
Natomas Co.	November 13, 1928	California
Network Appliance	November 1, 2001	Delaware
North Amer. Mtge. Investors SBI Dec of Trust	November 1, 1968	Massachusetts
N.Y. State Electric & Gas Co.	October 28, 1852	New York
Oklahoma Natural Gas Co.	November 10, 1933	Delaware
Olinkraft. Inc.	November 7, 1966	Delaware
Oneida, Ltd.	November 20, 1880	New York
Owens-Corning Fiberglass Corp.	October 31, 1938	Delaware
Paccar, Inc.	November 19, 1971	Delaware
Pacific Southwest Airlines	November 15, 1945	California
Pamida, Inc.	October 26, 1962	Nebraska
Paine Webber Inc.	October 26, 1973	Delaware
Philadelphia Electric Co.	October 31, 1929	Pennsylvania

Company	Date of Birth	Place of Birth
Philadelphia Suburban Co.	November 14, 1968	Pennsylvania
Pittsburgh Forging	October 28, 1927	Delaware
QLogic Corp.	November 16, 1992	Delaware
Questor	October 27, 1923	Delaware
Redman Industries, Inc.	November 14, 1960	Delaware
Reichold Chemicals, Inc.	November 5, 1930	Delaware
Revlon, Inc.	November 1, 1955	Delaware
Rosario Resources Corp.	November 17, 1880	New York
Ryan Homes, Inc.	November 12, 1948	Pennsylvania
St. Joseph Light & Power Co.	November 8, 1895	Missouri
Seafirst Corp.	October 24, 1973	Washington
SEars Holding	November 23, 2004	Delaware
Schlumberger, Ltd.	November 7, 1956	Netherlands
S.C.M. Corp.	October 30, 1924	New York
Scudder Duo-Vest Inc.	November 21, 1966	Delaware
Sheller Globe Corp.	November 14, 1946	Ohio
(Reincorporated February 23, 1929, Ohio)		
Sirius Satellite Radio	November 9, 1999	Delaware
Smith (A.O.) Corp.	November 11, 1916	New York
Southern Co.	November 9, 1945	?
Southern Natural Resources	October 30, 1935	Delaware
(Formerly Southern Natural Gas, merged parent s/s January 25, 1973 Delaware)		
South Jersey Industries, Inc.	November 12, 1969	New Jersey
Sperry & Hutchinson	October 25, 1900	New Jersey
Square D Co.	October 24, 1903	Michigan
Staley (A.E.) Mfg.	November 12, 1906	Delaware
Starbucks Corp.	November 4, 1985	Washington
Sterling Precision Corp.	October 24, 1955	Delaware
Stride Rite Corp.	November 4, 1919	Massachusetts
Superior Oil Co.	October 31, 1936	California
(Merged s/s parent February 18, 1963, Nevada)		
Sybron Corp.	November 1, 1965	New York

Company	Date of Birth	Place of Birth
Thiokol Corp.	November 18, 1930	Delaware
(Merged parent s/s September 28, 1973, Virginia)		
TransUnion Corp.	November 21, 1968	Delaware
UMET Trust SBI Dec of Trust	November 17, 1969	California
Unilever N.V.	November 9, 1927	Netherlands
Union Carbide Corp.	November 1, 1917	New York
United Jersey Banks	October 31, 1969	New Jersey
United Telecommunications	November 15, 1938	Kansas
US Life Corp.	November 15, 1966	New York
US Life Income Fund	October 27, 1972	Maryland
US Shoe Corp.	November 10, 1931	Ohio
Warner Lambert	November 8, 1920	Delaware
(Merged s/s parent November 1, 1976, Delaware)		
Xtra, Inc.	November 7, 1957	Massachusetts
Zapata Corp.	October 25, 1954	Delaware

Sagittarius Stocks (November 22-December 21)

Company	Date of Birth	Place of Birth
AlcoStandard	November 24, 1952	Ohio
Allegheny Power System, Inc.	December 11, 1925	Maryland
Allied Chemical Corp.	December 17, 1920	New York
American Bakeries Co.	December 1, 1924	Delaware
American Dual Vest Fund Inc.	December 2, 1966	Delaware
American Electric Power Co., Inc.	December 20, 1906	New York
Apache Corp.	December 6, 1954	Delaware
Arlen Realty & Development Corp.	November 23, 1970	New York
Ban Cal Tri-State Corp.	November 22, 1971	Delaware
Beckman Instruments, Inc.	November 26, 1934	California
Beech Aircraft	November 23, 1932	Kansas
(Merged parent s/s September 1, 1936, Delaware)		
Beker Industries Corp.	December 1, 1971	Delaware
Berkey Photo, Inc.	December 6, 1960	Delaware
Biomat	November 30, 1977	Indiana

Company	Date of Birth	Place of Birth
Campbell Soup Co.	November 23, 1922	New Jersey
Centex Corp.	November 27, 1968	Nevada
Champion Spark Plug Co.	December 5, 1938	Delaware
Cincinnati Milacron, Inc.	November 21, 1922	Ohio
Cisco Systems	December 10, 1984	California
Citicorp	December 4, 1967	Delaware
Citizens & Southern Realty SBI Dec of Trust	December 12, 1970	Maryland
City Investing Co.	December 2, 1904	New York
(Merged parent s/s October 31, 1967, Delaware)		
Clorox Co.	December 14, 1972	California
Cole National Corp.	December 2, 1949	Ohio
Community Public Service Co.	December 10, 1934	Delaware
(Merged parent s/s April 18, 1963, Texas)		
Continental Air Lines, Inc.	December 17, 1934	Nevada
Continental Telephone Corp.	December 16, 1960	Delaware
Crouse-Hinds Co.	November 30, 1903	New York
Crown Cork & Seal Co., Inc.	December 19, 1927	New York
Cutler-Hammer, Inc.	December 7, 1928	Delaware
Daniel Industries, Inc.	December 17, 1965	Texas
DiGiorgio Corp.	December 13, 1920	Delaware
Dow-Jones & Co., Inc.	November 23, 1949	Delaware
Duke Energy	November 27, 1963	Delaware
DuquesneLight Co.	November 25, 1912	Pennsylvania
El Paso Co.	November 28, 1928	Delaware
(Merged parent El Paso Natural Gas s/s February 27, 1974, Delaware)		
Eltra Corp.	December 16, 1895	New York
Ennis Business Forms, Inc.	December 10, 1909	Texas
Enserch	December 12, 1942	Texas
(Formerly Lone Star Gas)		
Esmark, Inc.	December 12, 1972	Delaware
(Merged Estech-Vickers-Swift & Co.)		
Equifax, Inc.	December 20, 1913	Georgia
Fairchild Camera & Instrument Corp.	November 23, 1927	Delaware

Company	Date of Birth	Place of Birth
Federated Department Stores, Inc.	November 25, 1929	Delaware
First Wisconsin Corp.	December 10. 1929	Wisconsin
Fleming Co., Inc.	December 6, 1915	Kansas
Fuqua Industries, Inc. December 12, 1929	Pennsylvania	
(Merged parent 2 for 1 split March 1, 1968, Delaware)		
Gannett Co., Inc.	December 19, 1923	New York
(Merged parent s/s February 28, 1972, Delaware)		
Gemini Fund, Inc.	November 23, 1966	Delaware
(Reincorporated January 10, 1973, Maryland)		
General Steel Industries	December 11, 1928	Delaware
Graniteville Co.	December 15, 1845	South Carolina
Great Northern Iron Ore Properties Trust	December 17, 1906	Minnesota
created Grumman Corp., December 6, 1929, New York		
Hardee's Food Systems, Inc.	December 7, 1960	North Carolina
Harris Intertype Corp.	December 6, 1926	Delaware
Heublein, Inc.	December 2, 1915	Connecticut
High Voltage Engineering Corp.	December 19, 1946	Massachusetts
H.M.W. Industries, Inc.	December 14, 1892	Pennsylvania
(Formerly Hamilton Watch Co.)		
I.C.N. Pharmaceuticals, Inc.	December 7, 1960	California
I.N.A. Corp.	December 4, 1967	Pennsylvania
Income & Capital Shares, Inc.	November 22, 1966	Massachusetts
Inspiration Consolidated Copper	December 18, 1911	Maine
Inter Capital Income Securities	December 21, 1972	Delaware
Inter Continental	December 11, 1970	Panama
International Flavors & Fragrances, Inc.	December 6, 1909	New York
International Multifoods	December 2, 1969	Delaware
International Tel & Tel	December 8, 1937	Delaware
(Merged parent ITT-Rayonier December 12, 1967, Delaware; former parent ITT)		
Itel Corp.	December 6, 1967	Delaware
Jonathan Logan, Inc.	December 13, 1954	Delaware
Jones & Laughlin Steel Corp.	December 19, 1922	Delaware
Kaiser Aluminum & Chemical Corp.	December 9, 1940	Delaware

Company	Date of Birth	Place of Birth
Kaiser Steel Corp.	December 1, 1941	Nevada
Kansas Gas & Electric Co.	December 11, 1909	West Virginia
(Reincorporation April 3, 1973, Kansas)		
Kellogg Co.	December 14, 1922	Delaware
Kirsch Co.	December 6, 1928	Michigan
Kraft Corp.	December 8, 1923	Delaware
Lear Siegler, Inc.	December 21, 1950	Delaware
Level3 Communications	December 10, 1985	Delaware
Lennar Corp.	November 24, 1969	Delaware
Levi Strauss	November 23, 1971	Delaware
(Merger of all Levi Strauss companies)		
Liberty Corp. (The)	November 27, 1967	South Caorlina
Liberty Loan Corp.	December 1, 1932	Delaware
Ligget Group	November 24, 1911	New Jersey
(Merger parent Ligget & Myers s/s April 22, 1968, Delaware)		
Masco Corp.	December 16, 1929	Michigan
Medenco	November 26, 1956	Delaware
Morgan (J.P.) & Co., Inc.	December 20, 1968	Delaware
Montana Power Co.	December 12, 1912	New Jersey
(Reincorporated April 19, 1961, Montana)		
Montgomery Str. Income Securities, Inc.	December 11, 1962	Delaware
Murray Ohio Mfg. Co.	December 4, 1919	Ohio
Natsushita Electric Industrial Co., Ltd.	December 15, 1935	Japan
National Fuel Gas Co.	December 8, 1902	New Jersey
N.I.C.O.R.	November 25, 1953	Illinois
(Merged parent Northern Illinois Gas Co. s/s January 12, 1976, Illinois)		
N.L. Industries	December 8, 1891	New Jersey
(Formerly National Lead Co.)		
Northern Central Railway Co.	December 16, 1854	Maryland, Penn.
Pacific American Income Shares, Inc.	December 21, 1972	Delaware
Penney (J.C.) Co., Inc.	December 15, 1924	Delaware
Pennsylvania Co.	December 13, 1958	Delaware
Perkin Elmer Corp.	December 13, 1939	Delaware

Company	Date of Birth	Place of Birth
Pixar	December 9, 1985	California
Publicker Industries, Inc.	December 16, 1913	Pennsylvania
Purex Corp., Ltd.	December 16, 1927	California
Ramada Inns, Inc.	December 16, 1955	Delaware
Revere Copper & Brass, Inc.	December 1, 1928	Maryland
Rockower Bros., Inc.	December 11, 1956	Pennsylvania
Rockwell International	December 6, 1928	Delaware
Rorer Group, Inc.	December 21, 1927	Pennsylvania
(Merged parent s/s July 1, 1968, Pennsylvania)		
Rowan Companies, Inc.	December 15, 1947	Delaware
Santa Fe Industries, Inc.	December 4, 1967	Delaware
Santa Fe Int. Corp.	December 19, 1946	California
(Schering merged with Plough Corporation July 28, 1970, New Jersey)		
Scott Fetzer Co.	November 30, 1917	Ohio
Scott Paper Co.	December 5, 1922	Pennsylvania
Shakespeare Co.	November 18, 1905	Michigan
(Reincorporated December 13, 1968, Delaware)		
Signode Corp.	December 19, 1928	Delaware
Simmons Co.	December 14, 1915	Delaware
Simplicity Pattern Co., Inc.	December 19, 1927	New York
Sonesta Intl Hotels	December 6, 1923	New York
Southern Union Co.	December 13, 1932	Delaware
Southland Corp.	December 10, 1924	Delaware
(Reincorporated November 21, 1961, Texas)		
State MutualInvestors SBI Dec of Trust	December 1, 1970	Massachusetts
State Mutual Securities, Inc.	December 11, 1972	Massachusetts
Stewart-Warner Corp.	December 20, 1912	Virginia
Surburban Propane Gas Corp.	November 27, 1945	New Jersey
Systron-Donner Corp.	December 10, 1956	California
Tampa Electric Company	December 2, 1899	Florida
Tesora Petroleum Corp.	December 14, 1939	California
(Merged parent s/s December 26, 1968, Delaware)		
Texas Gas Transmission Corp.	December 7, 1945	Delaware

Company	Date of Birth	Place of Birth
Thrifty Corp.	December 14, 1935	California
Time, Inc.	November 28, 1922	New York
Timken Roller Bearing Co.	December 16, 1904	Ohio
Union Electric Co.	November 22, 1922	Missouri
Universal Foods Corp.	December 4, 1882	Wisconsin
Upjohn Company	November 26, 1958	Delaware
U.S. Tobacco Co.	December 4, 1911	New Jersey
V.F. Corp.	December 4, 1899	Pennsylvania
Vornado, Inc.	December 3, 1941	Kansas
(Merged parent s/s April 15, 1965, Delaware)		
V.S.I. Corp.	December 2, 1907	Illinois
(Merged parent s/s August 18, 1967, Delaware)		
Vulcan Materials	November 24, 1956	New Jersey
Wabash, Inc.	December 7, 1947	Indiana
Wachovia Realty Investments SBI Dec of Trust	December 10, 1969	South Carolina
Watkins-Johnson Co.	December 6, 1957	California
Weis Markets, Inc.	December 18, 1924	Pennsylvania
Wheelabrator-Frye, Inc.	November 23, 1935	Delaware
Wheeling & Lake Erie R.R.	December 14, 1916	Ohio
Wilshire Oil Co. of Texas	December 7, 1951	Delaware
Woolworth (F.W.) Co.	December 15, 1911	New York
Wyle Laboratories	December 9, 1953	California
Zurn Industries, Inc.	December 20, 1927	Pennsylvania

Capricorn Stocks (December 22-January 19)

Company	Date of Birth	Place of Birth
Ahmanson (H.F.) & Co.	January 17, 1928	California
Aileen, Inc.	January 16, 1948	New York
Albertson's, Inc.	December 26, 1958	Nevada
(Merged parent s/s April 3, 1969, Delaware)		
Allen Group	January 13, 1928	Michigan
(Merged parent s/s May 1, 1969, Delaware)		
Amalgamated Sugar Co.	January 15, 1915	Utah

Company	Date of Birth	Place of Birth
Ambac Industries, Inc.	January 9, 1919	New York
Amcord Ins.	December 31, 1957	Delaware
AmFinance Systems, Inc.	December 31, 1947	Delaware
AMREP Corp.	December 27, 1955	Oklahoma
Anderson Clayton & Co.	December 31, 1921	Delaware
APL Corporation	January 12, 1959	New York
Armstrong Cork Co.	December 30, 1891	Pennsylvania
Arvin Industries, Inc.	December 31, 1921	Indiana
ATO, Inc.	December 27, 1963	Ohio
Ball Corp., Inc.	December 22, 1922	Indiana
Bank of Virginia, Inc.	January 11, 1962	Virginia
Bard (C.R.), Inc.	December 28, 1923	New York
(Merged parent s/s February 3, 1972, New Jersey)		
Barry Wright Ins.	January 3, 1946	Massachusetts
Bea Systems, Inc.	January 20, 1995	Delaware
Big Three Industrial Gas & Equip. Co.	January 16, 1956	Texas
Bliss & Laughlin Industries, Inc.	December 24, 1919	Delaware
Boston Edison Co.	January 8, 1886	Massachusetts
Brown Group, Inc.	January 2, 1913	New York
Brunswick Corp.	December 31, 1907	Delaware
Brush Wellman, Inc.	January 9, 1931	Ohio
Bunker Ramo	December 31, 1958	Delaware
Burlington Northern	January 12, 1961	Delaware
(Merger Northern-Pacific. Great Northern, Chicago Burlington & Quincy RR)		
Burroughs Corp.	January 16, 1905	Michigan
California Financial Corp.	December 29, 1958	Delaware
Career Education	January 5, 1994	Delaware
Cascade Natural Gas Corp.	January 2, 1953	Washington
Castle & Cooke. Inc.	December 29, 1894	Hawaii
Ceco Corporation	December 30, 1955	Delaware
Celonese Corp.	January 5, 1918	Delaware
Central Hudson Gas & Electric Corp.	December 31, 1926	New York
Central Louisiana Electric Co.	December 23, 1934	Louisiana

Company	Date of Birth	Place of Birth
Chemantron Corp.	December 29, 1933	Delaware
Chicago Pneumatic Tool Co.	December 28, 1901	New Jersey
Cities Service Company	September 2, 1910	Delaware
Clark Equipment Company	December 27, 1916	Michigan
(Merged parent s/s May 8, 1968, Delaware)		
Coachmen Industries. Inc.	December 31-64	Indiana
Codura Corp.	January 6, 1966	California
(Merged parent s/s May 26, 1972, Delaware)		
Columbus & Southern Ohio Electric Co.	December 26, 1906	Ohio
Columbia Pictures Industries, Inc.	January 10, 1924	New York
(Reincorporated October 14, 1969, Delaware)		
Continental Group. Inc.	January 17, 1913	New York
(Formerly Continental Can Corp.)		
Cooper Industries. Inc.	January 8, 1919	Ohio
Corning Glass Works	December 24, 1936	New York
Corron & Black Corp.	December 27, 1928	Delaware
Credithrift Financial. Inc.	December 22, 1927	Indiana
(Merged parent s/s February 26, 1974, Indiana)		
Delta Air Lines. Inc.	December 31, 1930	Louisiana
(Merged parent s/s March 16, 1967, Delaware)		
Detroit Edison Co.	January 17, 1903	New York
Diamond International Corp.	December 26, 1930	Delaware
Diamond Shamrock Corp.	December 28, 1928	Delaware
Dravo	December 31-36	Pennsylvania
Dun & Bradstreet, Inc.	December 23, 1930	Delaware
(Merged parent s/s February 6, 1973, Delaware)		
Eagle Picher Industries, Inc.	January 10, 1867	Ohio
Echlin Mfg. Co.	January 13, 1959	Connecticut
E Systems, Inc.	December 28, 1964	Delaware
Evans Products Co.	December 26, 1923	Delaware
Falcon Seaboard	December 27, 1948	Delaware
Falstaff Brewing Corp.	January 16, 1933	Delaware
Fastenal	December 24, 1968	Minnesota

Company	Date of Birth	Place of Birth
Federal Signal Corp.	January 9, 1905	New York
(Merged parent s/s January 31, 1969, Delaware)		
Fisher Scientific Co.	January 10, 1907	Pennsylvania
Florida Power & Light Co.	December 28, 1925	Florida
Food Fair Stores, Inc.	December 24, 1935	Pennsylvania
Foote, Cone & Belding	December 29, 1942	Delaware
G.D.V. Inc.	January 13, 1928	Delaware
General Medical Corp.	January 15, 1965	Virginia
Gidding & Lewis, Inc.	December 23, 1895	Wisconsin
Hall Printing Co.	January 10, 1893	Illinois
(Merged parent s/s April 14, 1971, Delaware)		
Harnischfeger Corp.	January 7, 1910	Wisconsin
(Merged parent November 3, 1971, Delaware)		
Helene Curtis Industries, Inc.	January 18, 1928	Illinois
Hesston Corp.	January 5, 1949	Kansas
Hudson Bay Mining & Smelting Co., Ltd.	December 27, 1927	Canada
Inland Container	January 17, 1930	Indiana
International Harvester Co.	December 22, 1965	Delaware
Jefferson Pilot Corp.	January 3, 1968	North Carolina
Jewel Companies, Inc.	January 14, 1916	New York
Johns Manville Corp.	December 28, 1926	New York
Jorgensen (Earl M.) Co.	January 7, 1924	California
Kidde (Walter) & Co.	January 2, 1917	New York
(Merged parent s/s March 5, 1968, Delaware)		
Lawter Chemicals, Inc.	January 6, 1958	Delaware
Leverage Fund of Boston	December 31, 1966	Massachusetts
Lilly (Eli) & Co.	January 17, 1901	Indiana
Loctite Corp.	December 26, 1953	Connecticut
Long Island Lighting Co.	December 31, 1901	New York
Louisiana Land & Exploration Co.	January 19, 1926	Maryland
Lukens Steel Co.	January 17, 1917	Pennsylvania
Lykes Corp.	January 3, 1925	Delaware
(Merged parent Lykes-Youngstown Sheet s/s February 20, 1969, Delaware)		

Company	Date of Birth	Place of Birth
Magic Chef, Inc.	January 7, 1932	Delaware
Marvell Technology Group	January 11, 1995	Bermuda
McGraw Hill, Inc.	December 29, 1925	New York
McLean Trucking Co. Measurex Corp.	January 9, 1940	North Carolina
MCI	December 29, 2003	Delaware
Mercantile Stores, Inc.	January 10, 1919	Delaware
Michigan Consolidated Gas Co.	January 12, 1898	Michigan
Millennium Pharmaceuticals	January 13, 1993	Delaware
Mohasco Industries, Inc.	December 31, 1873	New York
Mohawk Rubber	January 6, 1913	Ohio
Munford, Inc.	December 30, 1924	Georgia
Murphy (G.C.) Co.	December 31, 1919	Pennsylvania
N.C.R.	January 2, 1929	Maryland
New England Electric System	January 2, 1929	Massachusetts
New England Gas & Electric Dec of Trust	December 31, 1926	Massachusetts
NLT Corp.	January 1, 1981	Tennessee
Norfolk & Western Railway Co.	January 15, 1896	Virginia
Northeast Utilities Dec of Trust	January 15, 1924	Massachusetts
Northern Telecom, Ltd.	January 5, 1914	Canada
Northgate Exploration, Ltd.	January 7, 1919	Ontario
Nucor Corp.	January 2, 1940	Michigan
(Merged parent s/s March 28, 1958, Delaware)		
N.V.F. Co.	December 23, 1904	Delaware
Pacific Tel & Tel Co.	December 31, 1906	California
Panhandle Eastern Pipe Line Co.	December 23, 1909	Delaware
Pargas, Inc.	January 2, 1904	Maryland
Parker-Hannitin Corp.	December 30, 1938	Ohio
Petroleum Resources Corp.	January 16, 1929	Delaware
(Merged parent s/s February 4, 1977, Maryland)		
Pittston Co.	January 13, 1930	Delaware
Portland General Electric Co.	January 13, 1930	Delaware
Ralston Purina Co.	January 8, 1894	Missouri
Reeves Brothers, Inc.	December 28, 1922	New York

Company	Date of Birth	Place of Birth
Republic Financial Services	January 14, 1969	Texas
Robertshaw Controls Co.	December 23, 1926	Delaware
Russ Togs, Inc.	January 3, 1946	New York
Schering-Plough	January 16, 1971	New Jersey
Sierra Pacific Power Co.	January 15, 1964	Nevada
Smith International, Inc.	January 18, 1937	California
Smith Transfer Corp.	January 1, 1949	Virginia
Southwest Bancshares, Inc. (Chartered May 1, 1907)	January 6, 1970	Delaware
Standex International (Merged parent s/s May 22, 1975, Ohio)	January 5, 1955	Ohio
Standard Motor Products, Inc.	December 30, 1926	New York
Standard Oil Co. (Ohio)	January 10, 1870	Ohio
Stevens (J.P.) & Co., Inc.	December 29, 1923	Delaware
Stone Container Corp.	December 31, 1945	Illinois
Sun Electric	January 4, 1946	Delaware
Super Valu Stores, Inc.	December 28, 1925	Delaware
Tektronix, Inc.	January 2, 1946	Oregon
Teleprompter Corp.	January 3, 1951	New York
Texas Commerce Bankshares, Inc. (Chartered January 17, 1964 National Bank Act)	November 30, 1970	Delaware
Texas Gulf, Inc. (Formerly Texas Gulf Sulphur)	December 23, 1909	Texas
Texas Instruments, Inc.	December 23, 1938	Delaware
Thomas Industries, Inc. (Merged parent s/s August 31, 1953, Delaware)	December 28, 1928	Delaware
Ticor	December 30, 1893	California
Trans-World Airlines. Inc.	December 27, 1934	Delaware
Tri-Continental Corp.	December 31, 1929	Maryland
U.S. Gypsum (Merged parent s/s February 4, 1966, Delaware)	December 27, 1901	New Jersey
U.S.I. Industries, Inc. (Reorganized parent PSCC July 24, 1946)	January 12, 1899	New Jersey

Company	Date of Birth	Place of Birth
Veritas	January 6, 1997	Delaware
Walker Goodeham & Worts Ltd.	December 31, 1926	Canada
Wallace-Murry Corp.	December 27, 1936	Delaware
Warner Communications, Inc.	December 26, 1961	New York
(Merged parent Kinney Services s/s December 30, 1971, Delaware)		
Warner-Swassy Co.	January 18, 1900	Ohio
(Merged parent sls May 26, 1928, Ohio)		
Westinghouse Electric Corp.	January 8, 1886	Pennsylvania
Weyerhaeuser Co.	January 18, 1900	Washington
White Consolidated Industries, Inc.	January 11, 1926	Delaware
White Motor Corp.	December 23, 1915	Ohio
Winn-Dixie Stores, Inc.	December 26, 1928	Florida
Woods Petroleum Corp.	December 27, 1954	Delaware
WUI, Inc.	January 12, 1961	Delaware
(Merged WICO Corp. into WU International, Inc. April 3, 1972, Delaware)		

Appendix II
New and Full Moons, 2000-2050

2000

January 6	New Moon	15 Capricorn
January 21	Full Moon	0 Leo
February 5	New Moon	16 Aquarius
February 19	Full Moon	0 Virgo
March 6	New Moon	15 Pisces
March 20	Full Moon	29 Virgo
April 4	New Moon	15 Aries
April 18	Full Moon	29 Libra
May 4	New Moon	14 Taurus
May 18	Full Moon	27 Scorpio
June 2	New Moon	12 Gemini
June 16	Full Moon	26 Sagittarius
July 1	New Moon	10 Cancer
July 16	Full Moon	24 Capricorn
July 31	New Moon	8 Leo
August 15	Full Moon	22 Aquarius
August 29	New Moon	6 Virgo
September 13	Full Moon	21 Pisces
September 27	New Moon	5 Libra
October 13	Full Moon	20 Aries
October 27	New Moon	4 Scorpio
November 11	Full Moon	19 Taurus
November 25	New Moon	3 Sagittarius
December 11	Full Moon	19 Gemini
December 25	New Moon	4 Capricorn

2001

January 9	Full Moon	19 Cancer
January 24	New Moon	4 Aquarius
February 8	Full Moon	19 Leo
February 23	New Moon	4 Pisces
March 9	Full Moon	19 Virgo
March 25	New Moon	4 Aries
April 8	Full Moon	18 Libra
April 23	New Moon	3 Taurus
May 7	Full Moon	17 Scorpio
May 23	New Moon	2 Gemini
June 6	Full Moon	15 Sagittarius
June 21	New Moon	0 Cancer
July 5	Full Moon	13 Capricorn
July 20	New Moon	28 Cancer
August 4	Full Moon	12 Aquarius
August 19	New Moon	26 Leo
September 2	Full Moon	10 Pisces
September 17	New Moon	24 Virgo
October 2	Full Moon	9 Aries
October 16	New Moon	23 Libra
November 1	Full Moon	8 Taurus
November 15	New Moon	23 Scorpio
November 30	Full Moon	8 Gemini
December 14	New Moon	23 Sagittarius

2002

January 13	New Moon	23 Capricorn
January 28	Full Moon	9 Leo
Feruary 12	New Moon	23 Aquarius
February 27	Full Moon	8 Virgo
March 14	New Moon	23 Pisces
March 28	Full Moon	8 Libra
April 12	New Moon	23 Aries
April 26	Full Moon	6 Scorpio
May 12	New Moon	21 Taurus
May 24	Full Moon	5 Sagittarius
June 10	New Moon	20 Gemini
June 24	New Moon	3 Capricorn
July 10	New Moon	18 Cancer
July 24	Full Moon	1 Aquarius

Date	Phase	Sign	Date	Phase	Sign
August 8	New Moon	16 Leo	May 19	New Moon	28 Taurus
August 22	Full Moon	29 Aquarius	June 3	Full Moon	13 Sagittarius
September 7	New Moon	14 Virgo	June 17	New Moon	27 Gemini
September 21	Full Moon	28 Pisces	July 2	Full Moon	11 Capricorn
October 6	New Moon	13 Libra	July 17	New Moon	25 Cancer
October 21	Full Moon	27 Aries	July 31	Full Moon	9 Aquarius
November 4	New Moon	12 Scorpio	August 18	New Moon	23 Leo
November 20	Full Moon	27 Taurus	August 30	Full Moon	7 Pisces
December 4	New Moon	11 Sagittarius	September 14	New Moon	22 Virgo
December 19	Full Moon	27 Gemini	September 28	Full Moon	5 Aries
			October 14	New Moon	21 Libra

2003

Date	Phase	Sign	Date	Phase	Sign
January 2	New Moon	12 Capricorn	October 28	Full Moon	5 Taurus
January 18	Full Moon	28 Cancer	November 12	New Moon	20 Scorpio
February 1	New Moon	12 Aquarius	November 26	Full Moon	5 Gemini
February 16	Full Moon	28 Leo	December 12	New Moon	20 Sagittarius
March 3	New Moon	12 Pisces	December 26	Full Moon	5 Cancer
March 18	Full Moon	27 Virgo			

2005

Date	Phase	Sign	Date	Phase	Sign
April 1	New Moon	11 Aries	January 10	New Moon	20 Capricorn
April 16	Full Moon	26 Libra	January 25	Full Moon	5 Leo
May 1	New Moon	10 Taurus	February 8	New Moon	20 Aquarius
May 16	Full Moon	25 Scorpio	February 24	Full Moon	6 Virgo
May 31	New Moon	9 Gemini	March 10	New Moon	20 Pisces
June 14	Full Moon	23 Sagittarius	March 25	Full Moon	5 Libra
June 29	New Moon	7 Cancer	April 8	New Moon	19 Aries
July 13	Full Moon	21 Capricorn	April 24	Full Moon	4 Scorpio
July 29	New Moon	5 Leo	May 8	New Moon	18 Taurus
August 12	Full Moon	19 Aquarius	May 23	Full Moon	3 Sagittarius
August 27	New Moon	4 Virgo	June 6	New Moon	16 Gemini
September 10	Full Moon	17 Pisces	June 22	Full Moon	1 Capricorn
September 26	New Moon	2 Libra	July 6	New Moon	14 Cancer
October 10	Full Moon	16 Aries	July 21	Full Moon	28 Capricorn
October 25	New Moon	1 Scorpio	August 5	New Moon	13 Leo
November 9	Full Moon	16 Taurus	August 19	Full Moon	27 Aquarius
November 23	New Moon	1 Sagittarius	September 3	New Moon	11 Virgo
December 8	Full Moon	16 Gemini	September 18	Full Moon	25 Pisces
December 23	New Moon	1 Capricorn	October 3	New Moon	10 Libra
			October 17	Full Moon	24 Aries

2004

Date	Phase	Sign	Date	Phase	Sign
			November 2	New Moon	10 Scorpio
January 7	Full Moon	16 Cancer	November 16	Full Moon	24 Taurus
January 21	New Moon	1 Aquarius	December 1	New Moon	9 Sagittarius
February 6	Full Moon	17 Leo	December 15	Full Moon	24 Gemini
February 20	New Moon	1 Pisces			

2006

Date	Phase	Sign
March 6	Full Moon	16 Virgo
March 20	New Moon	0 Aries
April 5	Full Moon	16 Libra	January 14	Full Moon	24 Cancer
April 19	New Moon	29 Aries	January 29	New Moon	9 Aquarius
May 4	Full Moon	14 Scorpio	February 13	Full Moon	24 Leo
			February 28	New Moon	9 Pisces

March 14	Full Moon	24 Virgo		*2008*	
March 29	New Moon	8 Aries	January 8	New Moon	17 Capricorn
April 13	Full Moon	23 Libra	January 22	Full Moon	2 Leo
April 27	New Moon	7 Taurus	February 7	New Moon	17 Aquarius
May 13	Full Moon	22 Scorpio	February 21	Full Moon	2 Virgo
May 27	New Moon	6 Gemini	March 7	New Moon	17 Pisces
June 11	Full Moon	20 Sagittarius	March 21	Full Moon	1 Libra
June 25	New Moon	4 Cancer	April 6	New Moon	16 Aries
July 11	Full Moon	18 Capricorn	April 20	Full Moon	0 Scorpio
July 25	New Moon	2 Leo	May 5	New Moon	15 Taurus
August 9	Full Moon	16 Aquarius	May 20	Full Moon	29 Scorpio
August 23	New Moon	0 Virgo	June 3	New Moon	13 Gemini
September 7	Full Moon	15 Pisces	June 18	Full Moon	28 Sagittarius
September 22	New Moon	29 Virgo	July 3	New Moon	11 Cancer
October 7	Full Moon	14 Aries	July 18	Full Moon	26 Capricorn
October 22	New Moon	28 Libra	August 1	New Moon	9 Leo
November 5	Full Moon	13 Taurus	August 16	Full Moon	24 Aquarius
November 20	New Moon	28 Scorpio	August 30	New Moon	7 Virgo
December 5	Full Moon	12 Gemini	September 15	Full Moon	23 Pisces
December 20	New Moon	28 Sagittarius	September 29	New Moon	6 Libra
	2007		October 14	Full Moon	22 Aries
January 3	Full Moon	12 Cancer	October 28	New Moon	6 Scorpio
January 19	New Moon	28 Capricorn	November 13	Full Moon	21 Taurus
February 2	Full Moon	13 Leo	November 27	New Moon	5 Sagittarius
February 17	New Moon	28 Aquarius	December 12	Full Moon	21 Gemini
March 3	Full Moon	13 Virgo	December 27	New Moon	6 Capricorn
March 19	New Moon	28 Pisces		*2009*	
April 2	Full Moon	12 Libra	January 11	Full Moon	21 Cancer
April 17	New Moon	27 Aries	January 26	New Moon	6 Aquarius
May 2	Full Moon	12 Scorpio	February 9	Full Moon	20 Leo
May 16	New Moon	25 Taurus	February 25	New Moon	6 Pisces
June 1	Full Moon	10 Sagittarius	March 11	Full Moon	20 Virgo
June 15	New Moon	23 Gemini	March 26	New Moon	6 Aries
June 30	Full Moon	8 Capricorn	April 9	Full Moon	20 Libra
July 14	New Moon	21 Cancer	April 25	New Moon	5 Taurus
July 30	Full Moon	6 Aquarius	May 9	Full Moon	18 Scorpio
August 12	New Moon	20 Leo	May 24	New Moon	3 Gemini
August 28	Full Moon	4 Pisces	June 7	Full Moon	17 Sagittarius
September 11	New Moon	18 Virgo	June 22	New Moon	1 Cancer
September 26	Full Moon	3 Aries	July 7	Full Moon	15 Capricorn
October 11	New Moon	17 Libra	July 22	New Moon	29 Cancer
October 26	Full Moon	2 Taurus	August 6	Full Moon	13 Aquarius
November 9	New Moon	17 Scorpio	August 20	New Moon	27 Leo
November 24	Full Moon	2 Gemini	September 4	Full Moon	12 Pisces
December 9	New Moon	17 Sagittarius	September 18	New Moon	26 Virgo
December 24	Full Moon	2 Cancer	October 4	Full Moon	11 Aries
			October 18	New Moon	25 Libra

November 2	Full Moon	10 Taurus
November 16	New Moon	24 Scorpio
December 2	Full Moon	10 Gemini
December 16	New Moon	24 Sagittarius

2010

January 15	New Moon	25 Capricorn
January 30	Full Moon	10 Leo
February 14	New Moon	25 Aquarius
February 28	Full Moon	10 Virgo
March 15	New Moon	25 Pisces
March 30	Full Moon	9 Libra
April 14	New Moon	24 Aries
April 28	Full Moon	8 Scorpio
May 14	New Moon	23 Taurus
May 27	Full Moon	6 Sagittarius
June 12	New Moon	21 Gemini
June 26	Full Moon	4 Capricorn
July 11	New Moon	19 Cancer
July 26	Full Moon	3 Aquarius
August 10	New Moon	17 Leo
August 24	Full Moon	1 Pisces
September 8	New Moon	15 Virgo
September 23	Full Moon	0 Aries
October 7	New Moon	14 Libra
October 23	Full Moon	29 Aries
November 6	New Moon	13 Scorpio
November 21	Full Moon	29 Taurus
December 5	New Moon	13 Sagittarius
December 21	Full Moon	28 Gemini

2011

January 4	New Moon	13 Capricorn
January 19	Full Moon	29 Cancer
February 3	New Moon	14 Aquarius
February 18	Full Moon	29 Leo
March 4	New Moon	14 Pisces
March 19	Full Moon	28 Virgo
April 3	New Moon	13 Aries
April 18	Full Moon	27 Libra
May 3	New Moon	12 Taurus
May 17	Full Moon	26 Scorpio
June 1	New Moon	11 Gemini
June 15	Full Moon	24 Sagittarius
July 1	New Moon	9 Cancer
July 15	Full Moon	22 Capricorn
July 30	New Moon	7 Leo
August 13	Full Moon	20 Aquarius
August 29	New Moon	5 Virgo
September 12	Full Moon	19 Pisces
September 27	New Moon	4 Libra
October 12	Full Moon	18 Aries
October 26	New Moon	3 Scorpio
November 10	Full Moon	18 Taurus
November 25	New Moon	2 Sagittarius
December 10	Full Moon	18 Gemini
December 24	New Moon	2 Capricorn

2012

January 9	Full Moon	18 Cancer
January 23	New Moon	2 Aquarius
February 7	Full Moon	18 Leo
February 21	New Moon	2 Pisces
March 8	Full Moon	18 Virgo
March 22	New Moon	2 Aries
April 6	Full Moon	17 Libra
April 21	New Moon	1 Taurus
May 6	Full Moon	16 Scorpio
May 20	New Moon	0 Gemini
June 4	Full Moon	14 Sagittarius
June 19	New Moon	28 Gemini
July 3	Full Moon	12 Capricorn
July 19	New Moon	27 Cancer
August 2	Full Moon	10 Aquarius
August 17	New Moon	25 Leo
August 31	Full Moon	8 Pisces
September 16	New Moon	23 Virgo
September 30	Full Moon	7 Aries
October 15	New Moon	22 Libra
October 29	Full Moon	6 Taurus
November 13	New Moon	21 Scorpio
November 28	Full Moon	6 Gemini
December 13	New Moon	21 Sagittarius
December 28	Full Moon	7 Cancer

2013

January 11	New Moon	21 Capricorn
January 27	Full Moon	7 Leo
February 10	New Moon	21 Aquarius
February 25	Full Moon	7 Virgo
March 11	New Moon	21 Pisces
March 27	Full Moon	7 Libra
April 10	New Moon	20 Aries
April 25	Full Moon	6 Scorpio
May 10	New Moon	19 Taurus
May 25	Full Moon	4 Sagittarius

June 8	New Moon	18 Gemini
June 23	Full Moon	2 Capricorn
July 8	New Moon	16 Cancer
July 22	Full Moon	0 Aquarius
August 6	New Moon	14 Leo
August 21	Full Moon	28 Aquarius
September 5	New Moon	13 Virgo
September 19	Full Moon	26 Pisces
October 5	New Moon	12 Libra
October 18	Full Moon	25 Aries
November 3	New Moon	11 Scorpio
November 17	Full Moon	25 Taurus
December 3	New Moon	11 Sagittarius
December 17	Full Moon	25 Gemini

2014

January 1	New Moon	11 Capricorn
January 16	Full Moon	26 Cancer
January 30	New Moon	11 Aquarius
February 14	Full Moon	26 Leo
March 1	New Moon	10 Pisces
March 16	Full Moon	26 Virgo
March 30	New Moon	10 Aries
April 15	Full Moon	25 Libra
April 29	New Moon	9 Taurus
May 14	Full Moon	24 Scorpio
May 28	New Moon	7 Gemini
June 13	Full Moon	22 Sagittarius
June 27	New Moon	5 Cancer
July 12	Full Moon	20 Capricorn
July 26	New Moon	4 Leo
August 10	Full Moon	18 Aquarius
August 25	New Moon	2 Virgo
September 9	Full Moon	16 Pisces
September 24	New Moon	1 Libra
October 8	Full Moon	15 Aries
October 23	New Moon	0 Scorpio
November 6	Full Moon	14 Taurus
November 22	New Moon	0 Sagittarius
December 6	Full Moon	14 Gemini
December 22	New Moon	0 Capricorn

2015

January 5	Full Moon	14 Cancer
January 20	New Moon	0 Aquarius
February 3	Full Moon	14 Leo
February 18	New Moon	29 Aquarius
March 5	Full Moon	14 Virgo
March 20	New Moon	29 Pisces
April 4	Full Moon	14 Libra
April 18	New Moon	28 Aries
May 4	Full Moon	13 Scorpio
May 18	New Moon	27 Taurus
June 2	Full Moon	11 Sagittarius
June 16	New Moon	25 Gemini
July 2	Full Moon	10 Capricorn
July 16	New Moon	23 Cancer
July 31	Full Moon	8 Aquarius
August 14	New Moon	21 Leo
August 29	Full Moon	5 Pisces
September 13	New Moon	20 Virgo
September 28	Full Moon	4 Aries
October 13	New Moon	19 Libra
October 27	Full Moon	3 Taurus
November 11	New Moon	19 Scorpio
November 25	Full Moon	3 Gemini
December 11	New Moon	19 Sagittarius
December 25	Full Moon	3 Cancer

2016

January 10	New Moon	19 Capricorn
January 24	Full Moon	3 Leo
February 8	New Moon	19 Aquarius
February 22	Full Moon	3 Virgo
March 9	New Moon	19 Pisces
March 23	Full Moon	3 Libra
April 7	New Moon	18 Aries
April 22	Full Moon	2 Scorpio
May 6	New Moon	16 Taurus
May 21	Full Moon	1 Sagittarius
June 5	New Moon	15 Gemini
June 20	Full Moon	29 Sagittarius
July 4	New Moon	13 Cancer
July 19	Full Moon	27 Capricorn
August 2	New Moon	11 Leo
August 18	Full Moon	26 Aquarius
September 1	New Moon	9 Virgo
September 16	Full Moon	24 Pisces
October 1	New Moon	8 Libra
October 16	Full Moon	23 Aries
October 30	New Moon	7 Scorpio
November 14	Full Moon	22 Taurus
November 29	New Moon	7 Sagittarius
December 14	Full Moon	22 Gemini
December 29	New Moon	7 Capricorn

2017

January 12	Full Moon	22 Cancer
January 28	New Moon	8 Aquarius
February 11	Full Moon	22 Leo
February 26	New Moon	8 Pisces
March 12	Full Moon	22 Virgo
March 28	New Moon	7 Aries
April 11	Full Moon	21 Libra
April 26	New Moon	6 Taurus
May 10	Full Moon	20 Scorpio
May 25	New Moon	4 Gemini
June 9	Full Moon	19 Sagittarius
June 24	New Moon	2 Cancer
July 9	Full Moon	17 Capricorn
July 23	New Moon	0 Leo
August 7	Full Moon	15 Aquarius
August 21	New Moon	29 Leo
September 6	Full Moon	14 Pisces
September 20	New Moon	27 Virgo
October 5	Full Moon	12 Aries
October 19	New Moon	26 Libra
November 4	Full Moon	12 Taurus
November 18	New Moon	26 Scorpio
December 3	Full Moon	11 Gemini
December 18	New Moon	26 Sagittarius

2018

January 2	Full Moon	11 Cancer
January 17	New Moon	27 Capricorn
January 31	Full Moon	11 Leo
February 15	New Moon	27 Aquarius
March 2	Full Moon	11 Virgo
March 17	New Moon	27 Pisces
March 31	Full Moon	10 Libra
April 16	New Moon	26 Aries
April 30	Full Moon	9 Scorpio
May 15	New Moon	24 Taurus
May 29	Full Moon	8 Sagittarius
June 13	New Moon	22 Gemini
June 28	Full Moon	6 Capricorn
July 13	New Moon	20 Cancer
July 27	Full Moon	4 Aquarius
August 11	New Moon	18 Leo
August 26	Full Moon	3 Pisces
September 9	New Moon	17 Virgo
September 25	Full Moon	2 Aries
October 9	New Moon	15 Libra
October 24	Full Moon	1 Taurus
November 7	New Moon	15 Scorpio
November 23	Full Moon	1 Gemini
December 7	New Moon	15 Sagittarius
December 22	Full Moon	1 Cancer

2019

January 6	New Moon	15 Capricorn
January 21	Full Moon	1 Leo
February 4	New Moon	15 Aquarius
February 19	Full Moon	1 Virgo
March 6	New Moon	15 Pisces
March 21	Full Moon	1 Libra
April 5	New Moon	15 Aries
April 19	Full Moon	29 Libra
May 4	New Moon	14 Taurus
May 18	Full Moon	27 Scorpio
June 3	New Moon	12 Gemini
June 17	Full Moon	26 Sagittarius
July 2	New Moon	10 Cancer
July 16	Full Moon	24 Capricorn
August 1	New Moon	8 Leo
August 15	Full Moon	22 Aquarius
August 30	New Moon	6 Virgo
September 14	Full Moon	21 Pisces
September 28	New Moon	5 Libra
October 13	Full Moon	20 Aries
October 28	New Moon	4 Scorpio
November 12	Full Moon	20 Taurus
November 26	New Moon	4 Sagittarius
December 12	Full Moon	20 Gemini
December 26	New Moon	4 Capricorn

2020

January 10	Full Moon	20 Cancer
January 24	New Moon	4 Aquarius
February 9	Full Moon	20 Leo
February 23	New Moon	4 Pisces
March 9	Full Moon	19 Virgo
March 24	New Moon	4 Aries
April 8	Full Moon	18 Libra
April 23	New Moon	3 Taurus
May 7	Full Moon	17 Scorpio
May 22	New Moon	2 Gemini
June 5	Full Moon	15 Sagittarius
June 21	New Moon	0 Cancer
July 5	Full Moon	13 Capricorn
July 20	New Moon	28 Cancer
August 3	Full Moon	11 Aquarius

August 19	New Moon	26 Leo	May 30	New Moon	9 Gemini
September 2	Full Moon	10 Pisces	June 14	Full Moon	23 Sagittarius
September 17	New Moon	25 Virgo	June 29	New Moon	7 Cancer
October 1	Full Moon	9 Aries	July 13	Full Moon	21 Capricorn
October 16	New Moon	23 Libra	July 28	New Moon	5 Leo
October 31	Full Moon	8 Taurus	August 12	Full Moon	19 Aquarius
November 15	New Moon	23 Scorpio	August 27	New Moon	4 Virgo
November 30	Full Moon	8 Gemini	September 10	Full Moon	17 Pisces
December 14	New Moon	23 Sagittarius	September 25	New Moon	2 Libra
December 30	Full Moon	9 Cancer	October 9	Full Moon	16 Aries
			October 25	New Moon	2 Scorpio
	2021		November 8	Full Moon	16 Taurus
January 13	New Moon	23 Capricorn	November 23	New Moon	1 Sagittarius
January 28	Full Moon	9 Leo	December 8	Full Moon	16 Gemini
February 11	New Moon	23 Aquarius	December 23	New Moon	1 Capricorn
February 27	Full Moon	9 Virgo			
March 13	New Moon	23 Pisces		*2023*	
March 28	Full Moon	8 Libra	January 6	Full Moon	16 Cancer
April 12	New Moon	22 Aries	January 21	New Moon	1 Aquarius
April 27	Full Moon	7 Scorpio	February 5	Full Moon	16 Leo
May 11	New Moon	21 Taurus	February 20	New Moon	1 Pisces
May 26	Full Moon	5 Sagittarius	March 7	Full Moon	16 Virgo
June 10	New Moon	19 Gemini	March 21	New Moon	1 Aries
June 24	Full Moon	3 Capricorn	April 6	Full Moon	16 Libra
July 10	New Moon	18 Cancer	April 20	New Moon	29 Aries
July 24	Full Moon	1 Aquarius	May 5	Full Moon	15 Scorpio
August 8	New Moon	16 Leo	May 19	New Moon	28 Taurus
August 22	Full Moon	29 Aquarius	June 3	Full Moon	13 Sagittarius
September 7	New Moon	14 Virgo	June 17	New Moon	26 Gemini
September 20	Full Moon	28 Pisces	July 4	Full Moon	11 Capricorn
October 6	New Moon	13 Libra	July 18	New Moon	25 Cancer
October 20	Full Moon	27 Aries	August 1	Full Moon	9 Aquarius
November 4	New Moon	12 Scorpio	August 16	New Moon	23 Leo
November 19	Full Moon	27 Taurus	August 31	Full Moon	7 Pisces
December 4	New Moon	12 Sagittarius	September 15	New Moon	21 Virgo
December 19	Full Moon	27 Gemini	September 29	Full Moon	6 Aries
			October 14	New Moon	21 Libra
	2022		October 28	Full Moon	5 Taurus
January 2	New Moon	12 Capricorn	November 13	New Moon	20 Scorpio
January 17	Full Moon	28 Cancer	November 27	Full Moon	5 Gemini
February 1	New Moon	12 Aquarius	December 12	New Moon	20 Sagittarius
February 16	Full Moon	28 Leo	December 27	Full Moon	5 Cancer
March 2	New Moon	12 Pisces			
March 18	Full Moon	27 Virgo		*2024*	
April 1	New Moon	11 Aries	January 11	New Moon	20 Capricorn
April 16	Full Moon	26 Libra	January 25	Full Moon	5 Leo
April 30	New Moon	10 Taurus	February 9	New Moon	20 Aquarius
May 16	Full Moon	25 Scorpio	February 24	Full Moon	5 Virgo

March 10	New Moon	20 Pisces		*2026*	
March 25	Full Moon	5 Libra	January 3	Full Moon	13 Cancer
April 8	New Moon	19 Aries	January 18	New Moon	28 Capricorn
April 23	Full Moon	4 Scorpio	February 1	Full Moon	13 Leo
May 8	New Moon	18 Taurus	February 17	New Moon	29 Aquarius
May 23	Full Moon	3 Sagittarius	March 3	Full Moon	13 Virgo
June 6	New Moon	16 Gemini	March 19	New Moon	28 Pisces
June 22	Full Moon	1 Capricorn	April 2	Full Moon	12 Libra
July 5	New Moon	14 Cancer	April 17	New Moon	27 Aries
July 21	Full Moon	29 Capricorn	May 1	Full Moon	11 Scorpio
August 4	New Moon	12 Leo	May 16	New Moon	26 Taurus
August 19	Full Moon	27 Aquarius	May 31	Full Moon	9 Sagittarius
September 3	New Moon	11 Virgo	June 15	New Moon	24 Gemini
September 18	Full Moon	25 Pisces	June 29	Full Moon	8 Capricorn
October 2	New Moon	10 Libra	July 14	New Moon	22 Cancer
October 17	Full Moon	24 Aries	July 29	Full Moon	6 Aquarius
November 1	New Moon	9 Scorpio	August 12	New Moon	20 Leo
November 15	Full Moon	24 Taurus	August 28	Full Moon	5 Pisces
December 1	New Moon	9 Sagittarius	September 11	New Moon	18 Virgo
December 15	Full Moon	24 Gemini	September 26	Full Moon	3 Aries
December 30	New Moon	9 Capricorn	October 10	New Moon	17 Libra
	2025		October 26	Full Moon	2 Taurus
January 13	Full Moon	24 Cancer	November 9	New Moon	17 Scorpio
January 29	New Moon	10 Aquarius	November 24	Full Moon	2 Gemini
February 12	Full Moon	24 Leo	December 9	New Moon	16 Sagittarius
February 28	New Moon	9 Pisces	December 24	Full Moon	2 Cancer
March 14	Full Moon	23 Virgo		*2027*	
March 29	New Moon	9 Aries	January 7	New Moon	17 Capricorn
April 13	Full Moon	23 Libra	January 22	Full Moon	2 Leo
April 27	New Moon	7 Taurus	February 6	New Moon	17 Aquarius
May 12	Full Moon	22 Scorpio	February 20	Full Moon	2 Virgo
May 27	New Moon	6 Gemini	March 8	New Moon	17 Pisces
June 11	Full Moon	20 Sagittarius	March 22	Full Moon	1 Libra
June 25	New Moon	4 Cancer	April 6	New Moon	17 Aries
July 10	Full Moon	18 Capricorn	April 20	Full Moon	0 Scorpio
July 24	New Moon	2 Leo	May 6	New Moon	15 Taurus
August 9	Full Moon	16 Aquarius	May 20	Full Moon	29 Scorpio
August 23	New Moon	0 Virgo	June 4	New Moon	13 Gemini
September 7	Full Moon	15 Pisces	June 19	Full Moon	27 Sagittarius
September 21	New Moon	29 Virgo	July 4	New Moon	12 Cancer
October 7	Full Moon	14 Aries	July 18	Full Moon	25 Capricorn
October 21	New Moon	28 Libra	August 2	New Moon	10 Leo
November 5	Full Moon	13 Taurus	August 17	Full Moon	24 Aquarius
November 20	New Moon	28 Scorpio	August 31	New Moon	8 Virgo
December 4	Full Moon	13 Gemini	September 15	Full Moon	22 Pisces
December 20	New Moon	28 Sagittarius	September 30	New Moon	6 Libra
			October 15	Full Moon	21 Aries

October 29	New Moon	6 Scorpio
November 14	Full Moon	21 Taurus
November 28	New Moon	5 Sagittarius
December 13	Full Moon	21 Gemini
December 27	New Moon	6 Capricorn

2028

January 12	Full Moon	21 Cancer
January 26	New Moon	6 Aquarius
February 10	Full Moon	21 Leo
February 25	New Moon	6 Pisces
March 11	Full Moon	21 Virgo
March 26	New Moon	6 Aries
April 9	Full Moon	20 Libra
April 24	New Moon	5 Taurus
May 8	Full Moon	18 Scorpio
May 24	New Moon	3 Gemini
June 7	Full Moon	17 Sagittarius
June 22	New Moon	2 Cancer
July 6	Full Moon	15 Capricorn
July 22	New Moon	29 Cancer
August 5	Full Moon	13 Aquarius
August 20	New Moon	28 Leo
September 3	Full Moon	12 Pisces
September 18	New Moon	26 Virgo
October 3	Full Moon	11 Aries
October 18	New Moon	25 Libra
November 2	Full Moon	10 Taurus
November 16	New Moon	24 Scorpio
December 2	Full Moon	10 Gemini
December 16	New Moon	24 Sagittarius
December 31	Full Moon	10 Cancer

2029

January 14	New Moon	25 Capricorn
January 30	Full Moon	10 Leo
February 13	New Moon	25 Aquarius
February 28	Full Moon	10 Virgo
March 15	New Moon	25 Pisces
March 30	Full Moon	10 Libra
April 13	New Moon	24 Aries
April 28	Full Moon	8 Scorpio
May 13	New Moon	23 Taurus
May 27	Full Moon	6 Sagittarius
June 12	New Moon	21 Gemini
June 26	Full Moon	5 Capricorn
July 11	New Moon	19 Cancer
July 25	Full Moon	3 Aquarius

August 10	New Moon	17 Leo
August 24	Full Moon	1 Pisces
September 8	New Moon	16 Virgo
September 22	Full Moon	29 Pisces
October 7	New Moon	14 Libra
October 22	Full Moon	29 Aries
November 6	New Moon	14 Scorpio
November 21	Full Moon	29 Taurus
December 5	New Moon	13 Sagittarius
December 20	Full Moon	29 Gemini

2030

January 4	New Moon	13 Capricorn
January 19	Full Moon	29 Cancer
February 2	New Moon	14 Aquarius
February 18	Full Moon	29 Leo
March 4	New Moon	13 Pisces
March 19	Full Moon	29 Virgo
April 2	New Moon	13 Aries
April 18	Full Moon	28 Libra
May 2	New Moon	12 Taurus
May 17	Full Moon	26 Scorpio
June 1	New Moon	11 Gemini
June 15	Full Moon	24 Sagittarius
June 30	New Moon	19 Cancer
July 15	Full Moon	22 Capricorn
July 30	New Moon	7 Leo
August 13	Full Moon	20 Aquarius
August 28	New Moon	5 Virgo
September 11	Full Moon	19 Pisces
September 27	New Moon	4 Libra
October 11	Full Moon	18 Aries
October 26	New Moon	3 Scorpio
November 10	Full Moon	17 Taurus
November 25	New Moon	3 Sagittarius
December 9	Full Moon	18 Gemini
December 24	New Moon	3 Capricorn

2031

January 8	Full Moon	18 Cancer
January 23	New Moon	3 Aquarius
February 7	Full Moon	18 Leo
February 21	New Moon	2 Pisces
March 9	Full Moon	18 Virgo
March 23	New Moon	2 Aries
April 7	Full Moon	17 Libra
April 21	New Moon	1 Taurus
May 7	Full Moon	16 Scorpio

May 21	New Moon	0 Gemini	March 1	New Moon	11 Pisces
June 5	Full Moon	14 Sagittarius	March 16	Full Moon	25 Virgo
June 19	New Moon	28 Gemini	March 30	New Moon	10 Aries
July 4	Full Moon	12 Capricorn	April 14	Full Moon	25 Libra
July 19	New Moon	26 Cancer	April 29	New Moon	9 Taurus
August 3	Full Moon	10 Aquarius	May 14	Full Moon	23 Scorpio
August 18	New Moon	25 Leo	May 28	New Moon	7 Gemini
September 1	Full Moon	8 Pisces	June 12	Full Moon	22 Sagittarius
September 16	New Moon	23 Virgo	June 26	New Moon	5 Cancer
September 30	Full Moon	7 Aries	July 10	Full Moon	20 Capricorn
October 16	New Moon	22 Libra	July 26	New Moon	3 Leo
October 30	Full Moon	6 Taurus	August 10	Full Moon	18 Aquarius
November 14	New Moon	22 Scorpio	August 24	New Moon	2 Virgo
November 28	Full Moon	6 Gemini	September 9	Full Moon	16 Pisces
December 14	New Moon	22 Sagittarius	September 23	New Moon	1 Libra
December 28	Full Moon	6 Cancer	October 8	Full Moon	15 Aries
			October 23	New Moon	0 Scorpio

2032

January 12	New Moon	22 Capricorn	November 6	Full Moon	14 Taurus
January 27	Full Moon	7 Leo	November 22	New Moon	0 Sagittarius
February 11	New Moon	22 Aquarius	December 6	Full Moon	14 Gemini
February 26	Full Moon	7 Virgo	December 21	New Moon	0 Capricorn
March 11	New Moon	21 Pisces			
March 27	Full Moon	7 Libra		*2034*	
April 10	New Moon	20 Aries	January 4	Full Moon	14 Cancer
April 25	Full Moon	6 Scorpio	January 20	New Moon	0 Aquarius
May 9	New Moon	19 Taurus	February 3	Full Moon	14 Leo
May 25	Full Moon	4 Sagittarius	February 18	New Moon	0 Pisces
June 8	New Moon	18 Gemini	March 5	Full Moon	14 Virgo
June 23	Full Moon	2 Capricorn	March 20	New Moon	29 Pisces
July 7	New Moon	16 Cancer	April 3	Full Moon	14 Libra
July 22	Full Moon	0 Aquarius	April 18	New Moon	29 Aries
August 6	New Moon	14 Leo	May 3	Full Moon	13 Scorpio
August 21	Full Moon	28 Aquarius	May 18	New Moon	27 Taurus
September 4	New Moon	13 Virgo	June 2	Full Moon	11 Sagittarius
September 19	Full Moon	27 Pisces	June 16	New Moon	25 Gemini
October 4	New Moon	13 Libra	July 1	Full Moon	10 Capricorn
October 18	Full Moon	26 Aries	July 15	New Moon	23 Cancer
November 3	New Moon	11 Scorpio	July 31	Full Moon	8 Aquarius
November 17	Full Moon	25 Taurus	August 14	New Moon	21 Leo
December 2	New Moon	11 Sagittarius	August 29	Full Moon	6 Pisces
December 16	Full Moon	25 Gemini	September 12	New Moon	20 Virgo
			September 28	Full Moon	5 Aries
	2033		October 12	New Moon	19 Libra
January 1	New Moon	11 Capricorn	October 27	Full Moon	4 Taurus
January 15	Full Moon	25 Cancer	November 11	New Moon	18 Scorpio
January 30	New Moon	11 Aquarius	November 25	Full Moon	3 Gemini
February 14	Full Moon	25 Leo	December 10	New Moon	19 Sagittarius
			December 25	Full Moon	3 Cancer

2035

January 9	New Moon	19 Capricorn
January 23	Full Moon	3 Leo
February 8	New Moon	19 Aquarius
February 22	Full Moon	3 Virgo
March 9	New Moon	19 Pisces
March 23	Full Moon	3 Libra
April 8	New Moon	18 Aries
April 22	Full Moon	2 Scorpio
May 7	New Moon	17 Taurus
May 22	Full Moon	1 Sagittarius
June 6	New Moon	15 Gemini
June 20	Full Moon	29 Sagittarius
July 5	New Moon	13 Cancer
July 20	Full Moon	27 Capricorn
August 3	New Moon	11 Leo
August 19	Full Moon	26 Aquarius
September 2	New Moon	9 Virgo
September 17	Full Moon	24 Pisces
October 1	New Moon	8 Libra
October 17	Full Moon	23 Aries
October 31	New Moon	7 Scorpio
November 15	Full Moon	23 Taurus
November 29	New Moon	7 Sagittarius
December 15	Full Moon	23 Gemini
December 29	New Moon	7 Capricorn

2036

January 13	Full Moon	23 Cancer
January 28	New Moon	8 Aquarius
February 11	Full Moon	22 Leo
February 27	New Moon	8 Pisces
March 12	Full Moon	22 Virgo
March 27	New Moon	7 Aries
April 10	Full Moon	21 Libra
April 26	New Moon	6 Taurus
May 10	Full Moon	20 Scorpio
May 25	New Moon	5 Gemini
June 8	Full Moon	18 Sagittarius
June 24	New Moon	3 Cancer
July 8	Full Moon	16 Capricorn
July 23	New Moon	1 Leo
August 7	Full Moon	15 Aquarius
August 21	New Moon	29 Leo
September 5	Full Moon	13 Pisces
September 20	New Moon	27 Virgo
October 5	Full Moon	12 Aries
October 19	New Moon	26 Libra
November 4	Full Moon	12 Taurus
November 18	New Moon	26 Scorpio
December 3	Full Moon	12 Gemini
December 17	New Moon	26 Sagittarius

2037

January 2	Full Moon	12 Cancer
January 16	New Moon	26 Capricorn
January 31	Full Moon	12 Leo
February 15	New Moon	27 Aquarius
March 2	Full Moon	11 Virgo
March 16	New Moon	26 Pisces
March 31	Full Moon	11 Libra
April 15	New Moon	26 Aries
April 29	Full Moon	9 Scorpio
May 15	New Moon	24 Taurus
May 29	Full Moon	8 Sagittarius
June 13	New Moon	23 Gemini
June 27	Full Moon	6 Capricorn
July 13	New Moon	21 Cancer
July 27	Full Moon	4 Aquarius
August 11	New Moon	19 Leo
August 25	Full Moon	3 Pisces
September 9	New Moon	17 Virgo
September 24	Full Moon	1 Aries
October 9	New Moon	16 Libra
October 24	Full Moon	1 Taurus
November 7	New Moon	15 Scorpio
November 22	Full Moon	1 Gemini
December 6	New Moon	15 Sagittarius
December 22	Full Moon	1 Cancer

2038

January 5	New Moon	15 Capricorn
January 21	Full Moon	1 Leo
February 4	New Moon	15 Aquarius
February 19	Full Moon	1 Virgo
March 5	New Moon	15 Pisces
March 21	Full Moon	0 Libra
April 4	New Moon	15 Aries
April 19	Full Moon	29 Libra
May 4	New Moon	14 Taurus
May 18	Full Moon	28 Scorpio
June 3	New Moon	12 Gemini
June 17	Full Moon	26 Sagittarius
July 2	New Moon	10 Cancer
July 16	Full Moon	24 Capricorn
August 1	New Moon	9 Leo

August 14	Full Moon	22 Aquarius	May 26	Full Moon	6 Sagittarius
August 30	New Moon	7 Virgo	June 9	New Moon	19 Gemini
September 13	Full Moon	21 Pisces	June 24	Full Moon	4 Capricorn
September 28	New Moon	5 Libra	July 9	New Moon	17 Cancer
October 13	Full Moon	20 Aries	July 24	Full Moon	2 Aquarius
October 28	New Moon	5 Scorpio	August 8	New Moon	16 Leo
November 11	Full Moon	19 Taurus	August 22	Full Moon	29 Aquarius
November 26	New Moon	4 Sagittarius	September 6	New Moon	14 Virgo
December 11	Full Moon	19 Gemini	September 20	Full Moon	28 Pisces
December 26	New Moon	4 Capricorn	October 6	New Moon	13 Libra
			October 20	Full Moon	27 Aries
2039			November 4	New Moon	13 Scorpio
January 10	Full Moon	20 Cancer	November 18	Full Moon	27 Taurus
January 24	New Moon	4 Aquarius	December 4	New Moon	12 Sagittarius
February 9	Full Moon	20 Leo	December 18	Full Moon	27 Gemini
February 23	New Moon	4 Pisces			
March 10	Full Moon	19 Virgo	*2041*		
March 24	New Moon	4 Aries	January 2	New Moon	12 Capricorn
April 9	Full Moon	19 Libra	January 17	Full Moon	27 Cancer
April 23	New Moon	3 Taurus	February 1	New Moon	12 Aquarius
May 8	Full Moon	17 Scorpio	February 16	Full Moon	27 Leo
May 23	New Moon	1 Gemini	March 2	New Moon	12 Pisces
June 6	Full Moon	15 Sagittarius	March 17	Full Moon	27 Virgo
June 21	New Moon	0 Cancer	April 1	New Moon	11 Aries
July 6	Full Moon	14 Capricorn	April 16	Full Moon	27 Libra
July 21	New Moon	28 Cancer	April 30	New Moon	10 Taurus
August 4	Full Moon	11 Aquarius	May 16	Full Moon	25 Scorpio
August 19	New Moon	26 Leo	May 29	New Moon	9 Gemini
September 2	Full Moon	10 Pisces	June 14	Full Moon	23 Sagittarius
September 18	New Moon	25 Virgo	June 28	New Moon	7 Cancer
October 2	Full Moon	9 Aries	July 13	Full Moon	21 Capricorn
October 17	New Moon	24 Libra	July 28	New Moon	5 Leo
October 31	Full Moon	8 Taurus	August 12	Full Moon	19 Aquarius
November 16	New Moon	23 Scorpio	August 26	New Moon	3 Virgo
November 30	Full Moon	8 Gemini	September 10	Full Moon	18 Pisces
December 15	New Moon	23 Sagittarius	September 25	New Moon	2 Libra
December 30	Full Moon	8 Cancer	October 9	Full Moon	16 Aries
			October 25	New Moon	2 Scorpio
2040			November 8	Full Moon	16 Taurus
January 14	New Moon	23 Capricorn	November 23	New Moon	1 Sagittarius
January 29	Full Moon	9 Leo	December 7	Full Moon	16 Gemini
February 12	New Moon	23 Aquarius	December 23	New Moon	1 Capricorn
February 28	Full Moon	9 Virgo			
March 13	New Moon	23 Pisces	*2042*		
March 28	Full Moon	8 Libra	January 6	Full Moon	16 Cancer
April 11	New Moon	22 Aries	January 21	New Moon	1 Aquarius
April 27	Full Moon	7 Scorpio	February 5	Full Moon	16 Leo
May 11	New Moon	21 Taurus	February 20	New Moon	1 Pisces

March 6	Full Moon	16 Virgo		*2044*	
March 21	New Moon	1 Aries	January 14	Full Moon	24 Cancer
April 5	Full Moon	15 Libra	January 30	New Moon	10 Aquarius
April 20	New Moon	0 Taurus	February 13	Full Moon	24 Leo
May 5	Full Moon	15 Scorpio	February 28	New Moon	10 Pisces
May 19	New Moon	28 Taurus	March 13	Full Moon	24 Virgo
June 3	Full Moon	13 Sagittarius	March 29	New Moon	9 Aries
June 17	New Moon	26 Gemini	April 12	Full Moon	23 Libra
July 3	Full Moon	11 Capricorn	April 27	New Moon	8 Taurus
July 17	New Moon	24 Cancer	May 12	Full Moon	22 Scorpio
August 1	Full Moon	9 Aquarius	May 27	New Moon	6 Gemini
August 15	New Moon	23 Leo	June 10	Full Moon	20 Sagittarius
August 31	Full Moon	17 Pisces	June 25	New Moon	4 Cancer
September 14	New Moon	21 Virgo	July 10	Full Moon	18 Capricorn
September 29	Full Moon	6 Aries	July 24	New Moon	2 Leo
October 14	New Moon	21 Libra	August 8	Full Moon	17 Aquarius
October 28	Full Moon	5 Taurus	August 23	New Moon	0 Virgo
November 4	New Moon	20 Scorpio	September 7	Full Moon	15 Pisces
November 27	Full Moon	5 Gemini	September 21	New Moon	29 Virgo
December 12	New Moon	20 Sagittarius	October 7	Full Moon	14 Aries
December 26	Full Moon	5 Cancer	Octoer 20	New Moon	28 Libra
	2043		November 5	Full Moon	13 Taurus
January 11	New Moon	20 Capricorn	November 19	New Moon	28 Scorpio
January 25	Full Moon	5 Leo	December 4	Full Moon	13 Gemini
February 9	New Moon	21 Aquarius	December 19	New Moon	28 Sagittarius
February 23	Full Moon	5 Virgo		*2045*	
March 11	New Moon	20 Pisces	January 3	Full Moon	13 Cancer
March 25	Full Moon	5 Libra	January 18	New Moon	28 Capricorn
April 9	New Moon	20 Aries	February 1	Full Moon	13 Leo
April 24	Full Moon	4 Scorpio	February 16	New Moon	28 Aquarius
May 9	New Moon	18 Taurus	March 3	Full Moon	13 Virgo
May 23	Full Moon	2 Sagittarius	March 18	New Moon	28 Pisces
June 7	New Moon	16 Gemini	April 1	Full Moon	12 Libra
June 22	Full Moon	1 Capricorn	April 17	New Moon	27 Aries
July 6	New Moon	14 Cancer	May 1	Full Moon	11 Scorpio
July 22	Full Moon	29 Capricorn	May 16	New Moon	26 Taurus
August 5	New Moon	12 Leo	May 30	Full Moon	9 Sagittarius
August 20	Full Moon	27 Aquarius	June 15	New Moon	24 Gemini
September 3	New Moon	11 Virgo	June 29	Full Moon	8 Capricorn
September 19	Full Moon	26 Pisces	July 14	New Moon	22 Cancer
October 3	New Moon	9 Libra	July 28	Full Moon	6 Aquarius
October 18	Full Moon	25 Aries	August 12	New Moon	20 Leo
November 1	New Moon	9 Scorpio	August 27	Full Moon	4 Pisces
November 16	Full Moon	24 Taurus	September 11	New Moon	18 Virgo
December 1	New Moon	9 Sagittarius	September 26	Full Moon	3 Aries
December 16	Full Moon	24 Gemini	October 10	New Moon	17 Libra
			October 25	Full Moon	3 Taurus

November 8	New Moon	17 Scorpio
November 24	Full Moon	2 Gemini
December 8	New Moon	16 Sagittarius
December 24	Full Moon	2 Cancer

2046

January 7	New Moon	17 Capricorn
January 22	Full Moon	2 Leo
February 5	New Moon	17 Aquarius
February 20	Full Moon	2 Virgo
March 7	New Moon	17 Pisces
March 22	Full Moon	2 Libra
April 6	New Moon	17 Aries
April 20	Full Moon	1 Scorpio
May 6	New Moon	15 Taurus
May 20	Full Moon	29 Scorpio
June 4	New Moon	14 Gemini
June 18	Full Moon	27 Sagittarius
July 4	New Moon	12 Cancer
July 18	Full Moon	25 Capricorn
August 2	New Moon	10 Leo
August 16	Full Moon	24 Aquarius
August 31	New Moon	8 Virgo
September 15	Full Moon	22 Pisces
September 30	New Moon	7 Libra
October 14	Full Moon	21 Aries
October 29	New Moon	6 Scorpio
November 13	Full Moon	21 Taurus
November 27	New Moon	5 Sagittarius
December 13	Full Moon	21 Gemini
December 27	New Moon	5 Capricorn

2047

January 12	Full Moon	21 Cancer
January 26	New Moon	6 Aquarius
February 10	Full Moon	21 Leo
February 24	New Moon	6 Pisces
March 12	Full Moon	21 Virgo
March 26	New Moon	5 Aries
April 10	Full Moon	20 Libra
April 25	New Moon	5 Taurus
May 9	Full Moon	19 Scorpio
May 24	New Moon	3 Gemini
June 8	Full Moon	17 Sagittarius
June 23	New Moon	2 Cancer
July 7	Full Moon	15 Capricorn
July 22	New Moon	0 Leo
August 5	Full Moon	13 Aquarius
August 21	New Moon	28 Leo
September 4	Full Moon	11 Pisces
September 19	New Moon	26 Virgo
October 3	Full Moon	10 Aries
October 19	New Moon	25 Libra
November 2	Full Moon	10 Taurus
November 17	New Moon	25 Scorpio
December 2	Full Moon	10 Gemini
December 16	New Moon	25 Sagittarius

2048

January 1	Full Moon	10 Cancer
January 15	New Moon	25 Capricorn
January 31	Full Moon	10 Leo
February 14	New Moon	25 Aquarius
February 29	Full Moon	10 Virgo
March 14	New Moon	24 Pisces
March 30	Full Moon	10 Libra
April 13	New Moon	24 Aries
April 28	Full Moon	9 Scorpio
May 12	New Moon	22 Taurus
May 27	Full Moon	7 Sagittarius
June 11	New Moon	21 Gemini
June 26	Full Moon	5 Capricorn
July 11	New Moon	19 Cancer
July 25	Full Moon	3 Aquarius
August 9	New Moon	17 Leo
August 23	Full Moon	1 Pisces
September 8	New Moon	16 Virgo
September 22	Full Moon	29 Pisces
October 7	New Moon	15 Libra
October 21	Full Moon	29 Aries
November 6	New Moon	14 Scorpio
November 20	Full Moon	28 Taurus
December 5	New Moon	14 Sagittarius
December 20	Full Moon	29 Gemini

2049

January 4	New Moon	14 Capricorn
January 19	Full Moon	29 Cancer
February 2	New Moon	14 Aquarius
February 17	Full Moon	29 Leo
March 4	New Moon	14 Pisces
March 19	Full Moon	29 Virgo
April 2	New Moon	13 Aries
April 18	Full Moon	28 Libra
May 2	New Moon	12 Taurus
May 17	Full Moon	27 Scorpio

May 31	New Moon	10 Gemini
June 15	Full Moon	25 Sagittarius
June 30	New Moon	9 Cancer
July 15	Full Moon	23 Capricorn
July 29	New Moon	7 Leo
August 13	Full Moon	21 Aquarius
August 28	New Moon	5 Virgo
September 11	Full Moon	19 Pisces
September 27	New Moon	4 Libra
October 11	Full Moon	18 Aries
October 26	New Moon	3 Scorpio
November 9	Full Moon	17 Taurus
November 25	New Moon	3 Sagittarius
December 9	Full Moon	17 Gemini
December 24	New Moon	3 Capricorn

2050

January 8	Full Moon	18 Cancer
January 23	New Moon	3 Aquarius
February 6	Full Moon	18 Leo
February 21	New Moon	3 Pisces
March 8	Full Moon	18 Virgo
March 23	New Moon	2 Aries
April 7	Full Moon	17 Libra
April 21	New Moon	1 Taurus
May 6	Full Moon	16 Scorpio
May 20	New Moon	0 Gemini
June 5	Full Moon	14 Sagittarius
June 19	New Moon	26 Gemini
July 4	Full Moon	13 Capricorn
July 18	New Moon	26 Cancer
August 3	Full Moon	11 Aquarius
August 17	New Moon	24 Leo
September 1	Full Moon	9 Pisces
September 16	New Moon	23 Virgo
September 30	Full Moon	7 Aries
October 15	New Moon	22 Libra
October 30	Full Moon	7 Taurus
November 14	New Moon	22 Scorpio
November 28	Full Moon	6 Gemini
December 14	New Moon	22 Sagittarius
December 28	Full Moon	6 Cancer

Appendix III

Planetary Data

Mars

Dates	*Sign*
January 3-February 10, 2000	Pisces
February 11-March 21, 2000	Aries
March 22-May 2, 2000	Taurus
May 3-June 15, 2000	Gemini
June 16-July 30, 2000	Cancer
July 31-September 15, 2000	Leo
September 16-November 2, 2000	Virgo
November 3-December 22, 2000	Libra
December 23, 2000-February 13, 2001	Scorpio
February 14-September 7, 2001	Sagittarius
Retrograde, May 11-July 18, 2001	
September 8-October 26, 2001	Capricorn
October 27-December 7, 2001	Aquarius
December 8, 2001-January 17, 2002	Pisces
January 18-February 28, 2002	Aries
March 1-April 12, 2002	Taurus
April 13-May 27, 2002	Gemini
May 28-July 12, 2002	Cancer
July 13-August 28, 2002	Leo
August 29-October 14, 2002	Virgo
October 15-November 30, 2002	Libra
December 1, 2002-January 15, 2003	Scorpio
January 16-March 3, 2003	Sagittarius
March 4-April 20, 2003	Capricorn
April 21-June 15, 2003	Aquarius
June 16-December 15, 2003	Pisces
Retrograde, July 29-September 26, 2003	
December 16, 2003-February 2, 2004	Aries
February 3-March 20, 2004	Taurus
March 21-May 6, 2004	Gemini
May 7-June 22, 2004	Cancer

Mars Continued

Dates	Sign
June 23-August 9, 2004	Leo
August 10-September 25, 2004	Virgo
September 26-November 10, 2004	Libra
November 11-December 24, 2004	Scorpio
December 25, 2004-February 5, 2005	Sagittarius
February 6-March 19, 2005	Capricorn
March 20-April 29, 2005	Aquarius
April 30-June 10, 2005	Pisces
June 11-July 27, 2005	Aries
July 28, 2005-February 16, 2006	Taurus
Retrograde, October 1-December 8, 2005	
February 17-April 12, 2006	Gemini
April 13-June 2, 2006	Cancer
June 3-July 21, 2006	Leo
July 22-September 7, 2006	Virgo
September 8-October 22, 2006	Libra
October 23-December 4, 2006	Scorpio
December 5, 2006-January 15, 2007	Sagittarius
January 16-February 24, 2007	Capricorn
February 25-April 5, 2007	Aquarius
April 6-May 14, 2007	Pisces
May 15-June 23, 2007	Aries
June 24-August 6, 2007	Taurus
August 7-September 27, 2007	Gemini
September 28-December 30, 2007	Cancer
Retrograde, November 15, 2007-Januiary 29, 2008	
December 31, 2007-March 3, 2008	Gemini
March 4-May 8, 2008	Cancer
May 9-June 30, 2008	Leo
July 1-August 18, 2008	Virgo
August 19-October 3, 2008	Libra
October 4-November 15, 2008	Scorpio
November 16-December 26, 2008	Sagittarius
December 27, 2008-February 3, 2009	Capricorn
February 4-March 13, 2009	Aquarius
March 14-April 21, 2009	Pisces
April 22-May 30, 2009	Aries
May 31-July 10, 2009	Taurus
July 11-August 24, 2009	Gemini
August 25-October 15, 2009	Cancer
October 16, 2009-June 6, 2010	Leo
Retrograde, December 20, 2009-March 9, 2010	
June 7-July 28, 2010	Virgo
July 29-September 13, 2010	Libra

Mars Continued

Dates	Sign
September 14-October 27, 2010	Scorpio
October 28-December 6, 2010	Sagittarius
December 7, 2010-January 14, 2011	Capricorn
January 15-February 21, 2011	Aquarius
February 22-April 1, 2011	Pisces
April 2-May 10, 2011	Aries
May 11-June 19, 2011	Taurus
June 20-August 2, 2011	Gemini
August 3-September 17, 2011	Cancer
September 18-November 9, 2011	Leo
November 10, 2011-July 2, 2012	Virgo
Retrograde, January 22-April 12, 2012	
July 3-August 22, 2012	Libra
August 23-October 5, 2012	Scorpio
October 6-November 15, 2012	Sagittarius
November 16-December 24, 2012	Capricorn
December 25, 2012-January 31, 2013	Aquarius
February 1-March 11, 2013	Pisces
March 12-April 19, 2013	Aries
April 20-May 30, 2013	Taurus
May 31-July 12, 2013	Gemini
July 13-August 26, 2013	Cancer
August 27-October 14, 2013	Leo
October 15-December 6, 2013	Virgo
December 7, 2013-July 24, 2014	Libra
Retrograde, March 1-May 18, 2014	
July 25-September 12, 2014	Scorpio
September 13-October 25, 2014	Sagittarius
October 26-December 3, 2014	Capricorn
December 4, 2014-January 11, 2015	Aquarius
January 12-February 18, 2015	Pisces
February 19-March 30, 2015	Aries
March 31-May 10, 2015	Taurus
May 11-June 23, 2015	Gemini
June 24-August 7, 2015	Cancer
August 8-September 23, 2015	Leo
September 24-November 11, 2015	Virgo
November 12, 2015-January 2, 2016	Libra
January 3-March 4, 2016	Scorpio
March 5-May 26, 2016	Sagittarius
Retrograde, April 17-June 28, 2016	
May 27-August 1, 2016	Scorpio
August 2-September 26, 2016	Sagittarius
September 27-November 8, 2016	Capricorn

Mars Continued

Dates	Sign
November 9-December 18, 2016	Aquarius
December 19, 2016-January 27, 2017	Pisces
January 28-March 8, 2017	Aries
March 9-April 20, 2017	Taurus
April 21-June 3, 2017	Gemini
June 4-July 19, 2017	Cancer
July 20-September 4, 2017	Leo
September 5-October 21, 2017	Virgo
October 22-December 8, 2017	Libra
December 9, 2017-January 25, 2018	Scorpio
January 26-March 16, 2018	Sagittarius
March 17-May 15, 2018	Capricorn
May 16-August 11, 2018	Aquarius
Retrograde, June 26-August 26, 2018	
August 12-September 9, 2018	Capricorn
September 10-November 14, 2018	Aquarius
November 15-December 30, 2018	Pisces
December 31, 2018-February 13, 2019	Aries
February 14-March 30, 2019	Taurus
March 31-May 14, 2019	Gemini
May 15-June 30, 2019	Cancer
July 1-August 17, 2019	Leo
August 18-October 3, 2019	Virgo
October 4-November 18, 2019	Libra
November 19, 2019-January 2, 2020	Scorpio
January 3-February 15, 2020	Sagittarius
February 16-March 29, 2020	Capricorn
March 30-May 12, 2020	Aquarius
May 13-June 26, 2020	Pisces
June 27, 2020-January 5, 2021	Aries
Retrograde, September 9-November 12, 2020	
January 6-March 2, 2021	Taurus
March 3-April 22, 2021	Gemini
April 23-June 10, 2021	Cancer
June 11-July 28, 2021	Leo
July 29-September 13, 2021	Virgo
September 14-October 29, 2021	Libra
October 30-December 12, 2021	Scorpio
December 13, 2021-January 23, 2022	Sagittarius
January 24-March 5, 2022	Capricorn
March 6-April 13, 2022	Aquarius
April 14-May 23, 2022	Pisces
May 24-July 4, 2022	Aries
July 5-August 19, 2022	Taurus

Mars Continued

Dates	Sign
August 20, 2022-March 24, 2023	Gemini
Retrograde, October 30, 2022-January 11, 2023	
March 25-May 19, 2023	Cancer
May 20-July 9, 2023	Leo
July 10-August 26, 2023	Virgo
August 27-October 11, 2023	Libra
October 12-November 23, 2023	Scorpio
November 24, 2023-January 3, 2024	Sagittarius
January 4-February 12, 2024	Capricorn
February 13-March 21, 2024	Aquarius
March 22-April 29, 2024	Pisces
April 30-June 8, 2024	Aries
June 9-July 19, 2024	Taurus
July 20-September 3, 2024	Gemini
September 4-November 2, 2024	Cancer
November 3, 2024-January 5, 2025	Leo
Retrograde, December 6, 2024-February 22, 2025	
January 6-April 17, 2025	Cancer
April 18-June 16, 2025	Leo
June 17-August 5, 2025	Virgo
August 6-September 21, 2025	Libra
September 22-November 3, 2025	Scorpio
November 4- December 14, 2025	Sagittarius
December 15, 2025-January 22, 2026	Capricorn
January 23-March 1, 2026	Aquarius
March 2-April 8, 2026	Pisces
April 9-May 17, 2026	Aries
May 18-June 27, 2026	Taurus
June 28-August 10, 2026	Gemini
August 11-September 26, 2026	Cancer
September 27-November 24, 2026	Leo
November 25, 2026-February 20, 2027	Virgo
Retrograde, January 10-March 31, 2027	
February 21-May 13, 2027	Leo
May 14-July 14, 2027	Virgo
July 15-August 31, 2027	Libra
September 1-October 14, 2027	Scorpio
October 15-November 24, 2027	Sagittarius
November 25, 2027-January 2, 2028	Capricorn
January 3-February 9, 2028	Aquarius
February 10-March 18, 2028	Pisces
March 19-April 26, 2028	Aries
April 27-June 6, 2028	Taurus
June 7-July 19, 2028	Gemini

Mars Continued

Dates	Sign
July 20-September 3, 2028	Cancer
September 4-October 22, 2028	Leo
October 23-December 20, 2028	Virgo
December 21, 2028-April 6, 2029	Libra
Retrograde, February 14-May 4, 2029	
April 7-June 4, 2029	Virgo
June 5-August 6, 2029	Libra
August 7-September 22, 2029	Scorpio
September 23-November 2, 2029	Sagittarius
November 3-December 12, 2029	Capricorn
December 13, 2029-January 19, 2030	Aquarius
January 20-February 26, 2030	Pisces
February 27-April 7, 2030	Aries
April 8-May 18, 2030	Taurus
May 19-June 30, 2030	Gemini
July 1-August 14, 2030	Cancer
August 15-October 1, 2030	Leo
October 2-November 20, 2030	Virgo
November 21, 2030-January 14, 2031	Libra
January 15-August 24, 2031	Scorpio
Retrograde, March 28-June 12, 2031	
August 25-October 9, 2031	Sagittarius
October 10-November 19, 2031	Capricorn
November 20-December 28, 2031	Aquarius
December 29, 2031-February 5, 2032	Pisces
February 6-March 16, 2032	Aries
March 17-April 27, 2032	Taurus
April 28-June 10, 2032	Gemini
June 11-July 26, 2032	Cancer
July 27-September 11, 2032	Leo
September 12-October 28, 2032	Virgo
October 29-December 16, 2032	Libra
December 17, 2032-February 5, 2033	Scorpio
February 6-April 5, 2033	Sagittarius
April 6-July 25, 2033	Scorpio
Retrograde, May 26-July 31, 2033	
July 26-August 5, 2033	Sagittarius
August 6-October 16, 2033	Capricorn
October 17-November 30, 2033	Aquarius
December 1, 2033-January 11, 2034	Pisces
January 12-February 22, 2034	Aries
February 23-April 7, 2034	Taurus
April 8-May 22, 2034	Gemini
May 23-July 7, 2034	Cancer

Mars Continued

Dates	Sign
July 8-August 23, 2034	Leo
August 24-October 9, 2034	Virgo
October 10-November 25, 2034	Libra
November 26, 2034-January 10, 2035	Scorpio
January 11-February 24, 2035	Sagittarius
February 25-April 11, 2035	Capricorn
April 12-May 29, 2035	Aquarius
May 30-November 30, 2035	Pisces
Retrograde, August 15-October 14, 2035	
December 1, 2035-January 25, 2036	Aries
January 26-March 13, 2036	Taurus
March 14-April 30, 2036	Gemini
May 1-June 17, 2036	Cancer
June 18-August 4, 2036	Leo
August 5-September 20, 2036	Virgo
September 21-November 5, 2036	Libra
November 6- December 19, 2036	Scorpio
December 20, 2036-January 31, 2037	Sagittarius
February 1-March 13, 2037	Capricorn
March 14-April 23, 2037	Aquarius
April 24-June 3, 2037	Pisces
June 4-July 16, 2037	Aries
July 17-September 10, 2037	Taurus
September 11-November 11, 2037	Gemini
Retrograde, October 12-December 21, 2037	
November 12, 2037-February 3, 2038	Taurus
February 4-April 5, 2038	Gemini
April 6-May 28, 2038	Cancer
May 29-July 16, 2038	Leo
July 17-September 2, 2038	Virgo
September 3-October 17, 2038	Libra
October 18-November 30, 2038	Scorpio
December 1, 2038-January 10, 2039	Sagittarius
January 11-February 19, 2039	Capricorn
February 20-March 30, 2039	Aquarius
March 31-May 8, 2039	Pisces
May 9-June 17, 2039	Aries
June 18-July 30, 2039	Taurus
July 31-September 17, 2039	Gemini
September 18, 2039-May 1, 2040	Cancer
Retrograde, November 23, 2039-February 8, 2040	
May 2-June 24, 2040	Leo
June 25-August 13, 2040	Virgo
August 14-September 28, 2040	Libra

Mars Continued

Dates	*Sign*
September 29-November 10, 2040	Scorpio
November 11-December 21, 2040	Sagittarius
December 22, 2040-January 29, 2041	Capricorn
January 30-March 9, 2041	Aquarius
March 10-April 16, 2041	Pisces
April 17-May 25, 2041	Aries
May 26-July 5, 2041	Taurus
July 6-August 18, 2041	Gemini
August 19-October 7, 2041	Cancer
October 8, 2041-May 29, 2042	Leo
Retrograde, December 27, 2041-March 17, 2042	
May 30-July 23, 2042	Virgo
July 24-September 8, 2042	Libra
September 9-October 22, 2042	Scorpio
October 23-December 2, 2042	Sagittarius
December 3, 2042-January 9, 2043	Capricorn
January 10-February 17, 2043	Aquarius
February 18-March 27, 2043	Pisces
March 28-May 5, 2043	Aries
May 6-June 15, 2043	Taurus
June 16-July 28, 2043	Gemini
July 29-September 12, 2043	Cancer
September 13-November 2, 2043	Leo
November 3, 2043-January 18, 2044	Virgo
January 19-February 11, 2044	Libra
Retrograde, January 31-April 20, 2044	
February 12-June 23, 2044	Virgo
June 24-August 16, 2044	Libra
August 17-September 30, 2044	Scorpio
October 1-November 10, 2044	Sagittarius
November 11-December 19, 2044	Capricorn
December 20, 2044-January 26, 2045	Aquarius
January 27-March 6, 2045	Pisces
March 7-April 14, 2045	Aries
April 15-May 25, 2045	Taurus
May 26-July 7, 2045	Gemini
July 8-August 21, 2045	Cancer
August 22-October 8, 2045	Leo
October 9-November 29, 2045	Virgo
November 30, 2045-February 3, 2046	Libra
February 4-April 10, 2046	Scorpio
Retrograde, March 10-May 27, 2046	
April 11-July 14, 2046	Libra
July 15-September 6, 2046	Scorpio

Mars Continued

Dates	*Sign*
September 7-October 19, 2046	Sagittarius
October 20-November 28, 2046	Capricorn
November 29, 2046-January 6, 2047	Aquarius
January 7-February 13, 2047	Pisces
February 14-March 25, 2047	Aries
March 26-May 6, 2047	Taurus
May 7-June 18, 2047	Gemini
June 19-August 3, 2047	Cancer
August 4-September 19, 2047	Leo
September 20-November 6, 2047	Virgo
November 7-December 26, 2047	Libra
December 27, 2047-February 20, 2048	Scorpio
February 21-September 16, 2048	Sagittarius
Retrograde, April 30-July 9, 2048	
September 17-October 31, 2048	Capricorn
November 1-December 11, 2048	Aquarius
December 12, 2048-January 21, 2049	Pisces
January 22-March 3, 2049	Aries
March 4-April 15, 2049	Taurus
April 16-May 29, 2049	Gemini
May 30-July 14, 2049	Cancer
July 15-August 30, 2049	Leo
August 31-October 16, 2049	Virgo
October 17-December 2, 2049	Libra
December 3, 2049-January 19, 2050	Scorpio
January 20-March 8, 2050	Sagittarius
March 9-April 28, 2050	Capricorn
April 29-October 30, 2050	Aquarius
Retrograde, July 14-September 12, 2050	
October 31-December 22, 2050	Pisces

Jupiter

Dates	*Sign*
February 14, 2000-June 29, 2000	Taurus
June 30, 2000-July 11, 2001	Gemini
July 12, 2001-July 31, 2002	Cancer
August 1, 2002-August 26, 2003	Leo
August 27, 2003-September 23, 2004	Virgo
September 24, 2004-October 24, 2005	Libra
October 25, 2005-November 22, 2006	Scorpio
November 23, 2006-December 17, 2007	Sagittarius
December 18, 2007-January 4, 2009	Capricorn
January 5, 2009-January 16, 2010	Aquarius

Jupiter Continued

Dates	Sign
January 17-June 5, 2010	Pisces
June 6-September 8, 2010	Aries
September 9, 2010-January 21, 2011	Pisces
January 22-June 3, 2011	Aries
June 4, 2011-June 10, 2012	Taurus
June 11, 2012-June 24, 2013	Gemini
June 25, 2013-July 15, 2014	Cancer
July 16, 2014-August 10, 2015	Leo
August 11, 2015-September 8, 2016	Virgo
September 9, 2016-October 9, 2017	Libra
October 10, 2017-November 7, 2018	Scorpio
November 8, 2018-December 1, 2019	Sagittarius
December 2, 2019-December 18, 2020	Capricorn
December 19, 2020-May 12, 2021	Aquarius
May 13-July 27, 2021	Pisces
July 28-December 27, 2021	Aquarius
December 28, 2021-May 9, 2022	Pisces
May 10-October 27, 2022	Aries
October 28-December 19, 2022	Pisces
December 20, 2022-May 15, 2023	Aries
May 16, 2023-May 24, 2024	Taurus
May 25, 2024-June 8, 2025	Gemini
June 9, 2025-June 29, 2026	Cancer
June 30, 2026-July 25, 2027	Leo
July 26, 2027-August 23, 2028	Virgo
August 24, 2028-September 23, 2029	Libra
September 24, 2029-October 21, 2030	Scorpio
October 22, 2030-November 14, 2031	Sagittarius
November 15, 2031-April 10, 2032	Capricorn
April 11-June 25, 2032	Aquarius
June 26-November 28, 2032	Capricorn
November 29, 2032-April 13, 2033	Aquarius
April 14-September 11, 2033	Pisces
September 12-November 30, 2033	Aquarius
December 1, 2033-April 20, 2034	Pisces
April 21, 2034-April 28, 2035	Aries
April 29, 2035-May 8, 2036	Taurus
May 9, 2036-May 22, 2037	Gemini
May 23, 2037-June 11, 2038	Cancer
June 12-November 15, 2038	Leo
November 16, 2038-January 15, 2039	Virgo
January 16-July 6, 2039	Leo
July 7-December 11, 2039	Virgo
December 12, 2039-February 19, 2040	Libra

Jupiter Continued

Dates	**Sign**
February 20-August 4, 2040	Virgo
August 5, 2040-January 10, 2041	Libra
January 11-March 19, 2041	Scorpio
March 20-September 4, 2041	Libra
September 5, 2041-February 7, 2042	Scorpio
February 8-April 23, 2042	Sagittarius
April 24-October 3, 2042	Scorpio
October 4, 2042-February 28, 2043	Sagittarius
March 1-June 8, 2043	Capricorn
June 9-October 25, 2043	Sagittarius
October 26, 2043-March 13, 2044	Capricorn
March 14-August 8, 2044	Aquarius
August 9-November 3, 2044	Capricorn
November 4, 2044-March 25, 2045	Aquarius
March 26, 2045-April 3, 2046	Pisces
April 4, 2046-April 12, 2047	Aries
April 13, 2047-April 21, 2048	Taurus
April 22-September 22, 2048	Gemini
September 23-November 11, 2048	Cancer
November 12, 2048-May 4, 2049	Leo
May 5-September 26, 2049	Cancer
September 27, 2049-January 13, 2050	Leo
January 14-May 21, 2050	Cancer
May 22-October 17, 2050	Leo

Saturn

Dates	**Sign**
August 9-October 14, 2000	Gemini
October 15, 2000-April 19, 2001	Taurus
April 20, 2001-June 2, 2003	Gemini
June 3, 2003-July 15, 2005	Cancer
July 16, 2005-September 1, 2007	Leo
September 2, 2007-October 28, 2009	Virgo
October 29, 2009-April 6, 2010	Libra
April 7-July 20, 2010	Virgo
July 21, 2010-October 4, 2012	Libra
October 5, 2012-December 22, 2014	Scorpio
December 23, 2014-June 13, 2015	Sagittarius
June 14-September 16, 2015	Scorpio
September 17, 2015-December 18, 2017	Sagittarius
December 19, 2017-March 20, 2020	Capricorn
March 21-June 30, 2020	Aquarius
July 1-December 16, 2020	Capricorn

Saturn Continued

Dates	Sign
December 17, 2020-March 6, 2023	Aquarius
March 7, 2023-May 23, 2025	Pisces
May 24-August 31, 2025	ARies
September 1, 2025-February 12, 2026	Pisces
February 13, 2026-April 11, 2028	Aries
April 12, 2028-May 30, 2030	Taurus
May 31, 2030-July 12, 2032	Gemini
July 13, 2032-August 25, 2034	Cancer
August 26, 2034-February 14, 2035	Leo
February 15-May 10, 2035	Virgo
May 11, 2035-October 15, 2036	Leo
October 16, 2037-February 10, 2037	Virgo
February 11-July 5, 2037	Leo
July 6, 2037-September 4, 2039	Virgo
September 5, 2039-November 10, 2041	Libra
November 11, 2041-June 20, 2042	Scorpio
June 21-July 13, 2042	Libra
July 14, 2042-February 20, 2044	Scorpio
February 21-March 24, 2044	Sagittarius
March 25-October 30, 2044	Scorpio
October 31, 2044-January 23, 2047	Sagittarius
January 24-July 9, 2047	Capricorn
July 10-October 21, 2047	Sagittarius
October 22, 2047-January 20, 2050	Capricorn

Uranus

Dates	Sign
January 12, 1996-March 9, 2003	Aquarius
March 10-September 13, 2003	Pisces
September 14-December 29, 2003	Aquarius
December 30, 2003-May 26, 2010	Pisces
May 27-August 12, 2010	Aries
August 13, 2010-March 10, 2011	Pisces
March 11, 2011-May 14, 2018	Aries
May 15-November 5, 2018	Taurus
November 6, 2018-March 5, 2019	Aries
March 6, 2019-July 6, 2025	Taurus
July 7-November 6, 2025	Gemini
November 7, 2025-April 24, 2026	Taurus
April 25, 2026-August 2, 2032	Gemini
August 3-December 11, 2032	Cancer
December 12, 2032-May 21, 2033	Gemini
May 22, 2033-August 5, 2039	Cancer

Uranus Continued

Dates	Sign
August 6, 2039-February 24, 2040	Gemini
February 25-May 14, 2040	Cancer
May 15, 2040-October 5, 2045	Leo
October 6, 2045-February 7, 2046	Virgo
February 8-July 21, 2046	Leo
July 22, 2046-December 7, 2051	Virgo
December 8, 2051-January 30, 2052	Libra
January 31-September 10, 2052	Virgo
September 11, 2052	Libra

About the Author

Jack Gillen has been acclaimed as an extremely accurate astrologer and predictor of events by listening audiences and the media. These descriptions fit him well and he has carried this banner for his profession, as an astrologer and author, proudly and fearlessly throughout the country. His untiring efforts in enlightening people of all walks of life are directed toward the betterment of mankind through the understanding of the working principles of astrology.

Astrology has been studied for more than 50 centuries, perhaps even longer. A very selected few have dedicated themselves fully to this study and still fewer have achieved such degree in mastery of the art as Jack Gillen. He is a professional astrologer who has shown more than an amazing degree of accuracy in predicting changes in the world monetary structure, the stock exchange and other commodity markets.

The many years of research spent in the field of astrology led him to discover the keys of the Celestial Solar System, and his use of them has opened to the world and mankind information heretofore unknown except in the most primitive form.

Jack has made hundreds of predictions on a wide variety of subjects. He has proven beyond any doubt that he is the Nostradamus of this generation. His degree of accuracy is an amazing 96.5 percent. His predictions have been carried regularly by the *Miami Daily News*, *The National Enquirer*, *The Orlando Sentinal*, *The Express and Evening News*, *The Light Newspaper* and many radio stations throughout the country. Why does the news media carry the predictions of this astrologer? The answer is simple: accuracy.

One only has to take a look at a sampling of the variety of the many subjects that Jack Gillen has covered to realize the talent he possesses. Predictions on subjects such as individual stocks as listed on the New York Stock Exchange, the New York Stock Exchange as a whole, transportation accidents, airplane disasters, recession-inflation-depression, natural disasters, assassinations and deaths, political events and their outcome, astrological forecasts for the country and labor situations. For example, no one thought of recession in 1973; inflation fwas the problem, with prices rapidly rising and wages were galloping after them. But Jack's prediction was for a recession in 1974, because he was aware of several astrological factors, notable among them that 1974 was a year ruled by Saturn and that it coincided with the Saturn return in the United States chart.

The first part of the year was inflationary, jobs were plentiful and demands from all sectors of the economy were out of bounds; then came the last half of the year. It started with housing and construction trades, and then the auto plants, and gradually a large part of the manufacturing sector. Then followed the worst economic news in many years: the oil embargo by OPEC. Recession, and in some areas it could be called a depression, was a fact of life in late 1974 and continuing into 1975.

In his 1975 book, *Jack Gillen Predicts*, he predicted that during the week of April 21-26, 1978 the New York Stock Exchange would have extremely heavy trading. On the April 24, the exchange traded well over 63 million shares, breaking all previous records. Tapes were as much as one and one-half hours behind time as sales skyrocketed.

Those who have sought his advice and employed his methods have enjoyed piece of mind in personal matters and monetary rewards far beyond any expectations. His outstanding methods of communicating with all levels of humanity for the enrichment of all mankind place him in a category with many great men of the past.

During his career as an astrologer, Jack Gillen has written 48 books and countless articles and other publications. He was the first to present computer software on a hand-held computer as a tool for seminars on horse and greyhound racing, sports, commodities, stocks and lotteries. He was the first to do a national television special, and had his own radio talk show, *AstroView*, on *The Talk-America Radio Network*. In the 21st century, his predictions continue to be as accurate as they were in the 20th century.

www.ingramcontent.com/pod-product-compliance
Lightning Source LLC
Chambersburg PA
CBHW081807300426
44116CB00014B/2273